MUSICALLY

Yours

Monique
+
Rick
Jan 2021

A Duet's Memoir Of Life, Love, & Music

MONIQUE & RICK TREMBLAY

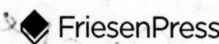

◆ FriesenPress

Suite 300 - 990 Fort St
Victoria, BC, V8V 3K2
Canada

www.friesenpress.com

ISBN
978-1-5255-7573-0 (Hardcover)
978-1-5255-7574-7 (Paperback)
978-1-5255-7575-4 (eBook)

1. BIOGRAPHY & AUTOBIOGRAPHY, COMPOSERS & MUSICIANS

Distributed to the trade by The Ingram Book Company

TABLE OF CONTENTS

FOREWORD

DURING THE 45 PLUS years that I have known Monique, I have marvelled at her tenacity and willingness to take on every mountain that threatened to derail her hopes and dreams. In circumstances where others would have quit, Monique has kept going, even in the darkest of nights after her beloved husband's stroke turned their world upside down.

It was a pleasure to read *Musically Yours*, a testament to Monique and Rick and their love song, sung as it were on paper by Monique, according to her unique style. In it, we get a glimpse of the heart and soul of a couple brought together by their passion for music. Monique has carefully transcribed the ebb and flow of the high times, the formative years when music captivated their interests, the passion of young love, the search for work and identity, and the thrill of entertaining audiences. And in the low times, the despair and struggle to regain a sense of balance and harmony in the midst of great uncertainty.

One of my earliest memories of Monique is from a high school city-wide track and field meet held in Sudbury, Ontario. We were both competing at the event. Monique chose to run in the 100m hurdles. Why you might ask, would the shortest person on the team be running hurdles? I don't know, but my guess is simply that she wanted to. She didn't perceive any handicap. And although she fell badly early on in the race, banging her head on the gravel track did not stop her from getting up and finishing her race.

The event of Rick's brainstem stroke in December 2005 forever changed the trajectory of their life together. The full weight of their future decisions now rested squarely on Monique's shoulders. Their song had changed. Initially, it was a dirge, a howling at the wind, as all the pieces needed to be collected, organized, and put back together again. It took years to regain some sense of equilibrium and stability. Even harmony. But they kept working at it, persisting, until eventually Monique and Rick were able to get back up on their feet and continue their race, their shared journey of love, adventure, and music.

I sense the ache of Monique's heart in writing this memoir. Will people remember Monique & Rick, the musical duo? Will they remember the songs we sang together? Will they remember Rick's brilliant musical mind? His songs. His performances. Will they remember us? It echoes the words Isak Dinesen penned in her book *Out of Africa*; "If I know a song of Africa, of the giraffe and the African new moon lying on her back, of the plows in the fields and the sweaty faces of the coffee pickers, does Africa know a song of me?"[1]

We all want to know that our life will be remembered in some small way; that we have touched people's lives as they have touched us; that what we have done "will not go unwitnessed." I believe Monique has accomplished her goal. Long after they are gone, *Musically Yours* will echo the song of *Monique & Rick*: the couple who loved well, lived well, and ran their race together to the end.

Lifelong friend,

Diane (Ramarr) Laakso
President, Graceland Africa Mission

DEDICATION

To Rick:

"You are my heart, my life, my song!"

To Monique:

"Only you can soothe my soul. Truly as I love your beauty I will always be in love with you!"

WITNESS OUR LEGACY

"We need a witness to our lives. There's a billion people on the planet, what does any one life really mean? But in a marriage, you're promising to care about everything. The good things, the bad things, the terrible things, the mundane things, all of it, all the time, every day. You're saying: Your life will not go unnoticed because I will notice it. Your life will not go unwitnessed because I will be your witness."[2]

When I first heard these words spoken by Susan Sarandon, as Beverley Clark in the movie *Shall We Dance*[3] – I was thrown into a tailspin of emotions. Each word rang true. I found myself on a roller coaster of sensations that brought tears to my eyes; pummelled my mind with flashbacks and made my heart beat so rapidly I thought it would explode.

I was dumbstruck! I replayed that scene again-and-again. Each time, things became clearer. I felt a weight lifting from my shoulders. Clarity was right around the corner.

I knew what I had to do! It was an idea I had thought about only fleetingly in the past. One I hadn't had the courage or the emotional strength to put it into action. The time had finally come. The mission was clear. It was time to tell the Monique & Rick life story.

Our memoir would document our roles as husband and wife, as a musical duo and life travellers so that our lives will not go unwitnessed! The desire to do this was driven by many different events like the movie. The time was right to write about the good, bad, terrible, mundane, and mysterious things that shaped our story.

The Monique & Rick Musically Yours memoir will focus on the stages of our lives, as illustrated in our Story Quilt: the Young Musicians, the Married Duo, and the Devoted Couple. Each stage of our story is a discovery of the adventures, the opportunities, and the challenges that we faced. There were growing pains, shared disappointments, and sometimes even some dark forces that tried to destroy us to our very core. The foundation, on which our life story has been built is solid. This foundation was purposefully built on our love of music, our commitment to champion each other's personal growth, and our intense love for each other.

Rick and I have embraced what really matters, which is love, respect and trust. We continue to witness each other's lives each in our own way. The scene script states: "In a marriage, you're promising to care about everything"—and we do!

This is the story of our legacy as we witnessed it through our eyes, our music, and our love. We hope this story touches and inspires you to reflect and share your own story with others.

Musically Yours

Monique & Rick

LOVE IS THE MUSIC

LOVE IS THE MUSIC is prominently displayed on our story quilt for a very good reason. Music and the love Rick and I have for it is a core part of our amazing journey together. Here are our stories, in our voices, about our musical way of being.

MANELLA HEMP —
HOME GROWN TALENT

Oh, the 70s. The clothes, the music, the TV shows, and the birth of the mullet! Rick and I were high school students and yes, we tried in our way to be cool. Like most high school kids across Canada, we were craving access to great music. We would save our money to buy vinyl records in 45 and 33-RPM[4] formats and the new technology quadraphonic sound on eight-track cartridges. We still have our collection. Yes, and the 8-tracks too!

Some of us wanted to create our own music, perform at school events and, if we were lucky enough, pull together a garage band. The guys latched onto that idea with dreams of being the next rock star or pop-rock artists. Maybe they could be the next Guess Who, Neil Young, Stampeders, Bachman Turner Overdrive (BTO), Rolling Stones, the Beatles, and the list is endless.

Of course, it was a great way to meet girls—because girls love boys that can sing and play. I fall into that category! Rick, like most teenagers, was not the exception as he chased the dream of being a musician and songwriter at the innocent and experimental age of 13.

Manella Hemp started with a few friends getting together to jam. In the beginning, it was Rick, Perry and Mike Guilbault, and Alvin (Junior) Erickson. They had three guitar players, so Perry ended up learning how to play bass, with Rick's help of course. Rick is a creature of habit because later in the 80s he helped Brian Crook to play bass for Aurora.

Rick Tremblay the cool rock and roller playing his Fender Mustang with the ever-popular baggy pants of the 70s. John Shaw on drums.

The jamming lasted a short while and they hooked up with John Shaw on drums and Marc St. Denis on rhythm guitar. This was when Manella Hemp was born. I asked Perry where the name Manella Hemp came from. He said, "It was during our Grade 8 science class." Now I'm curious what were they working on in chemistry class to come up with that name? Rick said he was in Grade 9 along with Mike Guilbeault so when Perry and the boys came up with the name Manella Hemp it sounded cool and the name stuck. Ah the 70s' education system feeding creativity.

Manella Hemp practiced at Rick's and John's houses and, naturally, they drove their parents crazy and may have caused early hearing loss. As newbie musicians, Manella Hemp didn't know that practicing at low volumes is much better than blasting the house down. But they were young and knew it all!

They were not alone in that misconception. *Spinal Tap*[5], a 1984 mockumentary brought this to life. In the film Nigel Tufnel the lead guitar player (portrayed by Christopher Guest), proudly bragged that his amplifier (amp) volume dial "goes to 11" proof of Spinal Tap's superiority over all other bands. When Rick and I watched this movie for the first time he was laughing so hard, with tears rolling down his cheeks, and said, "That's Manella Hemp. We wanted it loud. Real loud." For the non-musicians, the amp dial only goes to 10. If you haven't seen the movie, watch it and you'll be entertained and I'm sure it will conjure up memories of bands from your high school assuming of course, you were a teenager in the 70s.

Manella Hemp started to find their groove and before they knew it they found the nerve to play gigs outside of the parents' homes. Perry said, "It was Rick that led the band in singing and plucked (pardon the pun) the courage to get the band out of the basement to play at our high school, Chelmsford Valley District Composite School, or simply CVDCS."

I agree nothing is more nerve-wracking than performing live in front of your classmates. It is much easier to play for strangers—less peer pressure. Luckily, Manella Hemp played a few gigs at the Chelmsford Arena at weddings and other social functions. They got to play and that mattered most. Manella Hemp felt like they were on top of the world—even in the small town of Chelmsford.

Manella Hemp early jammers (Left to Right): Perry Guilbault (bass), Rick Tremblay (rhythm guitar), Mike Guilbault (lead guitar) and John Shaw (drums).

Manella Hemp played more middle-of-the-road music between rock and easy listening with songs from CCR (Creedence Clearwater Revival), Rolling Stones, Ike & Tina Turner and Santana. The song that was the most popular (and the longest) in their set was 'Black Magic Woman' by Santana because it got everyone up to dance. With more gigs under their belt, their rock-star confidence grew. "It was a great feeling to be playing in front of our classmates and we sure had a blast!" said Perry. He went on to say: "There was a point where Marc St. Denis was having so much fun, we had to get him off stage before he fell off. Just a tad too much to drink but he slept it off on the gym equipment. It was a great time in our lives to be stars in our minds for a short time, but we couldn't ask for better."

Yes, Manella Hemp a true definition of Home-Grown Talent—70s style! I wasn't living in Chelmsford at that time, but if I were, I would have loved to see Manella Hemp play. Better yet—I would have tried to join the group, as I would have rocked 'Proud Mary' as I did when I sang at CVDCS's Variety Night years later. Little did Rick and I know that our lives would collide because of our love of music.

YESTERDAY ONCE MORE

September 1974. New town—New home—New high school— New adventures! I remember my high school years clearly. Like 'It's Yesterday Once More'.

I was 15-years-old, the first child of three to go CVDCS. I didn't have an older brother or sister blazing a trail for me, showing me the ropes, and looking out for me. What made it even worse was that I didn't know anyone at CVDCS as I had attended Levack Public School, 40 km northwest of Chelmsford. Add to that, teenage angst and that feeling of "Ugh, I'm so misunderstood! What is life?"

Turns out I wasn't alone in these trials and tribulations. Another family had moved into the house across the street. Their daughter, Ruby Matthews, was also going to Chemmy high. We met two weeks prior and walked to school together. These newly minted Grade 9'rs now had each other's back and would have those backs until our late 30's.

I remember being dazed, confused, and intrigued. I enjoyed most of my classes with History and Music ranking at the top. In Grade 12, I won the History Award—I still have the trophy collecting dust in my home office. I worked hard to get good grades—they didn't come easy to me, especially those in math and science. That's when a kindred spirit came into my life—Diane Ramarr. She was in Grade 9 too, but she was a Chelmsford girl and knew pretty much everyone at school. She excelled in Sports, Music, and everything scholastic; she was self-confident with a beaming smile. Diane helped me with my science homework and projects. Diane often recalls the time she gave me her biology lab to copy. Which I reworded, because plagiarism wasn't my style, I also coloured the diagrams. The result was that I got a better mark than Diane. This proves that I had untapped 'marketing flare' because I took an idea, gave it polish and then made it sizzle. Despite that, it was the only time I got a better mark than Diane, I know I wouldn't have passed that class if it hadn't been for her patience and sense of humour. Diane continues to be a major part of my life and I'm very blessed to have her support—no matter what. Chemmy High gave me a lifelong friend!

Like every teenager, I wanted to fit in. That meant wearing cool clothes, especially Levi blue jeans. My parents were not fans of blue jeans. I did have a pair of those fake stretchy jeans from Sears, not very flattering and not cool. By earning money from babysitting jobs, I soon had enough saved to buy my first pair of bell-bottom jeans. Off I went to Sudbury to the jean store where they had a bonus special. Buy one pair at regular price, a second pair at half price and choose a free album! I still have Heart's *Little Queen* 1977 hit album in my collection.

I settled in and energetically participated in sports, the Girls Athletic Association (GAA), and the Student Council. I also played clarinet in the CVDCS school band. I maintained a high level of involvement all through high school. Hard work pays off. In Grade 13, I was presented with the Principals' Award of Merit for the student who showed exemplary commitment.

Another highlight of my high school years was Variety Night—a talent show. I remember meeting with our Guidance Counsellor Mrs. Peggy Salisbury when I started Grade 9. She had asked,

"What do you like to do? What makes you happy?" I replied, "I love to sing." Then she mentioned the auditions for Variety Night. She told me to speak to Mr. Tom McCool who was the teacher advisor for Variety Night and my history teacher.

I had never auditioned for anything before. I wasn't sure what to do but Mr. McCool urged me to try. I entered the gym on a Saturday afternoon. Mr. McCool and a few senior students were there. Nick Preyma and Stacey Castonguay, both singers, were part of the judging team. Nick had a band and played at local venues as well as Stag & Doe's. They knew their stuff.

I stood on the stage, no microphone, and no musical backup, as karaoke hadn't been invented yet. With only my voice to rely on, I channelled my inner Karen Carpenter and sang 'Yesterday Once More'.

To keep my legs from shaking and my bell-bottoms from quivering, I pictured myself practising this song accompanied by my record player which had a nickel taped to the playing arm for added weight. My pretend microphone was the cleaner stick for my recorder. Then I disappeared into the lyrics and sang acapella. When I was done there was unnerving silence! Then applause! Both Nick and Stacey spoke to me later and I was happy and surprised that they were so impressed. Nick was looking forward to learning the song so that his band could back me up on Variety Night. A real band, holding a real microphone, singing in front of a real audience? Wow!

The rehearsals as well as working out the arrangement for the song was most enjoyable. Now I had to find a dress. I found a maxi-dress with a stylish plaid pattern that was very popular in the '70s. It was the first of many maxi-dresses and I kept all five of them until 2015 when I donated them to a local theatre group for costumes.

Monique Dinel CVDCS Variety Night

Variety Night in 1974 was a special night. My parents, my brother Mike and sister Joanne were in the audience, as well as Diane and Ruby. When it was my turn to sing, I focused on the song and the thrill of singing with a rock & roll band. Karen Carpenter would have been proud. I now had a reputation as a singer and never again had to audition for Variety Night. As fate would have it a special someone had heard me sing that night and would soon become a part of: *"All the songs I loved so well. Just like before it's Yesterday Once More."*[6]

SESCOPEP SPIRIT

Do you know that expression "Fate brought us together?" You might roll your eyes and discount its value. You will have heard these words used over and over in movies, songs, and books. While it sounds made up, there is truth to it—It certainly applies to the tale of *Monique & Rick*.

In 1975, Serendipity came on the scene. The chance encounter happened at the annual Sescopep Spirit event for all high schools in Sudbury, Ontario. This event involved a senior boys' basketball tournament, cheerleader squad competition, and an overall explosion of school spirit. Five high schools were participating, and each school was asked to provide entertainment between games.

Mrs. Boyd was the faculty coordinator for CVDCS. She selected two students to provide our school's share of the entertainment. Steve Newman did a strip-tease cabaret-style comedy act as 'Stephanie' Newman. Monique Dinel—a 5' 2" Grade 10 student with a powerful voice, would provide one vocal solo. Monique Dinel!! That's me!

When Mrs. Boyd asked me to represent CVDCS, I was thrilled and concerned at the same time. I asked if there would be a back-up band available, but she said no. Oh, and karaoke wasn't an option. I was relatively new to the high school. Though I had a circle of friends, none of them were musicians that could play the guitar or piano. But Mrs. Boyd would take care of this.

She set up a meeting with Rick Tremblay, a Grade 12 student who played guitar. I didn't know too much about Rick except I had heard him play at Variety Night. We weren't in the same social circles. Now we had a month to learn a song for Sescopep and that meant Rick and I had to make time to practice.

The song I chose was by Diana Ross. In hindsight, I realize just how difficult this song was to learn to play on an acoustic guitar. It was also a challenge to sing but I knew I could do it. I played the 45 record over-and-over-again and sang with it. Soon I knew every note, every word, and every emotion by heart. I don't remember if I bought the *More 24 Carat Gold* songbook before or after I learned Rick was going to play. I do know that he borrowed this to get the chords down.

We usually practiced in his parents' basement after school. Rick worked at finding the right key for me to sing it in so that I could reach all the notes without too much strain. When we did our practice run, Rick's Dad Ernie listened in. "Not bad. But can you sing Country?" he asked after we were done. This was a challenge I could meet as I was raised on Country music. However back in the 1970's no teenager would be caught dead admitting that they sang or even liked it. Turns out, Rick had a repertoire of country crooning tunes under his belt as he too was raised on Country. He played guitar with his Uncle Rick and along with Ernie's vocals, they had a few Country standards they played at family get-togethers. The song I sang was 'Your Cheating Heart' by Hank Williams. I remember dialling-up the twang and the yodel notes to add effect. I got Ernie's seal of approval. I really could sing. This opinion held fast for years to come.

The Sescopep event took place at Hanmer High School which is a half-hour bus ride from Chemmy High. I was very nervous as this was the largest audience I had ever sung in front of. Rick was as steady as a rock. He made sure the microphone was set right and that the sound-guys didn't crank-up the volume just because

I was a girl. When I sang 'Touch Me in the Morning' I calmed my nerves by pretending I was singing in my bedroom. I turned off the noise in my over-active imagination and focussed on the lyrics and the melody. It helped that there were a few of my classmates in the audience. I know I did my high school proud. Even though there were no prizes for the entertainment, I'm convinced that my budding Diva performance contributed to CVDCS winning the 'School Spirit' award that year.

Rick too needs full credit for that Sescopep performance. He kept me grounded. Chord by Chord. Even back then, he was an anchor for me. Who knew that this was going to be his future role? Was this when Rick and I started dating? No. He had a girlfriend and I was single and stayed single throughout high school. We did hang out together at the dance that night but nothing more transpired and we went our separate ways. The next time Rick played guitar for me was in 1980—5 years later.

The Spirit of Sescopep came back to life when Rick and I went to see Diana Ross at the National Arts Centre (NAC) on October 3rd, 2018. She was incredible. A true diva. She sang songs from the Supremes, *Lady Sings the Blues* movie and yes, she sang 'Touch Me in the Morning'. I was catapulted in an emotional roller coaster. I had so many flashbacks, so many insights, and so many tears too.

Throughout her program, Rick held my hand and had his arm around my shoulder, my anchor then and now. So yes "Fate brought us together" all those years ago.

Yes, ours was and is a serendipitous love.

THE DAWN OF AURORA

Aurora! The common thought that will likely come to your mind is Aurora Borealis or if you are a Greek mythology buff you'll think of the Goddess Aurora who renews herself every morning and flies across the sky, announcing the arrival of the sun—the Dawn! Then only a select few, maybe you, will think of Aurora a Sudbury folk group. If that's the case then you know the band members: Marcel Bouchard, Brian Crook, Monique Dinel and Rick Tremblay.

The dawn of Aurora is a Chelmsford Ontario based quartet that was not premeditated. It was a combination of different musical journeys that finally came together. Like four single notes creating a perfect chord. Rick, Marcel, Brian, and I are the individual notes that eventually created the harmonious unique sound of Aurora that started in 1982.

Rick, the first unique note, brought forward his experience playing with his band Manella Hemp where he shared lead vocals and was the lead and rhythm guitar player. Though I went to the same high school, I never saw Manella Hemp play. I recently reached out to his bandmate, Perry Guilbeault about the Manella Hemp days. Perry said: "Thanks to Rick if it wasn't for his leadership, this band would have never made it out of the basement." Rick always led the charge to make things happen when music was involved. That held true with Rick & Marcel, Aurora, *Monique & Rick*, Null-Aids, and a series of Open Stages. I think Marcel and Brian would agree that Rick managed the business of getting Aurora off the ground.

Marcel Bouchard, Rick's cousin is the second unique note. Marcel was also a lead singer and rhythm guitar player for a band called Iron Chain. When I heard this band name, I heard heavy metal music playing in my head, but Rick said it was pretty much the same kind of pop-rock music Manella Hemp played. From Rolling Stones, Rod Stewart, Chuck Berry any rock and roll song that would get the girls dancing.

Sometime after college, Rick and Marcel got together and started to write their own music. Between them, they wrote a majority of the original songs that became a part of Aurora's setlist. They would record their music on Rick's Lloyds Stereo system on 8-track tapes. Raw and Real sounds.

Brian Crook, the third unique note, came into the mix when he returned to Chelmsford after graduating from the University of Western Ontario. Brian is a valley boy from Sheenboro-way and the musical influences from that area and his appreciation for Gordon Lightfoot, Murray McLaughlin, Stan Rogers, and John Prine became a source of inspiration for his songwriting and guitar playing. Brian also a singer enjoyed playing his 12-string guitar and yet he was quick to learn the bass when Aurora was forming.

To round out the Aurora Chord, the fourth note is yours truly. Rick and I were dating for two years at this point. During my high school years, I sang at the yearly Variety Nights and when I became a Country Radio Broadcaster, I was asked to be a guest vocalist at various country concerts in the Sudbury area. During this time, Rick was my manager of sorts making sure the sound guys knew about my projection and talked to the band about what key I sang my songs in, another example of Rick's leadership.

When asked why we chose the name Aurora, I could not remember. But Rick did and his explanation makes sense. He reminded me that I was trying to create an anagram using letters from all of our names and I came up with 'oria' (pronounced: ooh-rye-ah) but when I said it aloud it sounded like Aurora. I do indeed use anagrams to this day, to come up with team names. I simply don't remember and we never documented it. However, Rick being a gatekeeper of all things music in our lives and his clear recollection of it, therefore it must be true.

We performed in public only a few times at the New Sudbury Shopping Centre, the Northland Hotel in Chelmsford, and the Hotel Pontiac (aka The Fort) at Fort William, Ontario. The highlight for Aurora would be at the Sudbury Northern Lights Festival in July 1982. Rick and Marcel had prior experience as they did a duet concert the year before and Rick was also a panel member of the Northeastern Ontario Songwriters workshop. This, however, was a first-time experience for Brian and myself.

I clearly remember the promo shot, which we had only a few hours to get into the hands of the festival organizers. Rick's dad Ernie took a few pictures with his black and white Polaroid camera. Several posed shots were taken in the backyard of Rick's apartment. Most of us were in our early 20's trying to pull off the right look. We didn't have a PR team to add any extra polish as they do today.

Aurora (L–R): Rick Tremblay, Monique Dinel, Marcel Bouchard & Brian Crook. Photographer: Ernie Tremblay

To be honest, I don't recall being nervous that day but I do remember Rick being a bit fretful (pardon the pun) as he was making sure we had everything we needed like the setlist, the keys for each song and that Marcel, Brian and Rick's guitars were all in tune. I also recall Rick as Aurora's unofficial emcee and we followed his lead. We played semi-professionally for a year until the summer of 1983 with our last official concert at The Fort. We did have few chances to perform years later but it proved to be difficult as Marcel moved to Guelph and Brian, Rick and I were in Ottawa.

Aurora reflected the various musical experiences from Rick, Marcel, Brian, and I—like four notes in a chord of our lives. We have the recordings, the lyrics, the music, the posters, the pictures, and our memories to mark the dawn of our music in our time. That is the story of Aurora.

MONIQUE & RICK
MUSIC BIOGRAPHY — 1998

This memoir is our labour of love our written story to share with all of you who are curious to know about us. While researching our files, I came across various bio clips written by Rick to promote us during our performance career. This information would appear in press releases, newsletters and promotional packages sent to owners and managers of various entertainment establishments or festival organizers.

Rick, as always had several drafts of our biography handwritten with edits in the margin. Some were one or two paragraphs long and others were more comprehensive. When he was satisfied with the final version, he would make several copies to have on hand along with our business cards, which I designed and printed, and our latest 8" X 10" photo. This is the *Monique & Rick* Bio from 1998, word for word as I want to honour his words, his writing style, and his commitment to our musical journey.

Monique & Rick is an interesting and dynamic Neofolk-rock, singing and songwriting duet who has been entertaining audiences in Ottawa and area since the early 1980s. Their musical collaboration began in Northern Ontario, where each brought with them varied musical interests which ranged a pop spectrum from country to jazz and they were able to grow and evolve in a new environment in Eastern Ontario in the current sound and product that is available today.

Rick & Monique promotion photo. Photographer: Kevin Newman

In 1980, as Rick Tremblay fine-tuned his Folk-rock performing and songwriting skills, Monique Dinel was becoming known locally as a solo performer and radio personality who had a natural ability to sing both Country or Jazz with strength and style of her own. Their collaboration began during this period and they appeared at the Northern Lights Festival Boreal for three consecutive years. Also, during this time Monique continued to appear as a guest performer with many popular Canadian Country artists, such as The Family Brown, Anita Perras & Tim Taylor, Johnny Burke & the East Wind, and Harold MacIntyre with Area Code 705.

In 1983 they moved to Ottawa. Monique & Rick wasted no time re-establishing themselves in the city and surrounding areas, and Monique succeeded in becoming the only top ten finalists in the CKBY Talent Search that year who was to receive a spontaneous standing ovation for her powerful presence and delivery. Monique & Rick continued to perform Folk-Pop songs in Ottawa Clubs and Coffee Houses and this in turn, led to concert, club and Cable TV appearances, some of which include the: Magic In The Music Festivals and regular appearances at the Bank Street Café.

Monique & Rick could be seen and heard performing a broad and eclectic range of musical styles in and around the Ottawa area up until the mid-1990s. At this time public appearances dropped off (save a few) in favour of placing more time and emphasis on presenting themselves as a serious performing and songwriting partnership. Their repertoire now included original compositions of quality and depth and a several professional recordings were made available on Compact Disc. The Other Voices compilation CD from 1992, the earliest foray by the duo, included four songs by the pair which clearly showed a cross-section of their styles and enabled them to receive some airplay. In 1997 the demo-album entitled Renaissance was completed. It included two songs from the Other Voices project set in context with six new demos in such a way that the whole package could be presented as a cohesive and complete work in all aspects including Tempo, Key, Style, and overall Theme. All songs were written to work at a many levels from the basic story told to underlying philosophical themes without being dogmatic and while musically maintaining a Folk, Folk-Rock kind of sound and style.

Audiences with an appreciation for the dynamic vocals, interpretive harmonies, multi-layered lyrics, and just plain fun can be sure to enjoy their music.

As I read this again for the first time in 20-years, I am overwhelmed by Rick's impeccable, impactful, and remarkable communication style. He always chose his words carefully while also ensuring his message would be clearly understood. He did a spectacular job writing the *Monique & Rick* Bio as I'm sure you will agree.

THE CLIPPINGS

I have continued to work on my labour of love project, the Monique & Rick legacy. Right now, that means that I'm knee-deep in a collection of artifacts, collectibles and treasures that Rick and I have gathered over the years. Sometimes this is a little over-whelming. There's an old saying, "one man's trash is another man's treasure." We are enjoying strolling through delights from our past. To anyone else, these piles of memorabilia might look like worthless junk. In our particular 'junk' I continue to find cher-ished memories that capture key events in our time together. Case in point—the musical history of *Monique & Rick* as chronicled in newspaper clippings from the periods 1987 to 1995.

Ottawa Citizen Friday February 8, 1991

These clippings are important to us and worth keeping as they commemorate so many of the events we shared. We were leafing through a small collection of short clippings from the Citizen's Weekender edition and its 'Going Out' section. In this section, the Citizen regularly listed plays, art shows, festivals, etc., that were taking place in the Ottawa area over the weekend and the following week.

Looking closely, you can see the names of the entertainment providers listed. They represented various establishments that featured live music. While many of these bars and restaurants no longer exist many musicians in the '80s and '90s vied for a chance to play at these coveted locations, even for the paltry fee they offered. It was all about exposure, exposure, exposure! This was the only way to be noticed by scouts who might be in the 'music-biz'. YouTube, Google, Facebook, and the internet were not an option, at the time, for self-promotion. Word of mouth and grassroots marketing was the only way to hopefully grow a fan base. Making a buzz no matter what kind, no matter who with and no matter when was crucial.

Rick did 70% of the groundwork to get gigs for our folk-pop duo known as Monique & Rick. It wasn't easy. I initially wrote 80% for the groundwork effort but Rick, the co-author, insisted I change it to 70%. He reminded me of my additional efforts—creating posters on our Compaq computer using the Freelance application, a predecessor, to PowerPoint and word processing. Rick's 70% included talking to hiring managers, and finding additional contacts that might hire us as their musical entertainment.

He also wrote many letters of introduction to owners and managers describing our act. I have copies of two letters sent to Sue McLean the then Manager of The Bank Café. One letter is dated September 6th and the other October 23rd, 1990, another letter is to Joe at Ozzie's Eatery dated March 12th, 1991. Rick kept all his handwritten edited drafts the typewritten version that he had typed on our old Underwood typewriter and finally the word-processing version I'd created in DisplayWrite. In each letter, he carefully noted our experience, recent gigs we played, other services we provided including self-promotion, and he sometimes even listed our repertoire (Table 1).

Then we would wait and hope for the phone to ring. When there wasn't an early response, Rick would follow-up, with yet another letter, or would drop by for a chat when the manager was on-site.

(Table 1: Monique & Rick sample repertoire)

Song	Artist/Composer
Another You	The New Seekers
Try	Blue Rodeo
You Turn Me On (I'm a Radio)	Joni Mitchell
Ain't Misbehavin'	Fats Waller
I'll Feel A Whole Lot Better	The Byrds
Canadian Railroad Trilogy	Gordon Lightfoot
Creeque Alley	The Mamas and The Papas
Unsophisticated Time	Marti Jones
Round Midnight	Williams/Monk
You Were on My Mind	Sylvia Tyson

Like many musicians, we also had day jobs. We may have been dreamers but we also needed to manage the many demands of everyday life. We were 'Realistic Dreamers' trying to find a realistic balance between being secure and indulging our passion for our music. No living a hand-to-mouth existence for us even though we admired those who did brave the obstacles in search of fame and fortune. Some made it. Many more did not. Rick and I weren't die-hard musicians but that didn't stop us from imagining ourselves in starring roles.

These one-inch by one-inch clippings may seem insignificant to an onlooker, still, for us, each word, each ad and each gig is a visible and tangible testimony to our hard work and dedication.

The 'Folk-Pop' duo known as *Monique & Rick* was able to share their love of music with many small and not so small audiences. I like to think that you may have heard and seen us if you happened to wander into the right pub on an evening out.

THE GIGS

Rick and I were an important part of the Ottawa music scene from 1983 until 2005. Our act, *Monique & Rick* had evolved into a unique Folk-Pop combination that fits well into the circuit of solo artists or bands. Getting 'The Gig' and being re-booked for another, was proof that we were making our mark.

When Rick and I weren't at a gig, we busied ourselves by supporting our musical contemporaries. We watched. We learned. We were inspired. There were many musicians that we admired and we sought to analyze what it was that made them so good. Rick would focus on their songwriting and guitar playing. I would watch their delivery and their interpretation of cover songs. This was our 'must-see list' (Table 2) during the '80s and '90s.

(Table 2: Monique & Rick's locale entertainers list)

Catherine Arsenault	Phil Jenkins	Lynn Miles	Terry Tufts
Melwood Cutlery	Diane Jentes	Terry McCann	Toasted Westerns
Guy Del Villano	Russell Levia	Victor Nesrallah	Bruce Wittet
Shawn Ecano	Lisa Levesque	Susan Szathmary	David Wiffen

Sometimes we were present when they hosted open stages around town. We remember well the Jack Purcell Community Centre's Hootenanny. Held every Sunday night, this was an alcohol-free, family-friendly get together with a kitchen-a-la-granola ambiance. Home-baked goods, coffee, tea, and soda could be purchased at a modest price. The audience was genuine and happy to listen to anything. It was a perfect place for musicians to test their material on eclectic audiences of all ages, cultures, and life experiences.

Here we watched the magic unfold. Lynn Miles singing her newly penned heartbreaking songs is firmly etched in my memory. Lynn would become a Juno Award winner. I could claim I'd 'known her when' she was in her early years and still seeking her dream. Terry Tufts was another influence and Rick was blown away by his guitar playing prowess as well as his songwriting. Today he is a sought-after session musician for many Canadian performers. They and everyone listed had a major impact on the oh-so-impressionable *Monique & Rick*. When we sang our originals and covers with these musicians in the audience, it was nerve-wracking, humbling and encouraging, all at the same time. They took time to talk to us, gave us value-added advice and motivated us to continue. How much further would we have gone if we had grown up in Ottawa surrounded by musicians and mentors of this calibre?

Just the same we were lucky to be able to play Gigs at so many locations in the Ottawa area. Mostly we played Friday and Saturday from 9 p.m. to 12 midnight with three 15-minute breaks. We were paid in cash—$200. Some bar owners wanted to pay less and provide a bar-tab. We opted out of that arrangement and paid for our drinks.

Being paid with alcohol just didn't sit right with me. It wasn't a fair exchange for our talent. Though many a musician did accept a bar-tab, some paid the price for it later with slurred vocals, sloppy playing and unsavoury audience bantering. Eventually many became alcoholics, developed a bad reputation, and let their employment melt away. This is a road we avoided. As a vocalist, alcohol is not a recommended lubricant for the pipes. It was tough enough singing in a smoky bar. Adding alcohol to the mix wasn't a smart choice. Rick is an asthmatic and though he grew up in a household of smokers, singing in an oxygen-compromised setting was still tough to deal with. It wasn't until 2005 that bars became smoke-free.

Sometimes we hosted open-stages where we controlled the list of performers. Each would be allowed to play a maximum of three songs. It was a first-come, first perform system. Even so, there would be the odd musician who would try to squeeze in a fourth song, or play three long-winded anthologies stealing time from other performers. We soon learned the fine art of diplomacy especially when temperamental egos were involved. Rick was better at that than I was and could cheerfully get the wannabee-star off the stage to let the next performer have their turn.

There were a lot of trials and tribulations when we performed at a paying gig or on an open stage. One common issue involved the sound guys. Every time Rick and I would go to a bar that had their sound-guy, they would always put the volume up on my microphone. Why? Because I'm a girl. It was infuriating. I wondered how Janis Joplin, Ella Fitzgerald and KD Lang put up with that during their early years.

Monique & Rick performing at Magic in the Music, Ottawa Canada. Photographer: Mary Armellini

Despite Rick's efforts to get the sound-guy to leave the volume alone, they upped it anyway. Rick would shrug and I knew that the sound guy wouldn't listen. As soon as I belted a big note, say from Roy Orbison's 'Crying', the sound guy bolted his hand onto the master volume. It didn't take long for Rick and me to learn the difference between a sound guy and a sound engineer. A sound guy is usually on an ego-trip while a sound engineer is focused on the performance and the craft of music. Rick soon became a sound engineer in his own right. It came naturally to him. He always asked performers what they wanted from a technical standpoint. Rest assured, if a female singer did not want the volume on her microphone upped he would follow-through.

Another annoying issue was the quality of music systems bars had for the musicians versus the quality of the system for the juke-box-style music they played in-between breaks. The quality of the system for musicians was sub-standard, with dirty soundboards, busted up speakers, noisy jacks, damaged cables, and microphones that looked like they were dragged on the floor or used for a game of whack-a-mole. Nevertheless we worked with what we had. We started bringing our microphones for sound quality and hygiene. When the sound system quit or started shrieking with annoying piercing feedback, Rick knew how to troubleshoot. His electronics and electrical background came in handy. Electrical tape was added to our standard kit right along with guitar strings, guitar pics and guitar tuners.

During breaks, staff would up-the-volume on their music system, so much so that patrons had to raise their voices just to be heard. When we got back on stage, we were at a disadvantage because the crowd was now louder than we could be. How did we get around that? Simple! We sang our first song soft and low, keeping it hushed almost to a whisper, so much so that the crowd decreased their speaking volume to a normal conversational level. Gradually the room relaxed and we had their attention for the rest of the set but only until the next break. Then we had to repeat the process all over again, that is unless we were lucky enough to have a musician and part-time bartender behind the bar managing the sound system.

We did experience some quirky situations. In one bar, the stage was right beside the dartboards. Dart games continued while we played our music. As I was closest to the dartboard I was rather nervous, I kept my eye on each dart player and would step towards Rick or the audience just in case. The drunker the dart player, the more panicky I got. The pub owner's wife picked up on my distress and had the game stopped until it was our break. I think she wanted to hear me sing Patsy Cline's 'Crazy', not watch me go crazy with panic.

Then there was the time when the owners of a restaurant-bar asked us if we could cover the breakfast shift on Sunday morning. At first, Rick and I thought they wanted music for their breakfast crowd. Instead, they wanted us to be short-order cooks to make breakfast because they had to go to a funeral and had no staff to replace them. Hadn't they read our bio?

The 21st century arrived and the open stage environment changed. There were fewer places to play and some establishments didn't want to pay open stage hosts and only offered a bar tab. Truth be told, they were now getting free entertainment from musicians. Many installed karaoke machines and that changed the landscape of creativity at the grassroots level. Rick and I managed to maintain our local presence and made new friends along the way. During this time, Rick ventured out on his own, as sound engineer, song collaborator or to share writing co-hosting with other musicians. By now I was travelling a lot with work and couldn't participate. That was tough. In hindsight, I wish I had faced up to my employer and insisted on more flexibility. It's time I lost and can't get back. I couldn't have imagined that in

December 2005 our lives would suddenly take an entirely different direction with significantly different challenges.

I look back at our 25-year musical journey with a sense of pride and awe. *Monique & Rick* were a magical musical duo. Our music is an intensely beautiful element of our legacy. Our music was pure, simple, and genuine.

OTHER VOICES

How do I describe 14 minutes and 62 seconds—a mere soundbite from the *Monique & Rick* soundtrack? A stranger holding the CD *Other Voices – a Musical Cornucopia* may glance at the cover, looking at the local artists listed and they might be curious enough to listen to the music. Our music—our stories told in song.

It was 28-years ago when Alan Chrisman of Rock this Town productions asked Rick and me to be a part, of a project showcasing local artists. This was a low budget adventure on his part. On our part it meant investing in professional studio recordings of our original material. It's important to remember that in 1992 studio-quality recording equipment was hard to come by and costly. It's so much easier today with applications like YouTube, Garage Band, and iMovie, that is available to help musicians record and distribute their songs. Despite the technical challenges, Rick and I were excited to be a part of this project.

Though we were known as a duet act, the bulk of the behind the scenes work was Rick's responsibility. Music is his passion! He spent hours looking at our repertoire of original songs listening to live in-studio recordings taped on a basic Fostex 4-track system. From that effort, Rick came up with a shortlist of songs and between us, we selected the final four.

Being part of the local open stage scene, we met and jammed with other musicians who also dabbled in production. With this new project, Rick contacted Bruce Wittet and Victor Nesrallah at Free Flying Sound to see if they would be available to record our material. Bruce and Victor were very interested and had amazing production and arrangement ideas that would give our songs a professional boost.

I still remember the first day we walked into the studio. Bruce and Victor had laid down the drum and bass tracks working with the raw recordings Rick had given them. Then it was our turn to lay down the vocal and guitar tracks. After a few takes, we listened. Rick and I were truly blown away! It was better than we imagined. We were thrilled! (See The Recordings)

In the days that followed, the four of us explored new arrangements to showcase our material. Rick, who was often critical of his guitar playing, started to change his opinion when Bruce and Victor commented on his technical yet free-flowing playing style. As for me, I surprised myself with unusual intricate vocal harmonies during the recording of 'Yellow Room'.

When I listen to the 14 minutes and 62 seconds of our songs: 'Easy Now', 'She Dances to Dream', 'Magic Pleasure' and 'Yellow Room'—I can feel our energy in every note and I'm so grateful that we were able to capture our voices—our story. When I contacted Bruce Wittet, this was his memory he wanted to share.

Other Voices Bruce Wittet Producer's Diary

What I remember about Rick was: A twinkle in the eye, a look of wonder. And always a genuinely friendly, positive attitude. Rick's outlook was supremely positive and he seemed to exhibit an unconditional faith at what was happening around him, even if, on occasion, he was engaging in something that wouldn't have flowed from his natural druthers.

A rare, genuinely good soul whose questions were not challenges, as so many tend to be on studio sessions, wherein one's material often takes unanticipated directions. Instead, Rick was intent on understanding others' visions and in executing them.

Would that all freelance sessions be populated by the likes of Monique & Rick, happy people who are secure in what they do and yet are willing, and able, to change their approach and not feel as if they've been had; or as if their life's work has been tainted. I remember nothing smacking of artifice; all of it sincere and direct.

My diary revealed this impression "session with Monique & Rick, good folk."

MUSICAL CHRISTMAS WISHES

For hundreds of years on Christmas Eve, Santa and his reindeer have been pulling their magical sleigh as they travelled the globe. For a mere 22-years, Rick and I have travelled in our 4-wheel drive Subaru to North Bay and Chelmsford, Ontario to spend Christmas with family and friends. Only once have we stayed in our Nepean home for Christmas. Even so, I always put up our Christmas decorations in late November so we can enjoy our artificial tree. A real tree has been out of the question. Rick is allergic to evergreens. On the upside, the fake tree drops fake needles. Maybe because it doesn't get enough fake water?

I have always been proud to be a 'four-season kind of gal'. Yes—I love winter. Snowflake proud, I have always hoped that snow would fall by November 1st and continue until December

22nd. I hoped that if it snowed during this timeframe our chances of driving in a snowstorm for Christmas in Chelmsford and North Bay would be reduced. Wishful thinking! Still, I am like a kid thrilled when I see a fresh blanket of white fluffy snow blanketing everything on a fine Christmas morning.

In the past, Rick and I have had the usual pre-Christmas rush of activities, shopping, baking and merrymaking with office parties and pot-luck get-togethers. Decorating has always been more my thing. Rick was the troubleshooting light technician who could spot an offending light bulb within minutes. I wish I had paid more attention because I don't have the patience to fiddle around with lights and wires. Lights aside, the best part of our ritual is putting up our special ornaments, each of which evokes wonderful Christmas memories. Rick's favourites are the guitar, mandolin, harp, and a moose! My favourites are a Santa from 1960, our first Christmas ornament from 1983, icicles and mukluks from Iqaluit.

Once the transformation took place we would relax and watch Christmas movies—*White Christmas*, *It's a Wonderful Life*, *Miracle on 34th Street* and *Polar Express*. I love Polar Express so much that when we visited Santa's Village in 2017, I bought the 'I Believe' Reindeer Bell and the poem:

I Believe[7]

When you believe in Santa's Sleigh,
Miracles on Christmas Day.
That the North Pole's full of tiny Elves
Who make the toys and stock the shelves.
That magic happens Christmas Eve
When you hear the jingle and believe.
Then you're lucky through and through
Because when you believe…
Your dreams come true!

When I hear that and other famous songs or poems, I become a sentimental mush-ball. Rick chuckles when I start tearing up during these movies and is quick to give me a warm hug with a knowing twinkle in his eyes. While I was a Canada Post employee I had volunteered to answer letters to Santa. Between 1983 and 2008 working as Santa's helper, I always looked forward to this tradition. Rick and I would laugh and marvel at the imagination of children. At the same time, I arranged with their parents to have my niece and nephews' letters sent directly to me. Such fun! I had them fooled for years. Now they are adults, some with children of their own. Perhaps I will re-instate the letters to Santa tradition. Rick and I also had our own Christmas tradition. The night before leaving for Northern Ontario, we would open our stocking stuffers and enjoy our special time together.

Every Christmas, Rick and I entertained family and friends. This meant singing Christmas Carols. Rick's dad Ernie, Uncle Rick and Aunt Sue insisted that we do this. For them it wasn't officially Christmas until they heard us sing 'Happy Christmas -War is Over' by John and Yoko Lennon. In 2003, we made a CD called *Musical Christmas Wishes* and recorded our version of that song along with other Christmas standards. Rick suggested presenting this CD as a Christmas gift before we made our trek up north. The pressure was on. We broke into steps everything that needed to be done.

- Step 1:Buy a Christmas karaoke CD;
- Step 2: Lay down the instrumental tracks on the new Tascam recording system;
- Step 3: Determine the order of songs;
- Step 4: Record the vocal tracks;
- Step 5: Create the audio master;
- Step 6: Duplicate CDs; and
- Step 7: Buy a new printer to produce CD labels and covers.

We could have used an army of elves to give us a hand with this production. At the same time, we were babysitting our nephews Nicholas and Ryan. More chaos. Rick decided they should be part of the recording along with their parents' Norm and Joanne, my sister, to sing a few of the songs. We were sneaky. Joanne didn't realize we were recording our sister duet 'White Christmas'. 18 songs were recorded eight of which featured me as lead vocalist. This wasn't an easy undertaking. Karaoke is not flexible with the keys the songs are recorded in. No transposing allowed. At times it felt like vocal acrobatics were in play and you can hear that in our recording of 'Twelve Days of Christmas.'

As director, producer, editor and sound technician, Rick had the greatest responsibility of all. He was wearing many hats monitoring sound levels, adjusting dials, listening for any quirks, sound bleeds, etc. Of course, he also had the tough job of keeping the talent on track. Sometimes the talent can be a bit of a diva!

December 2019, sixteen years later and Rick and I are listening to this CD and the memories are flooding back. I hadn't listened to it in a long while, particularly during the early post-stroke years. Rick lovingly handled the CD case and I think he too is transported back in time. Now we are comforted by its magic—the *Musical Christmas Wishes* of our past still hold for our present as they will in our future. (See The Recordings)

COURAGEOUS CONTESTANTS — SONGWRITERS

Let's be honest, competitions are fun. At one point or another, each of us has probably enjoyed taking part in a competition. It's even better if you win. Unfortunately, contests are usually zero-sum games. Someone will win and others will lose. Guts and gumption will get you to the show and allow you to perform but the outcome is up to the judges.

Rick and I have always been ready to take on a challenge. We've competed in many events throughout our life together. Some were planned and others just happened. I was the one who was the most eclectic and the more intense of the two in acting, public speaking, athletics, scholastics but mostly singing. I worked hard and competed fiercely. Rick, on the other hand, had narrowed his focus to songwriting. His ultimate goal was to reach a level of perfection that would match his standards regardless of the outcome. To this end, he dedicated hours and hours to refining songs that would be worthy of sharing in a competition.

Rick playing his Martin guitar. Photographer: Monique Tremblay

Competition for us was a field of learning and yearning. Continually learning the tactics necessary for preparing and producing beautiful songs. Yearning always to find that perfect combination of sound and sense and message. Yearning always for a win and the potential benefits of that win – money, fame, personal satisfaction and validation of our skills, talent, and the labour required necessary to reach our highest level of achievement.

Rick's first official move into competitive songwriting was for the Sudbury Centennial Songwriting Contest held in February 1983. He and 38 other songwriters vied for a place in this event. The letter he received after the contest stated that: "The entries were very diverse in style, arrangement and lyrical adaptation. Because of the quality of the songs submitted, the song contest jury had a difficult time choosing a winner." But the winning song was 'Happy Birthday Sudbury' to be released in both French and English on a 45 RPM vinyl record with room for one song per side. I didn't get to hear this song, so I was unable to compare it to Rick's 'Sudbury Junction'[8]. The judges may have favoured a simple, catchy tune that would be easier to translate but this is speculation on my part. This leads to the ultimate songwriters' question: Do we write from our hearts or do we try to determine what judges will be looking for when we compete?

Rick had used a historical approach in telling Sudbury's story—similar to Gordon Lightfoot's storytelling style. Rick's 'Sudbury Junction' may not have had the commercial appeal the judges were looking for. Small consolation I suppose but if Gordon had written a song about Sudbury's Centennial it might have suffered the same fate as Rick's 'Sudbury Junction'. Here's the chorus of 'Sudbury Junction':

> A hundred years ago, in North Ontario
> The prospectors came, to strike their claims
> And they left their names in our past.
> Then settlers came also, and a town began to grow
> It began to function, at Sudbury Junction
> And a city started growing that would last.

While putting the original and cover tune lyrics into alphabetical order, I came across several versions of 'Sudbury Junction', further evidence of Rick's work ethic. To my surprise, I found that Rick had given me partial songwriting credit! There was my handwriting on a separate piece of paper. Rick had used a few of my lyrics in the final version. I also uncovered another song Rick had written called *Sudbury's Centennial Song*, one that was not submitted. He had taken lines from that and merged them into Sudbury Junction.

Songs from the Heart for the Ontario Council of Folk Festivals (OCFF) presented another songwriting opportunity for Rick and me in 1995 and 1996. Rick put together a program that included the following songs:

1995	1996
For Being Young and Being Free	For Being Young and Being Free (revised)
Magic Pleasure	Socio-Illogical Blues
She Dances to Dream	The Reception
Yellow Room	

This event was launched to encourage the craft of songwriting, especially for folk and roots music. Each year the jury selected four winning songs and awarded cash prizes for the top two—$300 and $200 respectively. Winners were invited to the annual awards ceremony. In the post-event newsletter, winners were announced and the financial details were shared. There had been 96 song submissions to the OCFF. Each songwriter paid $10 for each song they submitted to the contest. Again, we tried and we didn't win. So, what did we get for the $70? In retrospect, it was a combination of exposure and insight to feed our yearning.

Entering contests and performing original music created a need to protect our work. In 1993, Rick and I joined SOCAN (Society of Composers, Authors and Music Publishers of Canada). Part of their service was a song depository in which they would store up to ten years of our original material. In 1996 Rick submitted nine songs at a total fee of $55 and received a certified registration form. Twenty-four years have long since passed and I have no idea what happened to our songs. It will be another item on the to-do list to follow up with SOCAN to find out.

Between 1998 and 2002 Rick submitted nine songs to the Songwriters Association of Canada (SAC) along with a request for assessment:

Wild as Eden	Snowbound Road
How Many Times	Socio-Illogical Blues
She Dances to Dream	The Reception
Yellow Room	Between the Sun and the Moon

He received several letters and assessments before he wrote again: "I would like to have the songs from the Demo-Project assessed. The other songs that have already been reviewed by SAC, and although I do not fully agree with most of the earlier evaluations, I am still willing to submit the remainder of the project." He went on to describe the recording process as semi-professional because access to a professional studio was not an option. SAC's song critique form evaluated six elements. Each element was graded: Poor, Fair, Good or Very Good:

Packaging	Lyrics
Demo	Music
Structure	Commercial Appeal

Rick continued to write: "The program material presented on this disc is arranged in such a way that the songs follow a premeditated, albeit timeless theme where each tune is set with consideration toward its key, tempo and concept. Also, the lyric of any particular song can stand on its own, each with an individual blend of enigmas, abstractionisms, imagery, irony, metaphors, and euphemisms."

After reading the early assessments by the Songwriters Association of Canada I can see why Rick wanted to request a second assessment. This time the SAC responded with a more comprehensive and balanced review. Previous feedback had focused on professional production versus the songs themselves. Here are the positive highlights:

- Demo better than most. This is an artist's demo.
- Good sense of songwriting.
- Instead of a standard song, you have created a piece.
- Some of the best songs ever are enigmatic.
- The acoustic and voices sound great.
- There is a fierce, progressive nature and spirit at work here.
- Vocals are very passionately sung.

They did have concerns about:

- Low commercial potential.
- These are literary considerations but not commercial song considerations.
- The material defies assessment by the critique outline SAC offers.
- The material is not trying to be commercial. It defies the universal standards of mainstream material.

How does a judge evaluate 'commercial potential'? Leonard Cohen said: "I've done 12 albums very few of which were commercial successes. I'm not interested in an insurance plan for my work." In CBC's *From The Vaults*[9] there is a 50-year-old TV clip from *Take 30* when Cohen expanded this view, "The modern-day poet-minstrel is more interested in literary value versus monetary value in his work." Rick has the same mindset. I believe that Leonard Cohen would have empathized with or understood Rick's existential dilemma. Both would remain unbending regardless of popular appeal. More literary than commercial? So be it!

Eventually, Rick applied for a talent demo award with FACTOR (Foundation to Assist Canadian Talent on Records). Their feedback was similar to that of SAC. They too focused on sales potential and radio airplay.

We had no choice but to accept the decisions of our judges. We had worked to our criteria and they to theirs. Songwriter, his co-writer, and his favourite vocalist were left still well pumped with the courage to compete, to learn and to grow, and the gumption to make it happen regardless of the outcome.

COURAGEOUS CONTESTANTS
– SINGERS

The Oxford dictionary[10] defines a singer as a person who sings. That's me plain and simple. I sing. When I sing, I am in a dream world, a world where I am free to be me. Self-confidence radiates from every song, every note, every word, and every emotion. Singing has been my safety zone. 'I sing therefore I am.'

I found this refuge when I was 7-years-old. I didn't recognize it as such at the time and only became aware of its true significance as a teenager. Singing has always been my go-to position any time I felt uncertainty in my young and impressionable life. It is still my primary 'go-to' comfort zone.

In January 1966 my family moved from Val Caron to Levack, Ontario, towns that are 50 km apart. I was 7-years-old and had been in the Grade 2 class at the Notre Dame de L'Espérance French Catholic School. Now I was a student at Levack Public School. An English only school and a language I couldn't speak a word of! There I was, a new school, no friends, and no older siblings to guide me. Dad spoke both languages and Mom was French-speaking with minimal English. They did their best to help with my transition, but they also had my 5-year-old brother Mike and my 1-year-old sister Joanne to care for. Dad had a new job in a new town along with all of the usual challenges, of raising a young family. I struggled. The report cards from Val Caron were proof of my capabilities as a student. However, at Levack Public School I quickly went from A's & B's to C's & D's—with one exception. One grade stayed put—Music. Despite my serious scholastic challenges my singing was intact. I did not understand the lyrics but was able to memorize the words phonetically. Melodies were not a problem.

Mrs. Rita Zubak was the music teacher for several schools in the area, including St. Charles Public School and Rick was one of her students. She encouraged all of her students to participate in the school choir. As fate would have it both Rick and I did join the choir. Mrs. Zubak was my teacher, choirmaster, voice-coach and more importantly—my mentor. She was the one who convinced the school administrators to let me stay in Grade 2. I would have otherwise been put back to Grade 1. She leveraged my love for music to help me learn English. It was at that point, that I latched on to music as urgently as I would have grabbed the side of a swimming pool to save me from drowning. I worked hard and successfully graduated to Grade 3.

By the time I reached Grade 5 in 1970, Mrs. Zubak was certain that I was ready to compete at the Onaping-Levack Music Festival as a solo performer. I was thrilled. I remember practising the test piece 'On Counting Sheep'[11]. Today I still remember some of the lyrics and all of the melody.

When you are very tired and you cannot seem to sleep,
Have you ever tried to count a flock of woolly sheep?
You must close your eyes and try this very simple game,
Count a flock of sheep as they go running down the lane.

All contestants in the 10-years and under category had to sing that test piece in front of the Adjudicator. I can still see this bespectacled old gentleman sitting behind a table, music sheets in front of him and a red pen in his hand at-the-ready to circle every mistake. Just before I was to sing, he had peered over his glasses with a fixed stare and signalled Mrs. Zubac, my accompanist, to start playing. With my hands clasped in front of me, my back erect and my feet in a T-shape stance, I eased into the opening bars and my dream world. The beady-eyed adjudicator was now invisible. I was with a flock of woolly sheep.

I had been the first contestant to sing and I don't recall how many there were after me. What I haven't forgotten, however, is the tension I felt as we waited to hear who had won. Only when all of the runners up had been acknowledged then the winner named. Me? I had won! Mrs. Zubac hugged me and stunned as I was she had to push me onto the stage to accept my certificate.

I received a 1st place certificate complete with evaluation notes from Lorne Willets, the adjudicator: "Beautiful singing—lovely tone and words. Phrasing good—a very natural presentation of the song." I treasure these words to this day. There were other grade school competitions and I remember singing 'Queen Anne's Lace' in one of them but no other details. I never competed in another structured formal competition.

My singing safety zone came to my rescue once more the year our family moved to Chelmsford, Ontario. 'Déjà vu' here I was again, a new school, no friends, and no older siblings to guide me. The language barrier was gone but teenage angst had taken its place. In the *Yesterday Once More* chapter I further explored the role that singing has played in my life.

From 1979 to 1980 I attended Canadore College in North Bay, Ontario and enrolled in the Radio-Broadcasting program. It was a busy time. My schedule of courses and the On-Air shifts at CRTV left me little time for other activities. I did create a few commercial jingles for my copywriting class and these might still be on the reel-to-reel tapes that I have. What the jingles were about I can't remember. I guess being a budding radio announcer and producer of sorts fed my continued desire to be part of the performing arts.

With college over, I moved back to Sudbury and started my new job as the music programmer for CIGM-FM. I was behind the scenes at that time, no on-air shift yet, but I did have the opportunity to do commercial voice-over work. It was during this time that I reconnected with Rick and my music. Now I had a partner who shared my passion for music. When I finally got my on-air show, other opportunities to sing came forward in tandem with the master of ceremonies (MC) work I was expected to do, without pay I might add, for the radio station. There was the odd singing contest sponsored by local bars but mostly I sang as a guest host for country-based concerts. During this time, I continued to develop my performance personae—Home-Town Girl.

The Home-Town Girl days drew to an end when I was let go from CIGM-FM resulting from major lay-offs by INCO and Falconbridge mines. As in any one-industry town when it shuts down, everyone is affected. Off I went to follow my heart—Rick! We moved to Ottawa in 1983. Music continued to be my safety zone but this time Rick was by my side. *The Clippings* and *The Gigs* chapters of this memoir paint a picture of our early years.

I can't remember all of the singing contests I participated in but there are a few notable ones: CKBY Country Talent Search in 1983, Ontario Open Country Singing Contest in 1993, and Canada Post Idol Contest in 2004. Contests continued to be zero-sum games. Someone won and the rest lost. It's all about guts and gumption and the chance to perform—and perform I did.

I was one of the finalists at the CKBY Country Talent Search contest. The contest that year required all finalists to win a preliminary contest at one of the participating bars. I won a place and represented the Bayshore Hotel. Back then original music was discouraged and judging panels preferred cover versions. I provided two songs to the back-up band and was able to practise with them ahead of time. I can't remember with 100% certainty the songs I sang and neither can Rick, but our instincts say it was probably 'Two More Bottles of Wine' by Emmy Lou Harris and 'Blue Bayou' by Roy Orbison.

Monique competing at CKBY Country Talent Search contest. Photographer: Mary Armellini

I was competing against Lynn Miles who did cover songs as well, even though she had some solid original material in her repertoire. The judging criteria were based on overall talent, stage presence, and voice or instrumentation. When all the performances were completed, the judges deliberated and announced the winner. As you might expect they said it was a 'tough decision'. The winner that was selected was chosen not because he had won in each of the judging criteria areas but rather because he had played an original composition! Lynn and I shared a glance and knew then that a fix was on. Many of us complained because we had been told "no original material allowed" but that had not been in writing. In the following years of the contest, a fourth criterion was added—Originality. The process was also changed requiring contestants to submit tapes instead of winning a contest held at a local establishment. I don't remember trying to compete for the CKBY contest after that, as my trust in fair play had been severely shaken.

In August 1993, I competed in the Ontario Open Country Singing contest in Navan, Ontario. The female open category started at 19-years of age and up and there were 150 contestants registered. Most were from the Ottawa area, but 30% came from Southern Ontario. I was 34-years-old at the time, had experience and confidence, so I figured I had a good chance of winning.

I did one slow tempo and one fast tempo song as required. They had six judges scoring against nine criteria that fell into four major categories: Sound Quality, Interpretation, Presentation and Stage presence. Based on my scorecard for the two songs I was awarded 518.67 - 28.41 points above the average of 490.26 and 131.33 points short of perfect—650 points. However, all the judges had hit me with a 5-point deduction for a three-chord guitar break. This rule had not been posted. Other first-time contestants complained about this omission as well. My written feedback was direct – "Great strong voice!" I knew I had nailed it because after, each song that I performed, I received a standing ovation. Fans came by and asked me to sign their program. They expected me to be in the finals. Surprise—I wasn't.

This experience was similar to the 2002 Olympics when Jamie Salé and David Pelletier were robbed of gold due to suspicious judging. In the end, they got to share the Gold medal with Russia and the judging system was revamped. You may think that I have a case of sour grapes, but a seasoned performer knows when they have aced a performance; not just in their mind but also because of the audience's reaction. Of the eight judges, one had in particular recorded dramatically lower scores. I still have a computer-generated report. Rick was furious. Normally cool and controlled, he saw the injustice in this judging system. He wasn't the only one. Strangers followed us to the parking lot as we walked to our car. Many were angry and wanted to let us know. Then one particular person came forward after everyone else had left and explained why, based on his experience, this had happened. He pointed out that none of the finalists were first-timers. They all had had to pay their dues at other Ontario Open Country Singing contests. They had also been excluded from the finals until they had invested a certain amount in entry fees. The jig was up.

Had Facebook existed back then, this kind of contest rigging would have generated a lot of negative press for the organizers. I don't know how much longer they operated, or if there was even truth to the dues-paying accusations, but I never returned. I was angry not just for myself but also on behalf of the other contestants that I felt had deserved a better result. They were younger and may have had their dreams and their trust shattered. What I did know was that I was a winner in the eyes of the honest, country music fans. They'd enjoyed my songs and that would be reward enough for me.

I stopped competing for 11-years until the Canada Post Idol Contest on November 9 & 10, 2004. This was a quasi-version of the Canadian Idol contests popular between 2003 and 2008. The main purpose of the event was to raise funds for the United Way Campaign to highlight Canada Post talent and entertain employees.

While cleaning up our basement clutter, I came across the DVD of that contest and the Canada Post Rising Star Award I received. Rick and I sat down to watch the contest. Rick reminded me that he hadn't been there. Though he wanted to be he couldn't take the time off work. Only the second day of the contest was recorded. I had completely forgotten that it was a two-day contest. All 10 contestants were on stage, and the Top 5 were announced in alphabetical order. I said to Rick, I don't remember if I made the final. Tension all over again and then I knew I'd 'made the cut'. I have no idea why I had forgotten this.

When Tim McGurrin the MC introduced me as Ms. VentureOne™[12], he mentioned that the song I sang on Day 1 was 'Long Long Time' by Linda Ronstadt. Another blip in my memory so I'm grateful he mentioned it. The Day 2 song I chose to sing was 'Crying' by Roy Orbison, in which I had channelled my inner KD Lang. While watching my performance, I glanced over to Rick. He was focused, hand on his chin and I think he was holding his breath while I sang the big notes. When I was done, he simply looked at me with a proud smile on his face.

I received a standing ovation. The Day 2 Judges were Max Keeping from CTV, Jeff Mauler & Scott Rush from Hot 89.9 Radio, and Judy Follet the organizer of this event. Listening to their comments so many years later was both humbling and inspiring. Max said, "You just did an amazing job. I think you should use your marketing expertise to get into show business." Scott Rush added, "The main thing I really liked is that you looked like there was no other place you would rather be than performing." Then his co-host Jeff Mauler humorously added, "a little more passion next time." The best compliment came from Judy, "You nailed it. That was absolutely amazing."

After all, five contestants sang their songs and received their Canada Post Rising Star Award comments from the judges, it was up to the audience to vote. Vote they did, using electronic resolvers and they picked their favourite. I knew to go into this contest that winning would be based not only on talent but also on popularity. No, I didn't win, but I was proud of my performance.

Over the years, I have proved to myself over and over again that I am truly a singer. There is a part of me in every song I sing and it's a gift I treasure and I am glad to share with anyone who wishes to listen.

AURACALYPSE SOUND

Music and everything associated with it courses through Rick's veins. He has perpetually gravitated to music—inhaling it like fresh spring air. He sought out opportunities to play or to immerse himself in music's tantalizing pull. If he found none at hand he created it. In the 1990's Rick dabbled in a home-based indie production business. He was a wannabee self-taught music engineer, producer, and promoter, always aiming for the perfect mix. I don't think I'm exaggerating when I say that Rick spearheaded a movement to get musical talent out of kitchens and basements and into the local bar scene.

When asked what his number one takeaway from the various jam-sessions he had organized, his response was, "It was a lot of work, but worth it!" It was work that he loved. His primary reason for setting up a stage for musicians to perform on was to create a pleasant night out for family and friends to kick back and listen to live music. Of course, there was also the off chance that some local talent scouts might drop by and discover the new talent. Rick was a natural leader who excelled at making things happen. He never bragged and never sought compensation or recognition. I truly believe that if he hadn't instigated the four Null Aids, Eager Beaver Jam Session, and a series of Special Open Stages they would never have happened.

The work was relentless and selfless. There were many steps involved in finding a venue, selecting dates, negotiating payment for equipment rentals, contacting the musicians, finalizing the line-up, and promoting the event. Rick was continually on the phone with his musical contacts or meeting with them to go over the technical details. Many of the musicians he knew were itching to play outside of their kitchens, even for free. However, a free drink or two was also welcomed. I assisted with promotion by creating simple posters that Rick and I would put up around the venue. I also gave copies to the musicians encouraging them to further spread the word. Practice sessions often took place at our home but mostly in Bob & Joyce McKenna's kitchen on Delaney Street because it was central for those who lived in the Arnprior-Renfrew area.

There were four Null-Aid concerts during the '80s, the last one in 1989. The name Null-Aid was chosen as they were not a benefit of any kind. The idea came from Live-Aid. The main, yet small venues, were Den's Diner and one held at Zaphod Beeblebrox. Each time the bars were filled. Doug McKenna, a member of the Snortin' Roadhogs, remembers that Den's Diner ran out of alcohol for one of the Null-Aids. The Snortin' Roadhogs also included Bob McKenna, Rolly Bernier, Brian Crook, and Derick Fernie. All of the Snortin' Roadhogs wore pig noses, except Brian who sported a phallic member. Maybe he didn't get the memo? Also, in the line-up was Scott Wright, Michael Gaines & the Crying Cowboys, and of course *Monique & Rick* who were also the MCs.

Band names could change from year to year. The Snortin' Roadhogs repertoire was a combination of country bluegrass. When they changed their repertoire to Irish Celtic music they became Pagan Heart. Aurora also played at one Null-Aid when Marcel Bouchard made a special trip from Guelph, Ontario and reunited with Brian, Rick, and me. At the Eager Beaver Jam session, we created a quartet called the Canadian Tapestry that included Bob McKenna, Brian, Rick, and me. The poster describes our group as a cross-pollination of music that could be enjoyed in any Canadian kitchen.

At most of these events as at many others, Rick was involved with the sound equipment and made sure to rent the best choice for instruments like the violin and mandolin that needed special receptive conditions. We regularly loaded up our Subaru with amplifiers, mixers, speakers, speaker stands, microphones, stands, cables and recording equipment. So, I was a roadie as well as a singer. I was also a pro at setup and tear-down. I learned from the best—Rick!

Rick was a self-taught recording engineer. He wanted to record everything he could and mix the sound on the spot. He was quick to troubleshoot any technical problems, from feedback to buzzing strings or defective cables. Everything was done to make the playing experience problem-free for the musicians. He was always 'on it' nothing escaped his attention. Evidence of his recording commitment is found in the hundreds of cassettes, CDs, VHS tapes, Hi8 tapes and yes 8-track cartridges stored in our basement music room. I had no idea of the number of versions of recordings he had made until I went through all the special plastic boxes in our basement. Rick experimented with raw recordings, editing and remixing using different techniques. I was intensely concerned that many of these recordings, particularly those on cassette tapes, would be lost. I could not allow this to happen. Rick's legacy would need to be saved before it was too late.

I was fortunate to find out from Stella Castenada, a Management Development Program for Women (MDPW) Toastmaster, that her son Nick was a Music Industry Arts graduate from Algonquin College, and that he might be able to help. I wasn't sure what this would entail but Nick felt confident that re-recording Rick's work from several analog sources to a digital source could be done. It was quite a learning experience for all of us. Nick took the time to explain the process to both Rick and I. Rick was intrigued by the new digital recording technology. Now everything was in one place on a laptop instead of many individual physical pieces using a variety of recording mediums. Here's what Nick had to say about working on our project.

> *"Working with Monique & Rick's old recordings was an absolute pleasure. I was asked to convert analog recordings to digital, in a quest for Monique to back up and also rediscover the music they created over the years. The volume of recordings was extensive and predominantly included original compositions. There were some cover tunes, which were instantly recognizable as they both had good taste in covering the classics.*
>
> *Monique & Rick's musical endeavours came at a time when analog media was king and I got to learn some of the equipment that they used like an 8-track player. I had never used one before. It was really cool! Being able to digitize their old recordings was a unique experience for me. I used my high-end software and hardware to capture these recordings and I'm quite happy that I was given the opportunity. These recordings can now live on forever!"*

It is very comforting to know that most of our recordings have been converted and that they can still appeal to the younger generation.

In 2003, Rick had a dream. It was to start his own home-based indie production company and it would be called Auracalypse Sound. The name was derived from our folk group Aurora (*Aur*) and Apocalypse (*acalypse*) which is Greek for 'revelation of knowledge'. Only Rick the philosopher would come up with such a distinctive name. Auracalypse Sound appeared on the *Monique & Rick Soulessence Live '91* CD. Recently I discovered that Rick had never officially registered the name. Getting it registered has been added to the Monique & Rick Legacy Project 'to do' list. To quote Rick, "it will be a lot of work but it will be worth it." The songs of *Monique & Rick* will play on.

LOVE IS THE MUSIC

Love and Music have been bound together with the hearts of two people. *Monique & Rick's* story is infused with an intense love for each other and for the music we have performed or created. The stories I've shared with you about this love and this music can only go so far. Now you need to hear our songs and discover their depths and meanings in your way. Then you can draw your own conclusions as to the nature of our melodic alliance. Perhaps you have had a chance to hear us live or on a CD. Perhaps you weren't born yet during our most active period. Perhaps you will be amazed by what you now discover.

In previous chapters, I have related the story behind the *Other Voices* and *Christmas Wishes* recordings. We had also created other CDs that demonstrated our music from two unique perspectives, the *Soulessence Live '91* and *Renaissance* from 1996. These are two vastly different projects that demonstrate the range of our creativity. Recently I reviewed the liner notes on the *Soulessence Live '91* CD. Our descriptions have stood the test of time.

> *These LIVE recordings were cut at two separate venues March 23, 1991, at the Bank Street Café, and April 5-6, 1991 at the Hintonburgh Café. Monique and I had only recently agreed to re-emphasize folk and folk-pop, in our repertoire to help us secure downtown Ottawa gigs. It worked. These renditions come from sets that were still evolving and although more new songs were added and the sound got even better over the next few years, these are the only recordings that remain from that period. So, this cross-section of material gives a sample, or a sound byte of who and what we were at that place and time, even if it isn't as complete as I would have liked it to be. Hey, Live is Live. – Utterly Rick.*

> *Ditto to what Rick has written above. Equally important was the support we had from our family and friends before, during and after the Soulessence period. Sometimes they were our only audience. It was a musical bonding period that Rick and I will always appreciate and will never forget. Rick, I willingly and proudly admit, was the driving force behind the energy and tenacity needed to keep our musical duo alive and constantly striving for our personal best. To those who know him best it's the ultimate musical parking lot tour. As I type in my contribution to the liner notes, he is playing and practising in his musical sanctuary. Thank you, Rick, for being who you are and sharing the journey*

with me. As for you, dear reader (and hopefully fan), enjoy the music and hopefully, you will see the essence of the soul. Musically yours, Monique.

(See The Recordings)

After all these years, I am still mystified by the way Rick's mind works. My philosophical and complex husband looks at things with more intensity than I do. So, it wasn't surprising when he came up with a concept album featuring our original songs and focusing on a particular theme. He called it *Rational Intuition & Metaphysical Pragmatics*. That title went 'right over my head'. I had no clue as to his intentions. I had to ask questions as we discussed that title: "Who is going to understand this title? How can I explain its meaning to others, when I don't understand it myself?"

Having 'heady' discussions with Rick could be exhausting and eventually I pleaded my case and Rick considered simplifying the title. I recently came across a revised CD cover and the name was changed to Blue Horizon but that didn't make the final cut either. I forgot about that attempt. Rick felt it wasn't conceptually accurate to the theme. I agreed. So, Rick went back to his music room and he muddled over what the new title would be. Maybe the idea came to mind when he looked at the PEI Sunrise photo we had taken on one of our vacations. Or maybe the idea dawned on him while writing his *New Age Manifest* as the CD liner notes. Rick doesn't remember exactly how it happened but the Monique & Rick's first-ever concept album was entitled *Renaissance*. (See The Recordings)

With a simplified yet thought-provoking title, Rick wanted to provide a story behind each song and how they connected. I had never truly appreciated that each song was part of a larger story until I read his notes:

New Age Manifest by R.C. Tremblay

'Wild As Eden' *...the legacy of Prometheus.*

Whereas the Trickster brings fire and civilization to the creature, and this being is one man as he is all of woman and man, and whereas he begins to recognize himself and his plight, then he is fallen. However, Eden is not lost, only innocence, and consciousness is gained.

'How Many Times' *... can you be wrong?*

This he asks himself as he stumbles through his confusion and new-found ignorance. He grapples with his soul and his sensuality, reaching into the sky and falling again and again into the sand, to find the only peace is peace of mind through love.

'The Reception' *...she will receive him.*

She gives him a reason and he is inspired. This selection is natural and successful labour will provide rewards. Through generations, the river runs.

'For Being Young and Being Free' *...the dissolution of his rationale.*

The process of selection is perpetual and all newcomers may qualify. Someone falls from favour but spiritual love is not forgotten and remains eternal. Dreams and fantasy fill the void.

'Socio-illogical Blues' *...forty days and forty nights are insufficient.*

How many times can you be wrong before your soul is gone? Primal semi-spiritual confusion is replaced by semi-civilized socio-political cynicism. Disenchantment rules, but maturity brings a new peace and clarity of conscience via a new motif. The natural state of blues is now recognized as a cause for action as well as love.

'Yellow Room'...*the ideal prophetic intuitive.*

There are so many paths that lead him down to where demons must be purged and from which the way back is not always clear. Into the depths resonates the sound of the reasoned intuitive which helps to light the way back to that place where comfort may still exist. All is not lost.

'Between the Sun and the Moon'...*the vulnerable refuge.*

Here there is a plea for reassurance. Comfort appears to be attainable and it alone remains unchanged. All that we have is here before us and destiny is ours to decide.

'Magic Pleasure'...*without superstition there is but one magic.*

The pursuit of this magic is not without cost in the currency of the soul, but there is comfort here and life force resides here as well. Who should receive retribution who has harmed none but himself, for this he alone must achieve personal salvation.

So, if you are philosophically minded I will assume this New Age Manifest was an intriguing read for you, right? If you struggled, then welcome to Philosophical Enlightenment 101. Since 1996, I've grown in wisdom and understanding and now Rick's Manifest has become clearer.

As mentioned, *Soulessence Live '91* and *Renaissance* are two vastly different projects that exhibit the range of our creativity. Are you intrigued? Do you want to listen to these albums? I hope you do get the chance. As part of our Legacy project, I plan to make our music available through a social media platform and a website that will make our creative work available. Then you will be able to listen to our music and we hope that it will draw you into the magical world of our lifelong dedication to music and each other.

TAKE MY HEART

TAKE MY HEART IS entwined within every stitch of our story quilt. Every beaded song title, every detailed chord, and every black and white photo. It is the story of how we met and how we grew as a couple heartbeat by heartbeat. Our story as mirrored through the eyes of love.

BORN TO RUN IN A 10-CENT TOWN

It was Friday, June 6th, 1980 the night our Heart Song was *'Born to Run in a 10-cent town'* to an unsuspecting twosome. We didn't know it then, but we weren't simply memorizing songs by heart, but it was our hearts that was leading us to our unique song.

It happened at the Chelmsford's Western Day's inaugural event held at the local arena. The Master of Ceremonies was CIGM-FM's newest, youngest and first female Country radio personality. A Home-Town Gal, a CVDCS High School Alumni and a Canadore College Radio & TV graduate the one and only Monique Dinel. That's me the newly minted celebrity in Canada's Hard Rock Town.

I felt very comfortable on stage, introducing the performers, doing live commercial breaks and working with the event organizers. I was in my element as the Master of Ceremonies. I had recently moved back to my childhood home and it was five houses away from the arena so it would be like old times walking to the rink with my gear for figure skating and ringette. Except for this time, I am decked out in traditional western wear. Black cowboy hat, black-country boots by Boulet, tight-fitting boot cut jeans, western blouse 'a la Dolly Parton' and of course the big country hairdo! I could barely contain my excitement to meet the gang from Chemmy High and catch-up on the latest gossip.

My excitement was dialled down, like the volume on the radio, when I looked around the crowd and didn't recognize a single face. I felt like a stranger. My friends must have all moved away or stayed home or were working underground in the mines. But the show must go on. After all, I had a job to do as a bonus I was invited to be a guest vocalist. I never turn down the chance to sing.

The song I sang was 'It Doesn't Matter Anymore' written by Paul Anka and made popular by Buddy Holly. I preferred the 1974 country-rock version by Linda Ronstadt one of many of my make-believe vocal teachers. While singing and channelling my inner-Linda, I searched the audience to find someone, anyone, to feed my emotional connection with the song. Then a magic chord was struck, I locked eyes with a Chemmy High guitar player— Rick Tremblay. I had found 'my someone,' and Rick was with me— note for note, word for word!

Between MC breaks, Rick and I chatted about what we were up to since graduating from Chemmy High. Rick had been two grades ahead of me, so we hadn't run in the same social circles and had not been high school sweethearts. But he was my guitarist and I was his vocalist, for one song at the Sescopep School Spirit event that included all Sudbury area high schools.

The Chelmsford Western Days event was over that night—but we weren't. It felt like a new song was beginning and I had to follow my instincts and guarded optimism. Rick invited me to his apartment and I said YES—no hesitation, no second thoughts.

Rick and I were sitting on his well-worn plaid couch, drinking red wine and listening to music. We were captivated. We talked about everything. How certain songs and artists seemed to be able to say what we wanted to say in a song. Rick was sharing his song-writing experience and his dedication to find the right words to say, while I never even considered the possibility of writing. I was a vocal interpreter of songs. Next thing I knew, Rick was showing me some tips about songwriting and the artists that he wanted to emulate and I would point out variations on vocal delivery. It was as if we had created a language all of our own that night that only we understood.

We shared our dreams, our frustrations and our feelings through our musical tastes. I remember vividly when Rick introduced me to Bruce Springsteen's *Born to Run* album from 1975. He had an intimate knowledge of Bruce's songwriting style and the influences of Bob Dylan, Joe Cocker and Leon Russell. I felt I was in Songwriting School, being taught by a handsome, budding and enlightened songwriter and I was the eager student mesmerized by his passion. I shared my appreciation for Emmylou Harris's *Quarter Moon in a Ten Cent Town* album from 1978 that I had borrowed from the radio station where I was working on a segment to feature the album. Emmylou was another one of my make-believe vocal teachers and she had her style of interpreting songs. At that time, she hadn't tried her hand at songwriting yet, but she, like me, knew a good song when we heard it and made it her own. I remember showing Rick how to improve the projection of his voice.

Like a jukebox dropping one song at a time, Rick and I rattled on and on about Bruce Springsteen, Emmylou Harris, Bob Dylan, Leonard Cohen, Janis Ian, Joni Mitchell, Rod Stewart, Anne Murray, Ian & Sylvia Tyson, Mammas and the Pappas, Karen Carpenter and many more. We talked about everything and how sometimes we felt most at home sitting in our living room and simply listening to music and reading the lyrics.

Solitude in music soon became a joint partnership in music that eventually grew to a loving relationship. When asked what our favourite song is, it's like asking me which note I prefer to sing or which chord Rick prefers to play. One can't exist solely on its' own. It needs the complement of all musical influences to be a complete soulful repertoire that truly has a profound impression.

The *Monique & Rick* setlist contains many of the musical influences we spoke of that June night in 1980 and it's the foundation of our Heart Song. Our hearts led us to our unique song. 'Born to Run' with a 'Quarter Moon in a Ten Cent Town' is one example of that. Yes, the magic chord was struck for both Rick the songwriter, and Monique the vocal interpreter and it transformed the unsuspecting twosome into a genuine duet.

NINE YEAR TEST DRIVE

I wish I had had the foresight to be more consistent and dedicated to my diaries, my journals, and the stories of my earlier life. There have been many attempts and false starts to record our day-to-day stories. January 1st to September 1st, 1979; September 22nd to October 1st, 1983. Rick kept a diary in November 1979. We did keep two vacation diaries in July 1981 and July 1999.

Recently, I browsed through some of these early journals. At times I recall what Lucy-Maud Montgomery wrote about her early journals, those penned before the age of 9 and commented: "I burned these as they were full of drivel."[13] I think a similar fate is in store for my journals. The journals that I was more diligent with cover the Stroke Years starting from December 2005 to the present. At first, these were visitor's journals that were kept by Rick's bedside for when people came to visit. Then it changed into journals for medical care information as the number of Rick's visitors dwindled. The journals then evolved into a caregiver's insight and a wife's letters to her stricken husband. These journals tell a story that will be a separate memoir when I'm ready to write it.

I am digressing, so let's get back on track.

Rick and my writing styles are vastly different. Our songwriting is evidence of that. His style is more complex and contemplative while mine is simpler and more straightforward. One thing we do share is our love of detail. Our journal entries are full of details. Rick's entries would not only mention the date but the start and end times of particular tasks he undertook that day. I would mention what I was wearing, who I was with and what I was feeling.

As I write this memoir, I continue to wish we had kept better records of our early life together. Now I've realized that we do, indeed, have records. There are tons of stories languishing in storage boxes full of precious mementos—music posters, keepsakes, photo albums, VHS tapes, DVDs, Hi8 tapes, reel-to-reel, cassettes, 8-tracks, newspaper articles, yearbooks, set-lists, and letters. Our basement and guest bedroom accommodate a chaotic mess of paraphernalia. Now I'm trying to organize that mess into logical categories.

One thing that stands out is that Rick and I have two different viewpoints and two different life experiences. Yet we two became one, step-by-step, always careful not to tread on the other's independence. This partnership took time to build.

After reconnecting at Chelmsford Western Days in June 1980, Rick and I got to work knowing each other and ourselves simultaneously. Nine years of living together were our *Test Drive Years*. We didn't plan this; it just happened that way. Sometimes, when we couldn't clearly express our feelings, a song would do the job. It could be a cover tune or a self-penned composition. Rick excelled at composition. He'd built up volumes of material. That some songs were re-crafted at least 10 times was something I discovered when later I organized his files. Layers of complexity led the listener to contemplate the message. He had many mentors – especially Leonard Cohen, Bob Dylan, Neil Young and John Lennon. I am an interpreter. I will sing any style of music as long as I can connect with the lyrics and the emotions it brings out in me. My influences run the gamut, Billie Holiday, Ella Fitzgerald, Diana Ross, Emmylou Harris, Linda Ronstadt, Patsy Cline, Anne Murray, Karen Carpenter, and KD Lang. All of these women are interpreters of songs first-and-foremost.

Our test drive truly began when we started living together in 1982. We had moved to Ottawa. Life was exciting, frustrating, and frightening, all at the same time. Rick had moved to Ottawa earlier than I when Falconbridge Mines laid him off. Sudbury had become known as the Unemployment Capital of Canada. That is what happens in a one-industry hard rock town. There were hard times for everyone including Radio Announcers. Now I was faced with a decision. Would I suffer being laid-off or would I take a cut in pay? I was making $3.15 an hour and the minimum wage was $3.10. As a Nickel miner's daughter, my decision was worth a whopping 5 cents—pocket change. I followed my instincts and my heart. I packed up what little I owned and drove to Ottawa in my 4-speed bright blue Chevette.

Now Rick and I were both unemployed, taking a chance on a new city, a new career, and our mostly untested relationship. Our first apartment was at 883 Somerset Street West, shared with our roommate Kevin Newman, also a Chemmy High alumnus. The apartment building was in the middle of Chinatown and Little Italy on Preston Street.

Our 'Woomie' Kevin was a constant source of entertainment. His misadventures and sense of humour kept us on our toes. A fine example was when he discovered *The Joy of Cooking* and tried several culinary experiments. Our house rules dictated that whoever cooked didn't have to clean up or do the dishes. It seemed to be a fair rule, except when Kevin cooked. Kevin used every pot, pan, utensil in his culinary efforts. Despite the chaos, Kevin's feasts were a culinary delight to our pallets. Kevin would witness the early beginnings of *Monique & Rick*. He'd known us both during high school and had commented many times: "I can't believe you two are together!"

Less than a year later, Kevin moved to London. Now our relationship was put to another test. Whenever things went wrong, we had been able to blame Kevin. After he was gone it was another story. Rick had his quirks and I had mine. Sometimes we clicked and other times we clashed. It could be a little thing like washing dishes or a big thing as in family drama. Yes, we argued. Yes, we talked things out at length. Yes, we used our version of the 'cone of silence'. Eventually, we did listen, we did compromise and we did learn.

Having a healthy argument is better than having none. Over the years, Rick and I have seen many marriages and common-law relationships fall apart no matter how long they'd been together. Perhaps if they'd allowed each other to grow and be open to a healthy dialogue they would have stayed the course. Rick and I brought this understanding to our relationship. It is the foundation of our interdependent partnership. We never stopped each other from exploring and learning new things. If I wanted to work out at the gym or take flamenco dancing lessons, that was fine with Rick. If he decided to check out open stages or tinker for hours in his recording studio, I never protested.

Communication and expectations require a delicate balance in any relationship. Whether it's a spouse, a best friend, or a family member it comes down to trust, honesty, and love. Those three little words hold tremendous weight.

SNOWFLAKE PROPOSAL

The inside cover page of the white embossed binder reads: "This is the Wedding Keepsake of Monique Gaetane Dinel and Richard Charles Tremblay who were married on the 3rd day of June in the year 1989." This is a simple statement of fact but there is a back story. As with any relationship–the *Monique & Rick* story has its tale to tell.

The Wedding Keepsake binder holds an array of information that is standard for most nuptials. Some pages were filled, while others were not, because we did not follow all the traditions. The Proposal was the first evidence of that. I had no idea, not even a suspicion. It was all Rick's clever planning. Though we had been living together, during what I call the *Test Drive Years* we'd never really discussed marriage. On the engagement pages, I tell our story in the third person. I haven't changed a word, though I want to, but it has sentimental value and needs to stay as-is.

> *A very unusual yet remarkable event occurred on Saturday, December 19th, 1987.*
>
> *It was a beautiful wintery day. The sun was shining brightly on the freshly fallen snow, which sparkled like diamonds. Glistening snowflakes were falling ever so softly to the ground, creating such a delicate picture.*
>
> *Inspiration struck! Rick took hold of the moment. He woke Monique up and said, "Let's go for a walk, it's too nice a day to sleep in." Well, they both got dressed for the winter day and went for their little walk.*
>
> *They walked as far as the experimental farm gardens and stopped to look at the frozen pond. Monique likes this pond because in the summer a special frog makes its residence there. She calls this place the Frog Pond.*
>
> *It was at this special place when Rick asked in his unique way "Will you marry me?" and at the same time he opened his hand and a golden band caught Monique's gaze. Wonderment and shock are two*

words that best described what she was feeling at that moment. So shocked was she that she asked, "Is this what I think it is? I can't believe it!"

She said YES and then Rick placed the ring on her finger.

It was a most special day one that neither Rick nor Monique will ever forget!

Anyone who knows Rick would question the brevity of the actual proposal. Before he 'popped the question' a phrase he didn't like hearing, much less using, Rick offered a philosophical preamble. Which is what I meant by 'his unique way' in the above story. I recall him saying, "We seem to be working well together as a couple. That we both had our qualities and our faults." He briefly listed them and then said that he was working on his weaknesses and felt confident that I would be doing the same. Now at this point, I wasn't sure where he was heading with this conversation and I was feeling a bit uneasy. Then he said, "I think we can make our relationship work so I'm wondering if you feel the same? Will you marry me?"

I was in shock and wonder because for a brief millisecond I thought he had something else in mind. Having an overactive imagination has its tribulations. But when I saw the ring in his palm, I knew this moment was real. Rick's hazel-green eyes were staring into my deep brown eyes waiting for my answer. He didn't have to wait long.

Later, I realized the risk he took in giving me this ring outside in the snow. I can be a bit of a klutz sometimes, and there was a chance the ring could have been dropped into the knee-deep snow. He said he was ready for that. Rick had purchased the ring at Howard's Jewellery store in Ottawa even though it was more of a dinner ring than an engagement ring. He had wanted something distinctive and this was it. Later a gold wedding band was designed to fit the ring's shape, mission completed.

We promptly called our parents, siblings, and friends to tell them we were engaged. All were thrilled, with one exception. Joan, Rick's mother, warned, "Couples who live together before they tie-the-knot have a higher rate of divorce than those who wait to live together until after they marry." She didn't realize that she was on the speakerphone. Rick had heard her every word. He reacted, before I could, and said, "Mom you don't have to worry about that happening to us." Rick was right and still is after all these years.

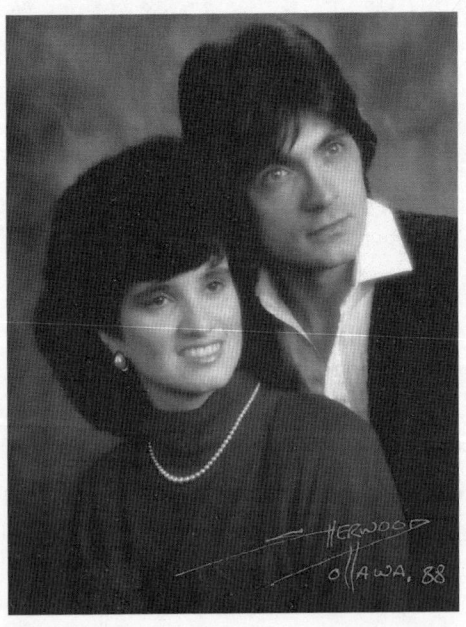

Monique & Rick Engagement photo 1988. Photographer: Sherwood Photography

A few months later, Rick and I had our picture taken at Sherwood Photography. This picture was our official engagement photo and we mailed it to all of our family and friends.

Every December 19th, Rick and I have celebrated our engagement anniversary in one way or another. It is especially magical if snow is falling. Our engagement date was harder to celebrate after December 22nd, 2005, the date of Rick's stroke. It has become easier, but I still struggle with the roller-coaster emotions associated with having the date of such a very happy memory being followed by the date of such a sad one.

By December 2018, the roller-coaster ride was less upsetting and I decided to arrange a romantic carriage ride with Cundell's Stables in the Ottawa Market for December 22nd at 7 p.m. I wasn't sure if we'd be able to go. The day before it had rained, washing away snow and icing the roads. However, Mother Nature changed her fickle mind, and the next day it snowed snowflakes glistening as they had on December 19th, 1987. Another magical moment in the making. We found Cundell's Stables on York Street, a place I had never noticed in all the years we had lived in Ottawa. I am surprised they have been able to stay in that location so long, since the 1940s. While we waited for the carriage to arrive from another trip, Rick and I visited with six miniature ponies in the stables. These black beauties all had braids in their manes and were excited to see us, just like little puppies. I wanted to take them home. Rick said "No!" with a chuckle.

John and Patty Cundell met us at the stable and were ready for Rick and me. They helped get Rick into the carriage and had provided extra blankets to keep us warm. Then off we went for our hour-long ride through the Market, to Parliament Hill, and the Justice Building, and back again.

We felt like royalty. When pedestrians and drivers waved at us, we waved back and called out 'Merry Christmas'. However, the real stars were probably Chip & Jake, the beautiful Belgian horses that clopped along the pavement on made-to-measure shoes to protect their hooves from cement, snow, ice, and street salt.

We could see the Christmas lights at Parliament Hill and the surrounding area. What we enjoyed most though was the sound of the sleigh bells as Chip & Jake moseyed along the streets. It inspired me to sing 'Silver Bells' and when I finished singing the song, Patty turned around from atop the driver's seat, next to John and said, "You have a beautiful voice." I was surprised she could hear me above the clatter of hooves and bells. The hour went by quickly and soon we were back at the stables. We waited in the carriage until they unhitched Chip & Jake, who could hardly wait to get back into their stalls. Then John and Patty helped Rick and me out of the carriage and held the wheelchair in place while I transferred Rick and he was safely seated.

Soon Rick and I were home on the loveseat in front of the fireplace, drinking champagne and looking at our Christmas Tree. I treasure the ornaments we have collected over the years and the memories they hold. Our engagement photo sits on the mantel. I remember the Snowflake Proposal on December 19th, 1987 and the road we have travelled since. Happy and sad memories have been blended into a simple steady, strolling pace with faint echoes of silver bells adding a touch of magic.

MUSICAL NEWLYWEDS

The Snowflake Proposal was a memorable moment soon to be outdone by our Wedding. On our day to *'share our lives, our love, and our hearts'* we sang our vows as Musical Newlyweds.

Most weddings then and now are planned by the Bride with the Groom responsible for tasks associated with the groomsmen.

Sometimes the parents of the Bride and Groom also get involved or even over-involved with the planning.

Rick and I have witnessed many weddings as guests, family and as wedding singers. We saw firsthand the chaos caused by family drama and communication breakdowns between Bride and Groom before the big day. To complicate things there was the 'wedding industry' happy to dictate what every couple must have at their wedding. We were determined not to alter our vision to appease anyone including family and friends. Whenever someone would say "You can't do that!" or "Why not get married in Chelmsford? Ottawa is not your real home!" our firm response was, "It's our wedding." If these unsolicited advisors continued to push, we pushed back with questions like: "Could it be that you didn't have the wedding you wanted? Maybe you should plan to renew your wedding vows and have a ceremony that makes you both happy." That usually stopped them, primarily women, in their tracks.

We planned everything together except for choosing my dress and Rick's suit. That surprised some people, but those who knew us best were not. It's the way we did everything in our day-to-day life, vacations, and gigs. Rick and I are planners and working out the details was always our thing.

I busied myself purchasing wedding magazines and attending bridal shows all the while gathering up information and ideas. Rick and I would go through each part of our ritual to create our master list—Ceremony, Reception, Honeymoon and most important—Budget. We would not let the planning of this event take over our lives. We patiently kept the chaos at bay right up until our Wedding Day—June 3rd, 1989.

The Ceremony

We designed our Wedding invitation and had them printed at Staples. On the front cover was an ink sketch of our engagement photo. We also designed a map showing where everything was located, directions, driving times and the RSVP card. Simple stock in simple black and white. We invited 70 people but anticipated 20 would not come, as they didn't like to travel.

"Take my heart ..."

Wedding Invitation sketch of Rick & Monique.

Rick and I are Catholic but not devout followers. However, we did consider getting married in the church. Unfortunately, that required taking a three-month course about marriage and living together. We didn't see the point since we'd been living together for eight years already. We also indicated that we would like to sing our wedding vows. The priest was firm, "This is not done and we have to approve any music you wish to have for the ceremony." Our decision was clear. We would not be marrying in the church.

We found that Reverend Hunter, the Chaplin at Carleton University, had no restrictions about the structure of our ceremony or its location. He did have one condition. He wanted to meet with us at least 2 or 3 times to get to know us and provide guidance if needed. In our Wedding Keepsake binder, we have a copy of Reverend Hunter's ceremony script that outlines our event from start to finish.

Our wedding ceremony included three songs and these were sung by the members of our folk group Aurora. As I walked up the aisle Brian Crook sang 'The First Time Ever I Saw Your Face' by Roberta Flack. Rick and I sang our song 'Take My Heart' as our wedding vows and Marcel Bouchard sang during the signing of the register – 'The First Words' written by Rick and Marcel.

Rick & Monique singing Take My Heart their wedding vows. Photographer: Mary Armellini

Rick and I were married at Vincent Massey's Bandstand in Ottawa. We had booked the bandstand with the city for free including the parking lot. The only thing we needed to do was to build a temporary sidewalk bridge and an outdoor carpet. Just in case, we had planned a 'storm location' at Macie's Ottawan, where the reception would be. We kept our fingers crossed that Mother Nature would be on our side. She was to a certain degree.

Just before the ceremony was to start the sun was still shining, but then the wind made its presence known and balloons started to sway. It blew harder and the balloons were soon smacking against each other. Guests' hairdos were becoming windswept, except for the Bride. My bridal coiffure was cemented in place with Ice hairspray. The Farmer's Almanac and the weather forecast had predicted a clear and cool day but the sky turned dark and it poured buckets of rain, as soon as we safely entered into the hotel for the reception.

Rick and I had done our best to plan for everything. We had Rick's youngest brother Tim drive his parents to the park. Rick and his brother Gary, the best man, were busy getting the guests settled for the ceremony. I was with my parents and Diane Laakso (*nee* Ramarr), the matron-of-honour, in the rental Cadillac. I know its customary for the Bride to be late, but not me. I was early but Rick's parents were late. So, there we were waiting until they finally showed up. I noticed Tim pop the trunk and took out two beers. Dad lost no time in walking over to the car and soon the unopened beer was placed back in the trunk. A crisis had been averted, though I was annoyed, to say the least. That feeling dissipated, when some little girls, playing in the park nearby stopped to look in the car and exclaimed, "Mom! Oh, it's a Princess Bride!" I did indeed feel like a princess.

Rick and I kept our wedding party simple, no ushers, no bridesmaids, no flower girls, no ring bearers. We did ask for help from Mary Armellini as a wedding photographer and my brother

Mike Dinel as the videographer. Mike is a cameraman by trade so he knew exactly what to do and would later edit his footage into a final cut. There was one little glitch. Mike was standing behind Reverend Hunter while filming the wedding party. You can see Rick and Gary, being distracted by something and then I was distracted too. Turns out, they'd spotted a daddy-long-legs spider climbing up the Reverend's arm. I saw it too and my eyes went big as saucers. Mike was so focused on the spider, that when the Reverend said, "You may kiss the Bride," Mike was filming Gary knocking off the spider but then quickly panned to the kiss. We hadn't planned for spiders but it was funny to see our moment almost upstaged by an arachnid.

The Reception

Our menu was simple–salad, entrée chicken and beef and our wedding cake for dessert. This was not a conventional wedding cake. We had gone to Reggina Patisseria on Preston Street and after several cake tastings over several months (hard work!) we had chosen Mocha Custard cake. It melted in your mouth and straight to your hips. Every anniversary until four years ago, Rick and I have ordered this cake. We also chose not to give out matches and those dreadful hunks of pre-wrapped fruit cake. Instead, we set aside take-home containers and people could help themselves to a piece of Mocha Custard Cake.

The reception dinner went smoothly, though we had to tell Macie's staff to add more bottles of wine as we had miscalculated amounts. We had planned for contingencies in our budget. We hadn't planned, however, for a four-legged wedding crasher. During the speeches, the door opened and running with determined speed was Daisy, Rick's parent's dog. Running frantically behind her, was Rick's, Aunt Lorraine. Daisy jumped onto Rick's mother's lap and there she stayed for the remainder of the evening. I guess I should have invited my furry four-legged 'sister-in-law' to the wedding.

The special part of our reception was the music. Rick and I had pre-recorded the music on three cassettes. I leveraged my radio programming skills and Rick's set-organization. We had a mix of all music genres to satisfy everyone. No Polkas—no Chicken Dance.

Monique & Rick performing live at their Wedding reception. Photographer: Mary Armellini

Most importantly, we had impromptu live music. Everyone who could play and sing was invited on stage. This included Ernie Tremblay, Rick Potvin, Debbie Williamson, Guy Morgan, Aurora, Brian Crook, Marcel Bouchard, Rick, and I had a reunion set, followed by the Musical Newlyweds who sang their joyous hearts out. The best gig ever! When we weren't singing, we were dancing. Rick and I had taken ballroom dancing lessons for about a year. We both loved the Viennese

Waltz, Tango and Foxtrot, and of course free-form dancing to any rock 'n' roll or pop music. During our planning stage selecting the song for our first dance had been difficult. Finally, it came down to 'Could I have this Dance' by Anne Murray and 'This Waltz' by Leonard Cohen. Let me say, that this was the only friction Rick and I had in planning our wedding. We certainly discussed the pros and cons of each song—a philosopher versus a starry-eyed romantic. I liked the melody of Leonard's song but the lyrics contained his trademark 'dark twist':

> *This waltz, this waltz, this waltz, this waltz*
> *With its very own breath of brandy and Death*
> *Dragging its tail in the sea.* [14]

Versus:

> *Could I have this dance for the rest of my life?*
> *Would you be my partner every night?*
> *When we're together it feels so right*
> *Could I have this dance for the rest of my life?*[15]

In the end, we chose 'Could I have this Dance', because the sentiment of the lyrics was simple and it worked best with the reasons for getting married. It also resonated with our lyrical vows in *'Take My Heart'*[16]:

> *Share our lives*
> *Now we start*
> *Take my love*
> *Take my heart!*

It's funny how we remember some details and how we may have forgotten or somewhat altered others, based on selected memories. When I wrote this chapter, I honestly thought I remembered everything accurately, until Rick and I watched the raw video footage of our wedding in February 2019.

While we watched the Wedding and the Reception we had forgotten some funny speeches and other hilarity brought on by impromptu incidents. Gary the Best Man-made mention of Rick's indecisiveness, when it came to finding the right parking spot. He asked wedding guests to raise their hands if they were passengers of Rick's parking lot tours. Everyone raised their hands. He also teased Rick about putting his soup cans in alphabetical order and that he and Kevin would go out of their way to mix them up.

Tim was the Master of Ceremonies and he was given strict notes to follow that Rick and I had put together. He did mention the notes to all the guests and said he had to ration out his beer intake until his duties were over. What we forgot while watching the video that he 'went off script' several times but it was funny. There were speeches from some from the head table, our Parents, the Matron-of-Honour and of course the Bride and Groom. I was tasked with thanking everyone who came from my family and Rick from his. When it was his time to speak, he forgot his glass of wine and realized it was nearly empty so he poured more into his glass. Then asked if anyone else needed a topping off. Well, at least a dozen people came forward until the carafe was emptied and then a second one.

Then Rick spoke and commented on Gary's speech and said, "I used to be indecisive but I'm not that sure anymore!" Then he went on to say "Marriage has always been a bit of a mystery to me." Then guests erupted with laughter. "But I'm hoping as Monique and I continue in our life together, that our marriage will continue to be a mystery!" Then Rick looked at me and raised his glass and said, "To my Bride!"

When we finished watching the raw footage of our wedding I turned to Rick and asked, "So is our marriage still a mystery to you?" He decisively said, "Yes, it is still a mystery. I'm glad you are my Bride and that you are by my side." At that moment, I felt like a young Bride being admired and loved by my handsome Groom. We were simply savouring the moment in our unique way enraptured once more as Musical Newlyweds.

THE JUNE BRIDE

I love musicals. Everything about them. The simple mushy storyline, the costumes, the dancing, and the songs. So many songs that would touch my heart and trigger memories like the *Seven Brides for Seven Brothers* 1954 musical classic and the song June Bride.[17]

> *Oh, they say when you marry in June,*
> *You're a bride all your life.*
> *And the bridegroom who marries in June*
> *Gets a sweetheart for a wife.*

Yes, I am a June Bride and Rick agrees, that he has a sweetheart for a wife. I remember all the details leading up to our special day. Discovering the Wedding dress, fashioning the Trousseau and ultimately the Boudoir gift for my Bridegroom.

When it comes to clothing, I have a split personality. On one hand, I like practicality and on the other originality. Maybe it's the Gemini in me–a split personality. So, when I went shopping for a wedding dress, I was looking for a mix of practicality and originality. I tried on many dresses; some, the skirt was so wide you could fit a dinette set for four underneath it. Others, so form-fitting that it would be impossible to sit down let alone dance in it. Funny how salesclerks, would say anything to get you to buy a dress–even if it didn't suit you.

Mr. & Mrs. Rick & Monique Tremblay at the Frog Pond. . Photographer: Mary Armellini

I was about to give up and have one made until I found what I wanted at a bridal shop on Somerset Street, Ottawa. It wasn't what I had imagined, it was more. Just one drawback, the train–not at all practical, though very beautiful. To work around this, I asked the seamstress if we could lift the train and attach it along the seam. Luckily, I know how to sew and understood dressmaking so I was able to explain my idea. It worked perfectly. The train was left down when I walked up the aisle and lifted just enough above the ground so I could walk, dance, and perform on stage without tripping. The beadwork on this dress, was exquisite and unique: it accentuated my figure just right and it was eye-catching.

As for headpiece, well that was a challenge. Everything I tried did not work. Hair combs broke, headpieces too tight or if they fit the style didn't match the dress. Then the idea came to me. A simple bow made from the fabric from the dress and attached to a heavy-duty barrette for thick hair. The bow was made to match the one on the back of the dress. Perfection plain and simple.

Whether my clothes were practical or original the one constant was the vibrant shades of colour. I am a Winter Woman whose colour palette includes bright, distinctive, high contrast, intensity, and cool icy shades. When I wear fuchsia, purple, azure blue, emerald green, and ruby red colours I feel energetic and playful. There is nothing pastel about my personality. So, when I searched for items for my trousseau, my choices were limited and uninspiring.

It was then that I decided to see Iva Diane an Ottawa based haute-couture designer. She created two dresses each based on my vision. The first was made of silk in an unusual shade of cyan that shimmers with purple undertones. The bolero jacket and a classic form-fitting dress with a flared skirt that is reminiscent of the classic elegance made popular by Audrey Hepburn. This dress was made for our honeymoon in Québec City in June 1989 and I wore it to our special supper at le Restaurant aux Anciens Canadiens. The second dress was made a year later to celebrate our first wedding anniversary. This too was made of silk in a vibrant aquamarine blue in a classic retro-style. I loved the jewel neckline as it truly made me feel like a confident woman. In that dress, I knew who I was.

There is a time in every woman's life when she feels everything is right with her world. I can say that this was true for me from 1987 to 1991. Love life—Rock-solid; Career—soaring, and

Self-confidence—strong. I truly came into my own—a woman with vision, spirit, adventure and bravely bodacious.

I remember the day when that bold moment was captured on film in Anna Beaudry's Photography Studio on Dalhousie Street in Ottawa. Llynne Plante and I walked into the studio with suitcases filled with a variety of negligees, jewelry, shoes, and other sultry garments for our first Boudoir Photo session. The pictures, if they turned out, would be given as a wedding gift to our soon to be husbands. For the photo session, Anna made sure the scene was set to enhance the experience, with a hairstylist/make-up artist, champagne and strawberries and music to unleash the apprehensive divas within. After the photo session, Llynne and I left the studio with egos greater than Madonna could match. I was proud of my body.

Two weeks later we were back at the studio to look at the proofs. Our 'Madonna-like' confidence was a distant memory and our responsible selves were wondering "what did we get ourselves into." Anna sat us down and said, "I will show you six similar styled poses and I want you to pick the five you don't like, this will help you pick the best picture." Though unusual it worked. We picked the photos that would be enlarged to 24" X 30" and gift wrapped for our respective bridegrooms.

My bodacious photo has been hanging in our master bedroom since June 3rd, 1989 where my husband could see it before waking or going to sleep. Others have seen this photo and the reactions ranged from 'well she always had a young character' to 'Kathleen Turner eat your heart out'.

Monique the Bride and her vibrant bouquet. Photographer: Mary Armellini

Fast forward 30-years, the Wedding dress is in a special keepsake box and the designer dresses are hanging in my closet. I may not be able to wear them again, but they hold memories and they remind me of the vibrant spirit that is uniquely my own. A spirit that was dulled by dark challenges brought on by Rick's stroke, but that has been gradually lightened due to renewed personal strength. I am not ready to part with them. Who knows, I may lose the weight, and wear them once more. Or maybe, it's time to create another vision of my perfect dress, that will embrace the woman I have become and it will be a vibrant colour to match the spirit within. So, there is some truth to the lyrics 'when you marry in June—You're a Bride all your life.'

HONEYMOON SPIRIT

As Musical Newlyweds, we looked forward to our next adventure 'where the river narrows' in Québec City. There is something special about that place. We don't know what it is but Rick and I have always been drawn there like magnets to the Pole. Could it be that in that place the spirits of our ancestors call out to us? Is that why we continue to visit this wonderful and historic city? It just had to be our honeymoon destination.

On June 3rd and 4th we organized a mini-honeymoon at The Westin hotel in Ottawa. We also had a few post-wedding events with family and friends that took place at our home on Kingston Avenue. These were lively and informal, even goofy. We had the standard gift opening, live music, and a buffet. We girls pulled out a jump rope and tried to remember our grade school jumping rhymes—'Tinker Tailor' and 'Supercalifragilisticexpialidocious'. We tied the jump rope and would jump in and out with special footwork. When successful the rope went from our ankles to our knees. A sad attempt at double-dutch was good for lots and lots of laughter. Little girls on our block couldn't stop giggling at these 30' somethings trying to jump rope.

The real highlight was when Rick came home with the 30" X 40" Boudoir picture. As he walked past Jack Balez, his long-time friend challenged him, "I showed you mine now show me yours!" Llynne's boudoir photo had been shown a year prior at their wedding gift opening party. Llynne's photo was demure and more ladylike. Mine was a sassy "a–la–Mae–West" creation.

With all the revelry over, Rick and I were finally on our way to Québec City. We hit the road early on June 5th hoping to beat the Montreal traffic. Rick and I always shared the driving no matter where we went. It was a five-hour drive and we were able to find parking in Old Québec since we had planned on walking everywhere we needed to get to during our visit. We stayed at the Château de la Terrasse at $72 per night. Our room had a striking view of the Saint Lawrence River and the Château Frontenac. We couldn't stay at the Château because it was booked up and besides it was outside of our budget.

Once we were in our room and unpacked, we got ready for our ritual. We went to the aptly named Dépanneur Epicerie Richard on Rue des Jardins to pick up wine, cheese, pâté, and fresh croissants for our room. We hibernated in our room as honeymooners do but more so because Mother Nature had given us an additional reason. The temperature dropped to 9 degrees Celsius and with it came the snow! Luckily, being Northern Ontario bred stock, with our Ancestral blood running in our veins, we faced it head-on. Nothing was going to ruin our June honeymoon. Alas! We were compelled to spend more time huddling under the blankets. Oh, what hardship!

Eventually, we explored our old favourite places. We walked down the L'escalier Casse-Cou to Place Royal and the Notre-Dame-des-Victoires church built-in 1629. We then rode the Funiculaire back up to the Terasse and eventually made our way to Rue du Trésor also known as Art Alley. Here 'artistes' displayed their talented visions for sale. Paintings, carvings, jewellery and more. All shapes, sizes, and price ranges. Rick and I always searched for that perfect picture that spoke to us but we didn't find it during our honeymoon. We had better luck in 1993 when we celebrated our 4th Wedding Anniversary.

In 1993 it turned out that Rick and I each had our eyes out for pictures we wanted to buy for each other as Anniversary gifts. We somehow managed to shop separately, picked out our surprise gifts and snuck them back into our hotel room without each other knowing. Later we surprised each other with two copper-plate etchings. Rick's was a street view of Vieux Québec by Jacques Brousseau and mine was of a young girl sitting on a park bench near the Château Frontenac by Denise Godbout. Later we would find out that these artists were husband and wife. They shared their passion for art as Rick and I shared our passion for music. Our etchings were eventually framed and prominently displayed in our dining room.

We always looked for new sights and sounds when we went to Québec City. I remember Rick taking me by the hand on one of our nightly romantic walks down Rue Saint-Jean. He led me down a narrow obscure alley softly lit and accompanied by faint sounds of folk music. It was the bar Les Yeux Bleus where local musicians would go to highlight their original music. Les Yeux Bleus was built into hard rock very cave-like and yet as intimate as a living room. It became another of our traditional stops whenever we reconnected with our favourite city.

In keeping with our tradition, Rick and I enjoyed long walks along the walls of the Citadel and picnics on the Plains of Abraham. Weather permitting of course. We also relished scouting through the unique shops rimming the cobblestone streets. It was in one of these shops, Les Trois Colombes, that I spied a pink wraparound soft leather skirt. It was the creation of Jos Binne, a Huron Indigenous artist from Québec. Tattooed designs of blue and purple splashed about its leather and the fringe made a soft swishing sound when I tried it on. I loved it and considered buying it before returning to Ottawa. However, my Groom surprised his new Bride and purchased it for her as a honeymoon gift. I treasure it to this day.

No story about Québec City would be complete without mentioning the food. All calorie-free of course because when it's your

Honeymoon, Wedding Anniversary, Birthday, or other special event, calories just don't count. Every restaurant in Québec City delivers an exquisite cuisine designed for every palate. Besides all that walking around of 'Canada's Paris' helps burn off calories from decadent crepes bathed in chocolate at Le Casse-crêpe Breton or breakfast at Restaurant L'omellete. For Rick and me the magic is never complete until we dine in style at our favourite restaurant Aux Anciens Canadien, internationally known for its fine cuisine and warm hospitality. They have an impressive menu of Québecois traditional entrées. My favourite has always been Bourguignon de bison à la crème et au vin de bleuets and for Rick, it's Tourtière du Lac St-Jean aux gibiers, ragoût de boulettes et patte de cochon. Then we share Tarte au sirop d'érable et crème barattée. I have deliberately kept the entrées names in French because they sound more scrumptious and romantic in the language de l'amour!

Each year from 1980 to 2005, Rick and I made our way back to our special place to make new memories and embrace those of our past. Last year in 2018, I drove by Québec City on my way to a Toastmaster Conference in Bromont, Québec. There was the Château Frontenac in the background calling to me but I could not answer the call without Rick. I was driven to set plans in motion to celebrate our 30th Wedding Anniversary plus the 9-years Test Drive in Québec City in June 2019. Everything was in place. VIA Tickets purchased, the Château Frontenac was booked and dinner reservations were made 6-months in advance at Aux Anciens Canadien. We intended to visit all of our rendezvous spots at the place 'where the river narrows' and where the spirits of our ancestors look on. Here the Musical Newlyweds will re-embrace the magic of their honeymoon in their special way.

RENEW OUR PROMISE

It is June 3rd, 2019. International tourists stroll and stop along a historic terrasse. They are in wonder of an iconic Canadian city, at the place 'where the river narrows'! Tourists of a different mind have been drawn to an intimate event unfolding beneath the Victoria Gazebo that stands in the far corner of the Dufferin Terrasse in Québec City. Some are accidental witnesses who have stumbled upon an emotionally charged reality tableau. A couple holds each other closely. They are renewing a promise, a promise made 30-years ago when they were Musical Newlyweds.

When the ceremony is over, the audience applauds and then gradually fades away. Will they continue their stroll along the royal promenade with a renewed spark of romance? I wanted to believe that our Wedding Renewal ceremony was an unexpected but memorable parting gift for these visitors. On the surface, ours looked like a simple renewal ceremony. Maybe some wondered about the wheelchair parked a few feet behind the couple as they engaged in a peculiar secure and loving embrace.

In our previous life, Rick and I had travelled to Québec City every year until the fateful event of 2005. On Valentine's Day fourteen years later, I knew that we would want to go again. There were some major changes and the invaluable help from Katrina Khoury, our CAA Travel Advisor. On Saturday, June 1st, we arrived at the VIA Train Station on Tremblay Road—one hour early to make sure we caught our 10:15 a.m. train to Québec City. The ticket agent examined our voucher then peered at us with a quizzical expression on her face. She picked up her phone and spoke to a colleague. With the headset still squeezed between her neck and shoulder she declared, "It shows in our system that you cancelled your ticket!" I couldn't believe what I was hearing and protested determinedly that I had not cancelled. More keyboard clattering and chattering. Apparently, or so they said, it was an unfortunate error and they would try to find a solution. Wide-eyed and smiling through my clenched teeth I countered with, "If Rick and I have to go on the baggage car so be it." At 10:12 a.m. Rick and our luggage were on the train, with me still waiting at the counter for our tickets. I had been assured that the train would not leave without me. An overactive imagination and experience with Murphy's Law left me with no sense of comfort. Finally, at 10:14 a.m. with everything worked out I was on the train and snuggled with Rick. The train moved. We were truly on our way.

In my pink leatherette journal, I noted the first highlight of our trip. My handwriting is nearly illegible as the train jostled, bumped, and squeaked. It didn't help that Rick and I were sitting backwards on the train. What an odd sensation, watching the past disappear down the rails behind us, yet blind to the immediate future out of sight ahead of us. Small Ontario towns were soon replaced by Québec settlements. The train stopped at rural stations to drop off or pick up passengers headed for the big city of Montreal. Six hours later we reached the last stop at Gare du Palais Québec City. From there we took a cab to our final destination, the Château Frontenac. It was a surreal moment when we entered the lobby of this historic hotel. After a dreamlike day, we were finally here.

The Château Frontenac staff were amazing, professional, and genuine. When I needed help, they were there. Plans for our adventure had started months earlier with Jessy Fortier, the Event Coordinator at the Château. Not only did he provide a list of officiants that might be able to preside over our Renewal Ceremony, but he also suggested locations inside and outside the Château. I was very fortunate that Reverend Dr. Louis Lafrance was available as the wedding officiant from the Centre d'Amour et Marriage. Love the business name 'Centre d'Amour'. Reverend Lafrance had wanted to know more of our story so he could personalize the ceremony and so sent me a questionnaire. When I read it, I thought the draft memoir stories from the *Take My Heart* chapters would give him a real insight. I was right. I was touched by his feedback about our story. He worked on the ceremony framework and I sought out a photographer based on a list provided by the Reverend.

I soon found a photographer, at least I thought I had one until I saw the quote. There was a considerable disconnect between what I had expected and what he required as payment. I found myself scrambling for another photographer. Someone was looking out for Rick and me because our path connected with a kindred spirit–Xavier Dachez. On the phone, he wanted to know our story before deciding to take the job. This was a refreshing approach. He needed to connect to the story. Our story. After a 30-minute somewhat bilingual conversation, the deal was done. It was clear that he was looking forward to participating in our renewal ceremony.

Thinking about all the plans, the people involved I still couldn't believe it. Rick and I were in our romantic hotel suite. The sun shone and our spirits soared. I couldn't wait for our traditional promenade on the Terrasse Dufferin. Rick decided that he wanted to walk and not use the wheelchair. I understood. In his mind walking shouldn't be a problem. That's one of the challenges with a brain-stem stroke. Rick doesn't remember the stroke. He remembers his life as it was before. I convinced him that it wasn't safe to do so. He did try to walk the 6-foot distance from the chaise lounge in our room to the door. After a few solid strides, his gait started to drift left and reluctantly he sat down in the wheelchair. Then I hugged him to let him know all would be okay.

(Left to Right) Reverend Dr. Louis Lafrance, Rick & Monique. Photographer Xavier Dachez.

The Terrasse Dufferin still held the magic I'd remembered. Every so often I would stop next to the railing overlooking the Saint Lawrence River. Then I would help Rick stand-up so that he could grab the wrought iron railing while I propped him up by wrapping my arm around his waist and he wrapped his around my shoulders. We had transported to our past trips to Québec City all those years ago. It was then that the tears started to roll down my cheek. I was overwhelmed. Rick squeezed me gently, kissed my forehead and his eyes spoke the silent words, 'I know!'

We continued to explore of our old haunts in 'Vieux Québec' city. Along the way we stopped and listened to the street performers, each adding a certain character to this city. Strolling down cobbled streets with a wheelchair proved to be quite an adventure. I was thankful that I had bought a new air cushion for Rick as it softened the judders caused by the uneven streets. I knew there would be a lot of up-hills, down-hills and curb drops along our route. I could handle that. What I hadn't considered were the entrances into some of our favourite places. Most had 3 to 4 steps. No ramps. No portable ramps either. I guess I've been spoiled by the Ottawa restaurants, who have gone to a lot of effort to accommodate clientele with accessibility challenges. But as a caregiver, finding an alternative solution on-the-spot had become second nature to me. As I pushed Rick up a 45-degree hill for at least a city block, I kept visualizing the 'fitness tank' my trainer had me push during my workouts. I made it to the top and took a break. Rick heaved a sigh of relief. I started laughing and said, "I think I've earned a decadent dessert." A great way to end our first day!

Sunday, June 2nd was a day of rest. The torrential rain saw to that. There was no way we could go outside. The winds were blowing off the Saint Lawrence River and pummeling the brave tourists who held onto inverted umbrellas while clinging to their rain ponchos. Rick and I hibernated in our room for most of the day. We enjoyed the free champagne, chocolate-covered strawberries and a crudité platter provided by the Château. We managed to meet with Xavier and his daughter for an hour to discuss the ceremony and for a casual photoshoot. I knew right then that Xavier was going to capture the moment in the way I had hoped. Rick and I finally, able to go out on the Terrasse again. When the rain stopped, we went for what was to be an international stroll, meeting tourists from New Zealand, Tennessee, Seoul, and Denmark. We happily engaged in conversation and took each other's pictures. It was nice to hear about their experiences in Québec City. When we returned to our room, I thought again about our renewal ceremony and what adventures that would bring. I also hoped Mother Nature would be on our side.

The wake-up call rang the start of a new day. The room was dark. I rushed out of bed and walked to the window. I held my breath, crossed my fingers, and pressed and held the switch. Then the wide window blinds silently rose ever so slowly to reveal–Sunshine. Perfect! It was 8 a.m. with the ceremony only 7-hours away. Rick was way too comfortable in our king-sized bed so I let him sleep in while I updated my journal and enjoyed a nice strong cup of coffee and planned our morning leading up to the main event. Finally, we were out the door and heading for a local café for brunch. We shared a Québecois omelet and melt-in-your-mouth crepes smothered with 100% Canadian Maple Syrup. Then we took a much needed 'stroll and roll', as I needed to work off the extra calories. We then got onto the Funiculaire du Vieux Québec to bring us to la Rue du Petit Champlain. It's a neat sensation going up and down the 45-degree rail system to and from the lower town. I must admit I missed taking the L'Escalier Casse-Cou (Breakneck Steps) but that wasn't an option anymore. The cobblestones were a lot rougher on these streets and I had to slow down for fear that Rick would be propelled out of his seat. We did some window shopping and stopped to listen to a few street musicians. Then it was back to the Funiculaire and up we went. It was still too early to head back to our room so we went back to Les Allées des Art. We'd been there on Saturday and had seen an oil painting that caught our attention. It had been Rick's who saw it first as it was hanging at his eye level. We looked at it again, and its artist who was present looked very familiar. A unique coincidence. We had bought copper-based etchings from Jacques and his wife Josée during our honeymoon. We couldn't resist and bought yet another Josée Rousseau, Québec City inspired work of art to commemorate our anniversary.

We headed back to the Château with painting in hand. Again, I pushed Rick up that hill and couldn't help but notice that clouds were rolling in and challenging the sunny ceremony. Both the reverend and the photographer also saw the clouds and we agreed that we should move the ceremony from 3 to 2 p.m. Now we had less time to get gussied-up. I helped Rick dress first. Suit, shirt, tie, socks. I've become somewhat of a pro with making a Windsor knot. Rick was now in the suit he'd worn at our wedding 30-years ago. I wasn't as lucky. My figure has changed, the one thing I was disappointed with. However, I had found a dress with the freedom to move about and wore comfortable shoes, so important when pushing a wheelchair. The dress had a soft and vibrant floral pattern on the skirt and flowed like a garden in the St. Lawrence breeze. Fortunately, I had a suit jacket that matched the mauve colour pallet. I wore the pearl necklace and earrings that Rick had given me as a wedding gift all those years ago.

The scene was set. Xavier the Photographer became the Director of our mini-movie, Reverend Louis, the officiant became the narrator with Rick as Leading Man and me as Leading Lady. The Victoria Gazebo was the perfect romantic setting, with the Château Frontenac on one side and the St. Lawrence on the other. The renewal vows were tailor-made for our story. We sang our vows, 'Take My Heart' the song that we wrote for our June 3rd, 1989 wedding. This day we sang only one verse:

> *Share our lives*
> *Now we start*
> *Take my love*
> *Take my heart.*

We exchanged the words "I do" and did not remove our rings. I didn't want to take the risk of re-exchanging the rings for fear they would drop through the cracks in the Terrasse. Then we kissed. The spirits of the young couple from 1989 and the young-at-heart couple from 2019 were mingled into one. After that moment the Reverend continued, "Your first gift today after renewing your vows, will be two single roses tied together by a simple ribbon. The rose is a symbol of love and simply says 'I love you.' The ribbon represents the journey you share as a duet in perfect harmony." The dried roses and the ribbon are 'keepers'.

After our ceremony, a young violinist was preparing for his busking set on the Terrasse. Reverend Louis took advantage of that and asked if he could play for us. The young man spoke to me and asked if there was something we'd like to hear. "Do you know La Vie En Rose?" I asked. He was learning it and had the sheet music with him. I sang it to Rick and could barely contain the emotions I felt. My voice quivered on the last few lyrics. Luckily Xavier recorded this impromptu moment. Many well-wishers stopped to congratulate us and added sparkle for our special day.

True to his word Xavier went out of his way to 'capture our moment'. He drove us in his Subaru Outback to various locations for photos. The marina, the park, the fountain and finally our stroll to our favourite restaurant L'Ancienne Canadienne. It was a labour of love for Xavier as evidenced by every photo. So many to choose from. So many memories.

Memories of June 3rd, 1989 and 2019 from the place 'where the river narrows'! Where the Musical Newlyweds renewed the promise, they made 30-years ago.

LIFE IS A SONG

LIFE IS A SONG is a collection of stories about our life and our adventures, big and small, serious and humorous and everything in between. Each story reflects events and how they influenced us and our life choices along the way.

HALCYON YEARS AT
THE TREMBLAY'S

Our story would not be complete without documenting our childhood days of growing up with our families. As with many families, ours has had its share of drama and dysfunction that remains unspoken. Our story will focus on the Halcyon Years, the days of innocence, tranquillity, and discovery.

Richard Charles Joseph Tremblay was born in North Bay, Ontario on August 25th, 1957, the first-born to Ernest (Ernie) and Jeanne d-Arc (Joan) Tremblay (*nee* Potvin). Soon Rick would become a big brother to Gary born February 17th, 1959 and Tim February 17th, 1960. Eventually, the Tremblay family settled in Chelmsford, Ontario where the boys spent most of their formative years. Like most fathers in the Sudbury area, Ernie worked for Falconbridge Mines while Joan stayed home and managed the household. For the most part, they lived a regular life in a bungalow on Coté Street in Chelmsford. They did have one exceptional challenge and that was Rick's health.

Every Christmas in his early years, Rick would get sick. He'd have trouble breathing and the local hospital didn't know why. Rick's parents finally drove him to Sick Kids in Toronto in search of answers. Ultimately, it was discovered that Rick had asthma and was extremely allergic to real Christmas trees. Breathing in the pollen and dust enclosed inside a home with a forced-air furnace made matters worse. After this diagnosis, only artificial trees would adorn the Tremblay living room at

Christmas. Rick was given his bedroom and the door was kept closed to keep the air fresh from cigarette smoke. Second-hand smoke wasn't considered an issue back then. I often wondered why his parents didn't think to reduce their smoking habit for Rick's sake.

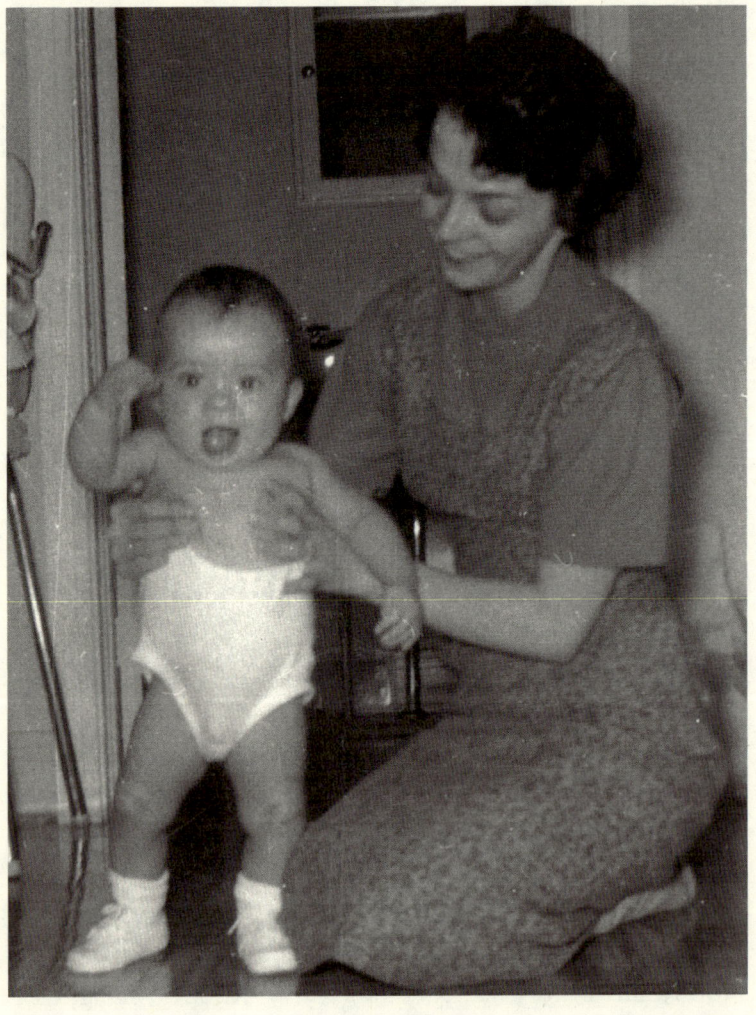

(Left to Right) Rick as a baby & Joan his mom keeping him steady on his feet.

For asthmatics, the rule of the day was to avoid physical activity. Therefore, Rick did not participate in sports. Instead, he participated in board games, built Meccano erector sets and became an avid reader. The first guitar in the Tremblay household belonged to Tim. Rick's youngest brother had a fleeting interest in it but then the acoustic 6-string Stella was forgotten. It was Rick who rescued Stella or maybe Stella rescued him. This guitar soon became a permanent appendage for Rick. He started to play guitar when his friend Michael Guilbeault started to strum the Guitar Boogie. Uncle Rick, Joan's youngest brother, also played guitar and taught Rick how to play the boogie. To learn how to play the up-tempo twelve-bar boogie-style instrumental piece is a rite of passage for any guitar player. My Mom and Uncle Harvey played the same guitar boogie when we lived in Val Caron. Both Rick and I were exposed to a lot of musical stimuli.

After a few years on the Stella, Rick graduated to an electric guitar with an amplifier purchased at Sears, not a name brand. No matter, it now belonged to Rick. A photo says it all. There is 12-year-old Rick with Beatle-like mop-top hairstyle, wearing striped bell-bottom jeans and a crew neck sweater with an extra-wide grin as he clutches his new guitar. Alongside him is his Dad sporting snazzy sideburns, a slicked-back a-la-Conway Twitty style and happily nursing a Molson's Canadian stubby.

Family gatherings were common at the Tremblay's. There was always music playing in the house whether it was the local radio station, hi-fi stereo player, or live music. Most times, Uncle Rick played country standards of the '50s and '60s. Ernie would chime in with his unique vocals and Auntie Sue (Rick's wife) would add her sweet voice to the mix. Their impromptu setlist ranged from 'A Wound Time Can't Erase' by Hank Snow, and 'Fraulein' sung by Bobby Helms. I would be there for these impromptu performances later on. I was always entertained as I watched Uncle Rick keep Ernie on time and on key. Once he steered him right, Ernie stayed true to the melody and stumbled only occasionally on the lyrics. Rick soon followed in his Uncle's footsteps when it came to accompanying his Dad and could adjust on the spot to add polish to the performance. We are fortunate to have recordings of these wonderful concerts.

(Left to Right) Rick with his new electric guitar & Ernie looking on at his happy son.

Other members of the Tremblay clan dabbled in music and regularly gathered about the kitchen table for 'jams'. Uncle Jean-Paul Robetaille, who also played guitar, and was married to Ernie's sister Carmelle. Uncle Yvon Bouchard played the harmonica. He was married to Ernie's oldest sister Lorraine. Yvon and Lorraine are Marcel Bouchard's parents, so he too was influenced by the family gatherings. Rick and Marcel continued with the family tradition and maintained this love of music in their lives.

At the time I didn't realize how close in age Rick was to Uncle Rick and Aunt Sue. This may explain why Rick was so close to his favourite Uncle and Aunt. Sue was 15-years-old and Uncle Rick 18-years-old when they babysat the "well behaved and quiet Tremblay boys" claimed Aunt Sue. Rick was 8-years-old at the time. I'm not sure about the well-behaved and quiet portrayal. There was a story about Rick, Gary, and a crochet needle. Joan had found these inquisitive lads sitting on the rug about to test their theory regarding the anatomy of the brain. They were convinced that there must be a tunnel between the left ear hole to the right. Gary was the patient and Rick the physician holding a crochet needle was set on confirming their belief. Luckily, Joan put a swift end to that experiment. The older Rick that I got to know was quiet, philosophical, and always more perceptive than his younger brothers. These are the qualities that attracted me to the man that I would first admire and then love.

Yes, there were Halcyon Years for the Tremblay's wrapped in innocence and with their identifiable music soundtrack.

HALCYON YEARS AT THE DINEL'S

The Dinel's travelled down their specific Halcyon country road. Like the Tremblay family, the Dinel family had its moments of innocence, tranquillity, and discovery. All my memories gather round those early childhood years when life was simple.

On June 17th, 1959 at 4:35 p.m. Monique Gaetane Dinel was born at the Sudbury General Hospital to Gerard (Gerry) Noe and Annabelle Claire Dinel (*nee* Pitre) proud first-time parents. According to the *Our Baby's First Years* notebook my Mom kept, she wrote that I weighed 6 pounds 3 ounces and I was 21 ½ inches long, I had big blue eyes that turned brown and light brown hair. I can prove that because my Mom kept the light brown curls from my first haircut when I was 3-years-old. My Mom also wrote in her enviable handwriting that I broke my soother on Christmas Day. Could it be that I was trying to spit it out so I can sing a Christmas Carol? Oh, if only I could tap into that innocent cherub's memory.

I often say to people I meet that "I am a Nickel Miner's Daughter" plagiarizing Loretta Lynn's famous 'Coal Miner's Daughter' song. When I do, I see one of my favourite pictures it's of my Dad wearing his red miner's hat and me sitting on his lap with my big one-tooth smile. Based on my Mom's note I cut my first tooth at 7-months-old.

The Nickle Miner's Daughter (Monique) with her Dad Gerry Dinel.

The Dinel family's first home was in Val Caron, Ontario next door to my Mom's family. In my formative years, I grew up with my grandparents Emile and Gaetane along with my Uncles Hervé (Harvey), David (Dave), Réjean (Pete), Gaetan (Gates), and Clarence (Kiki). My Uncle Kiki is only 2-years-older than me. I remember when I was old enough to walk on my own that I would pop in and visit. There was always something going on. My Grandmother and Mom would be sewing and mending on my Grandmother's Singer Treadle Sewing machine. I have a clear memory of sitting on the floor and using my hands to push the peddle up and down based on the beat of either my Mom or Grandmother's foot. My Uncle Dave still has this sewing machine and uses it too.

My other clear memory was of music. My Mom and Uncle Harvey both played guitar whenever there were family gatherings. They played country standards from the '50s and '60s. One song my Mom sang often was Kitty Wells' hit 'It Wasn't God Who Made Honky Tonk Angels'. I know that my love of music came from my Mom. That honky-tonk song would later become part of the *Monique & Rick* repertoire as a duet. Rick would sing Hank Thompson's 'Wild Side of Life' while I would answer back with Kitty's lyrics with 100% twang.

The Dinel family grew during the Val Caron years. I would become the big sister to Michel (Mike) born October 1st, 1961 and Joanne September 6th, 1965.

(Left to Right) Baby Brother Michel (Mike) Annabelle & Gerry (parents) and Big Sister Monique.

Like Rick's father, my Dad worked in the mines but he was employed by INCO instead of Falconbridge. My Dad worked underground during his early years but after a serious mining accident, he was reassigned to a surface job in the Mine Safety Department. This meant our family had to move to Levack, Ontario which was 44 kilometres away from Val Caron. This was a major change for our family and I think it was hard on my Mom. She was separated from her family and what few friends she had. Levack was an English town and not French and that presented us with unique cultural challenges. Despite this, my Mom would do her best and kept music alive by playing her guitar as we kids joined in. I remember Mike, Joanne and I would sing along to Mom's solid guitar bass-strum-strum beat of 'He's Got the Whole World In His Hands'. I didn't know it then but this song was a traditional African American 1927 spiritual, that became an international pop hit in 1957 by English singer Laurie London. I suspect my Mom heard this version on the radio and it inspired her to learn it then play it by heart on her sunburst, pearl adorned, Gibson guitar. Maybe that's why I always felt in my heart this was my Mom's song and no one else's.

The Dinel family was on the move again in 1973 to Chelmsford, Ontario. My Dad's job moved to Copper Cliff, Ontario and moving to Chelmsford made for a shorter commute. I started high school that year while Mike and Joanne attended Saint Charles Catholic elementary school. Each of us found our unique way in the new town. More about my experiences can be found in the *Education Exposé* chapter.

My parents continued to take us on camping trips, though not as frequently as they had during the Levack years because of our summer jobs or just life in general. What I do remember about all these road trips was the Backseat Trio (Joanne, Mike, and Monique). The family car, a green Dodge Coronet, only had a radio, no 8-track player, and no cassette player. Depending on where we were on the road the available radio stations would eventually fade away and replaced by annoying static. The Backstreet Trio would begin to sing songs. I tended to be the choir director, coming up with songs we all knew. Some popular ones like 'Joy to the World' (you know 'Jeremiah was a Bullfrog') by Three Dog Night, 'Take it Easy' by the Eagles, 'One Tin Soldier' by the Original Cast and of course we would sing 'He's Got the Whole World In His Hands' with Mom singing along from the front seat. My Dad didn't sing, though he did dabble with the Jew's harp now and then. Of course, he couldn't play that while driving. Not a hands-free task.

If I were to pick the Billboard Chart #1 song of the Backstreet Trio it was John Denver's 'Country Roads'. We would experiment with the harmonies each of us taking a turn singing lead. My sister Joanne sat in the middle, while Mike was sitting behind my Dad and me behind my Mom. While we were working out the arrangement, sometimes my sister would sing the melody or the harmony depending on what Mike and I were doing. I wish we were able to record those performances. I do have a photo from that timeframe. Here we are standing in front of our Tag-A-Long canvas tent trailer wearing the then fashion-able sombreros. My sister and I were wearing nautical bathing suits which conflicted with the sombreros. Maybe we were still discovering our fashion sense or we simply didn't care.

(Left to Right) The Backseat Trio Monique (growth spurt),
Joanne & Mike and the Tag-A-Long trailer.

Later in our adult lives, Rick recorded Mike and Joanne on different songs but regrettably, we never recorded 'Country Roads'. For the life of me, I don't know why we didn't. Maybe the Backseat Trio will find their harmony again, especially now that Jimmer Dinel, Mike's 3-year-old Grandson and our Great Nephew has been singing this song with his Mom (Michelle Dinel) & Dad (Steve Dinel). Who knows maybe we can join Jimmer and his little brother Nash along with the extended Dinel family on Smule an online karaoke application. Then we can recapture the moments of those Dinel Halcyon Years taking us home down our innocent country roads.

EDUCATION EXPOSÉ — RICK

Rick and I attended school in the '60s & '70s in the Sudbury area. Rick, two years older than I, went to grade school and high school in Chelmsford. I, on the other hand, went to grade school in Val Caron and Levack and High School in Chelmsford. Clap your eyes on the important intersection of Chelmsford in our story. Recently, I've looked more closely at our report cards and other relevant documents. All these years later I'm now armed with more discerning eyes and the insight brought on by many more years of experience. What might I discover by combing through our respective educational pasts? How were we alike and how were we different? Scrutinizing everything we had hoarded through the years I found many similarities and definite differences in our respective journeys.

Rick and I were at the tail-end of the Baby Boomer generation (1944-1965). In the '60's and '70s teachers were in short supply in Northern Ontario, so much so that they taught at different grade schools on a rotational basis. This was true for both Public and Separate school district school boards. The average class size was approximately thirty students. When we moved to Ottawa, we found out that Southern and Eastern Ontario schools offered more opportunities for their students. There was access to more teachers, more post-secondary institutions, more course options, more extra-curricular activities and in some cases more tailor-made solutions for gifted students and those with special needs. Were Rick and I gifted? That depends on the nature of the gift. We did have interests in the creative arts that the normal curriculum barely touched on.

Backing up a bit, Rick's Grade 7 progress reports from St. Charles Separate School reveals that he was a B+ (75-89) average student in Reading & Literature, Oral & Written English, and Social Studies (History/Geography). In Math and Sciences, he excelled as an A student (90-100). Non-graded subjects included Religion, Physical & Health Education, Art, French and Music. His teachers in Grade 7 were Mr. Legris and Mrs. Rita Zubac. Mrs. Zubac had been my music teacher at Levack Public School. Because there were very few music teachers in the district she taught at several schools. So here was another intersection in our journey. We both loved music. I came across a draft letter Rick had written to Mrs. Zubac. It was dated September 8th, 1969. He can't remember if he got a reply. When I read the letter to him recently, he chuckled at his 11-year-old-self. This is what he wrote, word for word:

> *Dear Mrs. Zubac:*
>
> *I'm the boy that sits four rows from the door in the (blank space) desk from the front. I think you are a good teacher in all subjects. I do think we should get more music though. I'd like to learn how to read music. If I'm already supposed to know how to read music, it's not my fault that I don't, because*

*I tried to learn. We do plenty of work and have fun
sometimes (he scratched that word out) and I like
that. But I think you give us too much homework.
I think that from either 3:00 or 3:15 to 3:30 you
should give us time to finish it.*

Yours sincerely Richard Tremblay

I had to laugh. I think all kids throughout many generations
have felt the same way–too much homework! Mrs. Zubac indicated in his report card: *Rick is skilled and always does his best in
all music and art activity.* Rick excelling in Art? This came as a
surprise. I found his 1970 Certificate of Merit from the Sudbury
and District Separate Schools Annual Art and Crafts Exhibition.
I asked him what had he created that merited 'a Worthy Piece of
Canadian Art' designation? He thinks it must have been something he built with his hands and that it would have had moving
parts. In Grade 7 Rick had started to excel in written compositions. Mr. Legris noted: *Richard's compositions are a pleasure to
read because he has a great variety of ideas and uses them.* That's all
I uncovered about Rick's grade school years, except for pictures. I
did find a final notation dated June 1970 from A.J. DeFinney, the
Principal, a terse note that read "Rick is promoted to Grade 8."
What an odd term "promoted" versus graduated too!

In September 1971 Rick went to Chelmsford Valley District
Composite School (CVDCS). It was only a 20-minute walk from
his family home on 137 Coté Street. Here Rick kept his report cards
from Grades 10 to 13 (1973 - 1976). His marks up to Grade 12
indicate that he was an average student in many of his subjects. He
was, however, more than average in English, Drafting, Residential
Planning, Geography and Data Processing. There was no mention
of music. When I asked Rick about music class, he said that in
Grade 9 he'd been assigned to learn the trombone when he would
have preferred playing guitar. The Guitar wasn't an option in the

school band. He also had a rough start with Mr. John MacNeil. I too found Mr. MacNeil a bit intimidating. However, I stayed with music throughout my five years of high school and played clarinet with the CVDCS High School Band. It wasn't until the college years, that I learned the school band had loosened up enough to include guitars, bass guitars, and keyboards. I think Rick would have stayed in music class and would have learned to tolerate Mr. MacNeil's teaching style if he could have played guitar.

Rick and I went to the same high school but we didn't know each other. I contacted some of his friends for their insights and memories of those early years. Wayne Golder is a close friend and he had this to share about their journey at CVDCS:

> *I first remember meeting Rick in Mr. Spears Grade 9 English class. At that awkward time of life, all the teenagers seemed to want to be part of groups and be cool, but I noticed Rick was different. He always seemed to have his own mind and his own opinions, yet somehow, he was very non-judgmental of others. That was an ideal I aspired to and I wanted to get to know him better. It seems we shared certain likes and dislikes of the same teachers and subjects. Examples being Mr. Ducharme the librarian or Mr. Wade the math teacher.*
>
> *We liked hanging out together because we were the same yet different. We both enjoyed a good debate and shared a similar viewpoint on many subjects. Rick is musical and I can't tell one note from the other. I recall often going to Rick's house, sometimes just him and I. Sometimes all the Tremblay's were there or sometimes there was a party happening. It was always fun at the Tremblay's and was different from the Golder's.*

When we were 16, I managed to buy an old '66 Chev and Rick and I used to cruise a bit in it. If I remember correctly, I think that is where Rick first started to learn how to drive. High school was a pretty good time, considering the stress of being a teenager.

I always knew Rick was unique in a way that I admired and aspired to. He was open in his thoughts and opinions; he tried to see the world from different angles. He was very welcoming to new people and old friends. Rick represented all of those things and has been my friend since we were 14 and I can't think of anyone I would rather have been my best man!

Wayne's words are evidence of Rick's genuine character. Rick is one of a kind.

There was an ominous blip during Grade 13. Rick's marks dropped below average and, in some cases, he even failed to hand in assignments. I noted that he was frequently late or even absent from school. Rick had mentioned that sometimes his asthma did make him sluggish but that wasn't the real reason for the drop in his marks. He was no longer motivated and wanted to leave high school and go to college. I asked if he'd sought help from the Guidance Counsellor. "No." This isn't surprising. Boys, and men for that matter, tended not to seek advice or help. I also knew that things at the Tremblay home had under-currents of family turmoil fuelled in part by alcohol dependencies. In the end, Rick did not complete Grade 13. I did find a partial lyric he wrote expressing his frustration: *"I guess you tried to be the teacher, but I wanted more than freekin' school."* I wonder what would have happened if he had sought guidance? I also wonder why his teachers and his parents didn't step in when his marks were dropping?

In 1977-78 Rick went to Cambrian College where he enrolled in the Electronics Engineering Technicians program. There were several courses in electronics, instrumentation, electrical fundamentals, and human resources management. He graduated with honours. Now he was motivated, even inspired!

In later years Rick enjoyed learning new subjects and earned several continuing education credits and certification courses at Algonquin College, to keep his skills up-to-date and to boost his résumé. He struggled with the time commitment required by these courses. Now he had less time for his music projects because he would have homework to do. The 11-year-old boy's opinion of homework was still alive and well in Rick's 48-year-old's mindset. Rick's need to learn on his own terms was now being met. The homework was to be tolerated as a peripheral nuisance.

What did I learn from my little investigation? Just how much were we alike? Just how much were we different? It was more than that. Let me explain.

EDUCATION EXPOSÉ — MONIQUE

When I began to survey our sheaves of paper and memorabilia from our educational years, it was obvious I hoarded more than Rick. Why had I hung onto these items for so many years? Am I a packrat? According to the Merriam-Webster dictionary, a packrat is 'a person who collects or hoards especially unneeded items.' How does anyone decide what to keep and what to toss? One man's trash is another man's treasure, in this case, this woman's treasure. Did I intuitively guess that someday I would need these artifacts? Now I'm thankful that I kept all of this unneeded stuff. It has triggered memories both fond and otherwise, and led me to penning yet another chapter in the 'Report Card of My Life.'

From September 1964 to January 1966, I attended Notre Dame de L'Espérance in Val Caron, Ontario. I was the only child in my family to attend a French Catholic school because my brother was a toddler and my sister was a baby. Reviewing the three report cards for kindergarten, 1st, and 2nd grade children, titled "bulletin scolaire for Jardin d'enfants and 1ère et 2ième années" I find that I was a good student in most subjects—lots of A's and B's. I enjoyed music class where we learned 'Savez-vous planter les choux', 'Sur le pont d'Avignon', 'Aloutte;' and of course 'Frère Jacques' I still remember the words to these songs. I still stumble on the English word for chou. Cabbage! Right?

My continued digging found my 'travail manuel' (manual work) marks for the first and second terms of kindergarten. The report cards started out merely "satisfactory" and then jumped to 'très bien' (very good) in the third term. 'Travail manuel' included colouring, painting, shaping, cutting, and gluing skills. I suspect that the jump in marks had a lot to do with finally being allowed to use my left hand. Initially, I had been coerced to use my right hand in my Catholic school. I remember going home with a note from the teacher indicating that I was having trouble colouring between the lines. Mom was skeptical because she knew I loved to colour. She asked me how I coloured when I was at school. I sat down, put my left hand in the back waistband of my school uniform, picked up a crayon with my right hand and started to colour. "Why are you doing that?" Mom asked. I replied "Dieu aime les enfants qui sont droitiers." Translation "God loves children who are right-handed." Mom said that this wasn't true and that I was to keep using my left hand. The next day my parents visited the school and I regained my freedom to be a south-paw. I marvel at the influence the Catholic school had over its students and how they used God as their licence to control innocent minds. Rick also had a brief encounter with this kind of licence during his kindergarten years. His Mom received a letter from the Priest saying that Rick was asking too many questions about God during religion class. He went on to say that "God didn't like children who questioned their elders." The next day Rick was enrolled in another school. Our parents had minds of their own and a willingness to step in and demand what was logical and best for their children's education.

I noticed a tagline on the front cover of the report card that reads 'Travail d'aujourd'hui'-succès de demain!' (today's work is tomorrow's success) I find that ironic because the work I put in at Notre Dame de L'Espérance barely kept me in good standing at Levack English Public School. My family moved to Levack because INCO had transferred my Dad's job to the Levack Mine. My marks plummeted just like the winter temperatures of January 1966. From Grade 2 to 8, I was in a perpetual state of catch-up with the class average. With each report card, there were 'Certificates of Achievement' and a unit of standing. For example, in Grade 2 there were two units and I needed to pass to move on to the next Grade. I was always behind, struggling between grades as I tried to learn a new language. I went home with yet another note for my parents. It read that if I didn't learn to speak English by the end of the year, I might have to go back to Grade 1. This was insane and unfair. I had 6-months to learn English or go back to Grade 1? To make matters worse I would be in the same grade as my baby brother. Good grief! I understood Charlie Brown's frustration. Maybe that's when I started to channel my inner Lucy Van Pelt? After years of hard work, I graduated from Grade 8 on June 26th, 1973. Maybe that's why I still keep this certificate. I certainly remember the effort it took to get it.

In September 1973, I was enrolled at CVDCS. It was only a 10-minute walk from my new family home on 245 Edward Street. This street ran parallel to Coté Street where Rick lived. We had moved again, this time from Levack to Chelmsford because of my Dad's job. So here I was in a new school, friendless and awash in the trials and tribulations of teenage-angst. I had no older brother or sister blazing the trail for me and the same was true for Rick.

I have all my CVDCS report cards from Grades 9 to 13 (1974-1978). Like Rick, I was an average student in several subjects. However, I excelled in History, Physical Education, Music, Home Economics and even English. The *lingual bête noire* from my grade school years no longer slowed me down. Math and Sciences were my weak points and I had to work hard to keep my marks up. I did additional homework, asked for support from the Guidance teachers and got help from friends who excelled in those subjects. I didn't mind homework or working on projects. I enjoyed the effort and sought creative ways in which to communicate what I had learned. I still have two of my projects from Grades 12 and 13 (1977-78). Recently I re-read them and shared them with Rick. The first was a comparison and contrast paper for Mrs. Lebel's English class where she had asked us to compare two songs. I picked 'I want to make you love me' by Janis Ian and 'Part-time Love' by Anne Murray. Mrs. Lebel wrote: "Quotes incorporated well, weak in some areas, but for the most part, well done!" (Mark 79%). Rick wasn't familiar with the songs so I played them while I tingled with flashbacks of listening to 45's on the family record player. I agreed with Mrs. Lebel's assessment. Now I am a more insightful interpreter of songs and understand what areas needed improvement. Rick was intrigued by the assignment and wished that he could have had a Mrs. Lebel as his English teacher.

The second project was a biography of a hero or heroine for Mr. McCool's Grade 13 History class. It may have been the 'Why Not?' campaign that encouraged girls to look at non-traditional roles and question gender inequities in the '70s that inspired me to do my report on Nellie McClung. I enthusiastically researched everything about *Windy Nellie*. Mr. McCool noted: "You have a somewhat awkward style, but your message comes through loud and clear. Your use of quotations was very skillful and your footnotes were correct. Well researched essay and interesting to read. An excellent effort." (Mark 86%). I was proud of that and the History Award I won at my Grade 12 graduation. Yes, I still have the trophy.

I continued to Grade 13 as did Rick but I was the more motivated. I kept my grades up and participated in various sports, Variety Night and in my fourth year was the President of the Girls Athletic Association (GAA). I became a member of the Student's Council, my first foray into leadership. My 'potential announcer' skills were discovered by accident. Mr. Joe Drago (of Sudbury Wolves fame) and also our high school principal asked if I would like to do the morning announcements. I was the first student to do this and took to it quite naturally. Like many of my Grade 13 classmates, I was struggling with what I wanted to do after high school. Although I was interested in teaching history and physical education, my true passion was performance arts–acting and singing.

The realist in me knew that the risks of failure were high in the music world. As for teaching, everyone I knew who was going that route had not been successful in finding jobs after they graduated. I also knew that I needed to go away to school. I needed my independence and that would not happen if I went to Cambrian College or Laurentian University. Mrs. Peggy Salisbury my gym teacher and more importantly my guidance counsellor helped me to explore my options. It was then that we discovered Radio & Television Broadcasting programs being offered in Ontario. The only post-secondary, college-level schools in Ontario were Ryerson University in Toronto and Canadore College in North Bay. I was accepted at both but I couldn't afford Ryerson and scholarships weren't available at that time. I did receive a grant and loan from the Ontario Student Assistant Program (OSAP) but it wasn't enough to pay for all expenses. However, I supplemented with the money I had saved from summer jobs. I could go to Canadore College. My parents questioned my educational choice and counseled me to go to the local college or university. Luckily for me, Radio & TV programs were not offered at either institution. My Grade 13 graduation was a double dose of encouragement: (1) I won the Principal's Award for best overall student and (2) It was announced that "Monique Dinel had been accepted to the Radio and TV Broadcasting program at Canadore College."

In 1978 and 1979, I was living in North Bay and learning to manage on my own. Almost. In the first year, I lived in a rooming house on 5th Avenue and shared a room with another Radio & TV student, who came from Temiskaming, Ontario, a 1½ hour drive north of North Bay. Every weekend she was expected to go home to help out with the family business. In the end, this demand on her time prevented her from completing On-Air shifts and other course expectations. In my 2nd year, I decided to stay at the College Residence. I had a private room in a town-house designed building that housed six students. The proximity to the college was perfect as my schedule was very demanding with odd hours seven days a week.

There were several courses in communications, politics, news writing, radio production, radio broadcasting, interviewing techniques and typing. I was surprised by the number of female students in the program, considering that this was traditionally a male-dominated profession. We were assessed equally in all of our courses, with one exception. Only the girls were tested for their vocal dB (decibel) levels. If the VU meter needle went into the red too often, we had to lower our natural speaking voice. It was believed by the industry at the time, that women's higher-pitched voices would be harmful to the public's hearing. We also weren't allowed to play two female songs back-to-back on the radio. It was still an old boys' domain and the CRTC (Canadian Radio & Television Commission) followed suit! In 1990, that all changed after *Lilith Fair* spearheaded by Sarah McLaughlin and the CRTC rule was taken off the books. I graduated with honours and won the INCO Radio Achievement Award. The trophy may be collecting dust but it still shines in my memory.

Like Rick, I enjoyed learning new subjects and earned several continuing education credits and certification courses at Algonquin College, Carleton University, Queen's University, and the Canadian Direct Marketing Association. This kept my skills up-to-date and expanded my résumé. Unlike Rick, I was fortunate enough to meet mentors along the way. They coached me and inspired me to expand my options.

What did I conclude from my little investigation? I think Rick and I did our best, rolled up our sleeves when we were motivated, and we were always open to learning. Just how much were we different? Rick was more introverted and worked out his challenges on his own, while I sought advice from mentors and then drew my own conclusions. Understanding ourselves and appreciating our respective successes was only possible because we were canny pack rats. Our sheaves of papers and memorabilia have allowed us to travel back in time, re-live our special memories and use them to strengthen our futures.

RICK'S CAREER PATH — OF SORTS

Rick and I do not recall making conscious decisions to follow specific career paths. We finished high school, went to college, and then hit the pavement to find work. Thinking 'Career' didn't become part of our vocabulary until the mid-1980s. We had moved from a one-industry mining hard-rock town into Ottawa, the Capital of Canada. Looking back perhaps we had followed a career path of sorts without realizing it.

During his high school years, Rick worked at the IGA grocery store on Errington Street in Chelmsford, Ontario. The IGA was the hub of 'Chemmy' and was conveniently located next to the Post Office, the Bank, and the Liquor Store. You were bound to bump into acquaintances regularly. Rick was a bag and stock boy and gofer for anything else that needed doing. Recently I came across Rick's elastic IGA bow tie and a cashier price list dated March 1st, 1976. Rick had kept it because he had written a song idea on the back of it. His scribbled notes give a glimpse into Rick the early songwriter: *Ignore time. On death, he held few regrets and I held none. I can't get used to love.* Price deals then were interesting: a 7lb bag of Five Roses Flour was on sale for $1.29 and a 2lb bag of McCain French fries was a deal at .69 cents. As an IGA employee, Rick learned many skills about customer service, how to pack groceries into a paper bag and how to pick up broken eggs using two pieces of cardboard, just to name a few. Eventually, he passed these skills on to me. I miss paper bags and now, in light of environmental concerns, I think it might have been a mistake to phase them out.

During 1977-78 Cambrian College years, Rick worked the odd Sunday shift at the IGA but then he secured a full-time summer job with Falconbridge Mines as an Electrical helper. He got to do the tasks the Electricians didn't like doing. Changing light bulbs underground is one such task. Sounds simple, doesn't it? Imagine a normal room with low light, then imagine absolute darkness. In the mines, it is so dark that if you hold your hand in front of your face and move it toward you, you will be surprised when you touch your nose. Miners are told that if their headlamp burns out and there is no light around them, they are to wait on-the-spot until someone finds them. Changing light bulbs is important for everyone's safety–with the possible exception of the changer. Rick had to climb up a 20 to 30-foot ladder in pitch dark to change burned-out bulbs. Rick was never afraid of heights after that job. Another helper task was to clean dashboard panels on mining equipment so that the knobs and levers would move freely.

In May 1978, Rick graduated from Cambrian College with his Electronics Engineering Technicians diploma. Like many other graduates, he was now looking for work. In a one-industry town, it was a tough search but he was finally successful and was hired at Cambrian Broadcasting (CKSO) in Sudbury. It turned out to be a short stint. Rick wrote in his journal: "Whoa boy! On Tuesday, August 29th, 1978 Chief Engineer Bill Scofield gave me the unexpected news that after 3 p.m. on September 15th, 1978 (the end of my probation period) my employment at CKSO would be terminated. Later on, Rick found there was an opening at the North Bay, sister location, and he moved there in October 1978.

Though Rick liked his work, he didn't enjoy the work environment. Full-time engineers had better shifts and more interesting work. Rick wrote: "My duties as an electronics technician were never clearly defined by my boss. I learned what I could from senior technicians. It was very difficult to learn anything at CKSO in North Bay. When I asked questions, the staff often seemed at a loss for answers." If Rick's first boss, Bill Schofield, had been given the proper tools of leadership then, he may have realized that Rick had much more to bring to the job. I had worked with Bill when I was a Radio Announcer at CKSO's sister station in Sudbury CIGM-FM, but luckily, I didn't have to report to him.

Rick found it difficult living in North Bay and commuting to Chelmsford every other weekend to visit his family and friends. It didn't help that the work was not satisfying. He wrote: "I saw very few good work habits here that would be beneficial to me, or that I would care to take with me to a new place of employment." In his résumé, he described his seven-month employment: "Responsible for maintenance and calibration of television broadcasting and transmission equipment as well as repair work that can be done at the station."

After one month in North Bay, Rick quit and moved back to his childhood home until he was able to find an apartment. He started a new job at Falconbridge Mines in the Instrumentation group on November 20th, 1978. Specifically, he worked at the Strathcona Mine in Levack Township, 22 km northwest of Chelmsford. Rick worked standard miner's shifts on weekly rotations. One week 'Days' (8 a.m. - 4 p.m.) the next 'Afternoons' (4 p.m. - 11 p.m.) and the following week the dreaded Graveyard shift (11 p.m. - 8 a.m.). Wannabee musicians didn't like the afternoon and graveyard shifts because this meant they would miss concerts or impromptu jam sessions.

From November 1978 to June 1979 Rick's résumé indicated: "As Technical Assistant I worked along with the technician on construction, and maintenance of various pneumatic and electronic instrumentation control systems from simple loops to computer interface." As a layperson, I don't completely understand what this means but it sounds impressive just the same.

Rick the Miner fourth from the right.

A few months after starting this job Rick heard about the Government of Ontario's Apprenticeship Electricians program. Rick applied and was accepted. As part of the Government of Ontario's apprenticeship program, he had to complete assignments and the required reading. Rick decided to read the materials during his lunch break. The Union Rep objected and insisted that he not bring his technical books into the mine. Reading Henry David Thoreau's *Civil Disobedience* and *Walden* was okay. Often, he was able to read well past his lunch hour while waiting for his next assignment. As an apprentice, he wasn't allowed to start any job unless told to. I teased Rick: "They pay you to read books? How lucky is that?"

Rick's apprenticeship program also included a two-month course covering the Electrical Code Book and other licence requirements. The course was held in Sault Ste. Marie, Ontario and Rick stayed at the Lincoln Motel paid for in part by the government and Falconbridge. At this point, I did my first solo long-distance drive in my Chevette. I was familiar with the 3-hour drive on Highway 17 up to the Little Current turn-off to Manitoulin Island because of family camping trips. This adventure gave me confidence for the future. Seeing my new boyfriend was a great motivator.

Rick finished all the required course elements for the apprenticeship program. All he needed now was to log in the required 'work hours'. This should have been straightforward but fate had a different plan. In 1982, Falconbridge reduced its workforce by 25% and Rick, as well as all other apprentices and full-time employees, were let go. INCO followed suit. Rick had only 3 months left until he completed the work hours required in the 4-year apprenticeship program and enabling him to write his final Electricians exam. Then he would have his 'ticket' as an Electrician. The Progressive Conservative government under Bill Davis's leadership did not allow the laid-off apprentices to write their exams. There would be no exceptions. Rick's only other option was to find an employer willing to take him on for 3-months so he could become a licensed electrician, a faint hope because Sudbury was now branded as the Unemployment Capital of Canada. Rick would never become a licensed electrician. The Ontario Government's apprenticeship program had failed Rick and many other hard-working young men of Northern Ontario.

During this frustrating time, Rick, along with his cousin Marcel Bouchard, wrote the Aurora signature song, 'The Ballad of Snowbound Road'[18], a lament of sorts about their unemployment. Their poignant verses explored that theme with a touch of humour tinged with irony.

> *Well she told me that I needed a job.*
> *I said, "Anything we need I can easily rob.*
> *Why must I stay within the criminal code?"*
> *Then, she said, "You can't have me!"*
> *I guess the best things in life they don't come free.*
> *I said, "Then get out and push 'cause I'm stuck on a*
> *Snowbound Road."*
>
> *So, I went out looking for work,*
> *But they made me feel like such a jerk.*
> *They didn't like the references I showed.*
> *It was just some friends of mine.*
> *And we all had ourselves a real good time.*
> *We were living on a Snowbound Road.*

Many left the Sudbury area to find work in Toronto, Hamilton, Windsor, or Ottawa. Late in 1982, Rick moved to Ottawa and lived with Kevin Newman and Brian Crook as he started his job search. Recently I found a Sucrets cough drop tin box with job postings from the Citizen that Rick snipped out with his pocketknife. He landed a brief contract with an Interconnect company, so brief that neither of us can remember the name. It involved wiring-up government and private sector office buildings.

His determination was finally rewarded when he found a job at Avtech Electrosystems Ltd. Rick was hired in September 1983 as an Electro-Mechanical Production Technician. His boss, a Ph.D. in Electronics, had started this company in 1975. He had a niche-market that created pulse generators that could measure things smaller than a Nano-second. Rick often referred to his boss as 'The Doctor' when he spoke of his work there to others. Eventually, Rick became the Senior Technician. He tested and calibrated Pulse Generator power supplies. He had specialized AutoCAD experience that leveraged the Vanguard 7000 computerized engraving system used to create the faceplates for the equipment. For nearly 20-years the relationship between The Doctor and Rick had been amicable. As long as Rick did what he was told and didn't try to be too proactive, things were fine.

In later years, their rapport became more strained. The Doctor and his wife were socially cordial at staff Christmas parties and yet they were elitist in their manner. Much like Sheldon Cooper in the Big Bang Theory, but colder and more calculated. I knew Rick had become unhappy, frustrated, and unappreciated at work. "It's the third Monday of the week." Translation: all days of the work-week were Mondays. I encouraged him to find something else but just as he was going to set the plans in motion, two-thirds of the Nortel workforce (60,000 staff) were laid off. Ottawa-based jobs in his field disappeared between 2001-2003. His options were now severely limited. He tried to find work as an electrical apprentice but nothing was available. The Doctor knew that and took advantage of this with his technical staff.

Then Rick found himself in an ethical dilemma. He had observed first-hand the disrespectful treatment of a young clerical employee. He couldn't just stand-by and so he voiced his carefully worded concerns with The Doctor. Had

Henry David Thoreau's *Civil Disobedience* influenced Rick's decision to act? Later that same day, I picked Rick up and noticed that he carried more personal stuff than usual. Rick told me then that the conversation with The Doctor had ended coldly with an "agree to disagree outcome." Rick didn't trust The Doctor, so he had decided to take his stuff home that Friday just in case. Rick's instincts were right. On Monday morning November 14th, 2003 as we were getting ready for work, Rick asked: "Are you going somewhere today, because there is a cab in the driveway?' I wasn't. The cab driver came to the door, asked for Rick, and gave him an envelope. It was from Avtech and it was formal notification of dismissal. The Doctor had not had the decency to dismiss Rick in person. He had also failed to follow Labour Board rules. Rick's lawyer set him straight. The Doctor had a Ph.D. but still had a lot to learn on many other fronts. His humanity meter was faulty.

Here was Rick at 46 with unique skills and work experience and again unemployed. We had always believed that years of faithful service with one employer had merit and would have value until we retired. Instead, we had learned that loyalty and quality work meant nothing. Nor could Unions protect you. Rick was seriously adrift and I didn't comprehend this until I myself, was set adrift in 2008. Maybe Rick was foreshadowing our outcomes when he wrote 'Honest Work' in 1993 on the back of an AutoCAD menu printout:

> *Looking for someone to take advantage of today—*
> *for Honest Work.*
> *Seems we gotta' sell our souls if we want to do—*
> *Honest work.*
> *Pay me for what I do, not for what I say I do—*
> *Honest work.*

Rick, with battered self-confidence, set out to find a new job—not a career. Eventually, he found contract work with the Spherion Employment Agency with short work assignments ranging from 1-3 months. The longest was 8-months with Med-Eng. Systems, which involved technical production line type of work. Here Rick was regularly exposed to a rubber drying agent that caused a severe case of Contact Dermatitis that damaged his skin on both hands. It looked like someone had taken an Exacto knife and cut his skin in deep gashes until it bled. Now he couldn't play guitar without pain and had difficulty holding anything in his hands. In September 2005, Rick went on medical leave and was on a waiting list with the Workplace Safety and Insurance Board (WSIB) for retraining in January 2006. Rick allowed himself to hope again that things were going to change for the better. However, fate derailed Rick's career or job track for good on December 22nd, 2005. The beginning of The Stroke Years.

MONIQUE'S CAREER PATH — OF SORTS

It's 2019 and I'm updating my résumé, once again documenting my experience and my accomplishments to market my skills to a potential employer. How did I get here? Some say, "Why aren't you retired yet?" That is a simple question. The answer is not simple. I haven't found it yet.

Like Rick, during my high school years, I worked for extra pocket money and started saving for college. The standard job for most teenage girls were babysitting. The pay was minimal by today's standards. There were few options for part-time jobs in Chelmsford, Ontario, particularly for girls. That changed when the Sudbury Downs racetrack opened in 1974. I was lucky enough to be hired as a pari-mutual cashier and then as a ticket seller. The harness racetrack was open Mondays, Wednesdays, and Saturdays and in summer between 7 p.m. and 11 p.m. The hours were perfect and the pay was more substantial than babysitting. Between races, we were allowed to do our homework. Bonus! Eventually, my father, brother and sister worked part-time at Sudbury Downs. I stayed there until I went to college.

I still wasn't making enough money to save up for college. That meant I had to find another part-time job in summer. As luck would have it a new opportunity emerged. The Summer Experience Program, funded in part by the Ontario Government and initiated by the municipalities kept high schools open in the summer for kids from 10 to 19 years of age. This gave them a place to go for arts and recreation during their school holidays. I was hired, along with Diane Ramarr, Maria Llana and Jane O'Link all CVDCS students, to run the afternoon and evening events at our high school. Diane and I were responsible for organizing tournaments, mini-workshops, and arts & crafts activities. We rounded out the end of the summer with a talent show.

The experience would turn out to be pivotal. Our team reported to the Rayside-Balfour Program Coordinator who was responsible for two high schools, Chemmy and Rayside. She was a first-year Laurentian University Student who had her ideas of leadership. When things went well, she took the credit. When things did not, she placed the blame. She was regularly unavailable when we needed her, leaving her employees to make do with what we knew. A boiling point was reached after a badminton tournament that we held at the school. Diane and I had opted for an elimination versus a round-robin tournament because of the time limitations and the number of participants involved. Competitors had a great time and we were proud of the outcome.

Imagine our surprise when at the staff meeting that night, when the Coordinator reprimanded us for choosing the elimination format. She listed our faults as she saw them, without knowing all of the facts. When she was through I spoke up. I reminded her that she had not been available to advise us. She had not been there for a single team member needing support. I asked how she would feel if we reported to the City Manager that she had been playing women's softball instead of being at work? Everyone knew this because the baseball field was near the high school and we had seen her playing there. Silence! The meeting ended abruptly with her storming out of the Student's Council Office. I had surprised myself as well as my colleagues. I had summoned sufficient nerve to take a risk and speak up. Meek Monique had morphed into Activist Monique. At age 17 my sense of justice was thrust into top gear. I had learned a valuable lesson. 'Stand your ground!'

After my first year of college in 1979, I was hired as the Summer Experience Program Coordinator and knew what to do and what not to do. Lead by example, listen, be present and provide encouragement for growth. These were skills I developed and practiced as I moved along my career path. I also learned to juggle responsibilities with other part-time jobs that same year. At times I was a roller-skating disc jockey at Roller Country in Sudbury and had to learn how to roller skate, a requirement for that job. Wearing roller-skates, playing records, taking requests, working the light-show, and announcing were simple enough tasks. What I didn't expect was that the job required that I clean the washrooms with my roller-skates on. This was not a part of my Radio program curriculum. I must note that the women's washrooms were worse than the men's. There was garbage on the floor, unflushed toilets among other disgusting habits. I was not impressed with my gender.

In my second year of college, I focused on my studies and job search simultaneously. Jobs in Radio & TV were few and there was a lot of competition. It was mostly a man's world but women were slowly penetrating the old boy's network. I can't remember how many résumés and audition tapes (cassettes & mini reel-to-reel) I sent out. In the end, I had contacted all stations in Ontario. There were many rejection letters. I still have copies of my cover letters, audition tapes and copywriting scripts.

Job prospects were looking grim until Gary Stevens, my instructor, gave me surprising news. CIGM-FM Radio of United Broadcasting was looking for a music programmer. They had reached out to him to find out if there were any students qualified and immediately available for the job. He gave them my name because I had the highest GPA. This meant that the college would allow me to finish my diploma on-the-job. At that point, I had three months left to complete before I could graduate. It was up to me to impress them at the interview. CIGM-FM was located in Sudbury as luck would have it. I returned to Chelmsford, stayed at my parent's house, and prepared for the interview. I was nervous and uncertain. It turned out to be a laidback interview more like a coffee house chat. We listened to my audition tape, reviewed my copywriting skills and then I did a cold read in the studio. That was it. I was offered the job. I couldn't believe it. Next thing I knew I was heading back to Canadore College in North Bay, to pack my belongings, say goodbye to my friends and fast forward into the adult workforce.

CIGM-FM was an adult contemporary format radio station. When I started in late 1979 as the Music Programmer, it was my job to complete the playlist for all radio shifts. There were several criteria I had to follow but the most notable was the CRTC regulations. Back then radio stations had to be regulated to play Canadian content (CANCON) because most stations only wanted to play Billboard chart-toppers. Primarily featuring US talent. Therefore, all songs played on-air had to be on playlists and in order, and I needed to indicate M-A-P-L criteria. M=Music, A=Artist, P=production and L=Lyrics. If you have albums at home, look at the labels for a circle with those letters in it. There has to be two of the letters blacked out to count as CANCON. Here's an example, Anne Murray is a Canadian Artist (A) but if the music (M), lyrics

(L), and production (P) were US-based, then that particular song would not count as having Canadian content. As the Music Programmer, I also had to make sure two out of every ten songs played met content guidelines.

Another CRTC regulation concerned female recording artists. It was against the rule to play two female songs back-to-back. The only allowable exception was if we were to feature a new album release and we had to keep that at to a minimum as well. This ruling stayed on the books until Sarah McLaughlin's Lilith Fair Tour in 1997 featuring only female artists. Sadly, things haven't changed much. When I heard about Jane Watson's 2019 study on *Gender Representation on Country Format Radio* found that in '2000 male to female artists were played at a ratio of 2.1 to one, and increasing to 2018 to 9.7 to one'[19] is evidence that there is still work to do on the 'equality front'.

I was behind the scenes at CIGM-FM. Occasionally, I read commercial copy but I didn't have an On-Air slot. There were no women announcers on this station or CKSO-AM, their sister station. One day, I spoke to Ron Smith, the morning announcer on CKSO, asking what I could do to get some air-time. He had an idea. First, I had to create a demo to share with the Station Manager. I would be the producer, researcher, writer, and host of *Growing Years*. This 30-minute pre-recorded segment would feature Sudbury's historical highlights and music popular at that time. For example, if I focused in 1959, I would play Country hits from the same year. When I recorded the demo, I had to remember to use my 'radio voice'. This meant speaking in the lower register to protect the hearing of my listeners, as I mentioned in the *Education Exposé*. Lately, I read Lloyd Robertson's memoir[20] where he acknowledged that "women were consigned to homemaker shows" and "at the CBC there was a general view that women's voices were not acceptable for general broadcast work." The odds were stacked against me but I had to try.

With the demo completed, it was presented to the management team and the senior announcers. The decision – it was a go! I was asked to produce five 30-minute segments that would be aired Monday to Friday and aired twice a day. My standard sign-off was, "I'm Monique Dinel, inviting you to join me again for *Growing Years* as you remember when you were there!"

There was one more goal I hoped to reach and that was to have my own 'live show.' When opportunities arose, I was passed over by male talent. The male contenders had better voices. I needed more experience. Then the unexpected happened. The 'drive-home' show announcer was at the microphone and was talking in circles with slurred speech. From my office, I could see him through the window. As I was checking the playlist for the next day, I heard a loud crash. The announcer had fallen backwards in his chair, feet up in the air and with a live micro-phone sprung up on the console. I acted quickly. I switched the mic off and the music on. He was passed out drunk on the floor. I paged the newsroom and two news announcers, includ-ing Ron Smith, came and helped him out of the studio. Ron came to my rescue and said: "Well Monique, you need to take over!" He gave me quick training on how to use the control board and that was it. "You're listening to CIGM-FM and I'm Monique Dinel!" The management team agreed to a three-week probation period. This meant I was working a split-shift from 6 a.m. to 10 a.m. as the Music Programmer and I was back from 5 p.m. to 10 p.m. for my on-air show. It was a perfect time too because CIGM changed to country format. As a singer, I was very familiar with country music and I had grown up listening to it at home. I had never admitted to liking it in high school. When the probation period was over, they gave me the show. I was the first female on-air radio personality in Sudbury.

CIGM-FM 1982 Superstars including Monique Dinel bottom centre. — Sudbury Star

I enjoyed the work, the people I worked with and the fans I met at various events. I was also amused by some of the comments from fans. One said, "You sound taller than you are!" Another fan called the station to complain about the new female radio announcer. She said, "my husband just started to listen to her show when normally he wouldn't listen to your station." I asked in my normal voice what the issue was? Her response? "She sounds too sexy for my taste!" I mulled that over for a bit and asked: "Who do you like listening to?" "Oh, I like Malo, what a soothing, romantic voice!" My response? "Does your husband complain about that?" Silence followed but I knew she understood double standard. When I revealed to her that I was the female announcer we both had a good laugh. I walked away with the attractive notion that I sounded sexy and taller on the air. Sadly, when there were major layoffs in the mining industry, my radio announcer days were over. I left CIGM-FM on April 22nd, 1983 and followed my soulmate as I headed for an unknown fork in my career path.

I had hoped to find work in radio when I moved to Ottawa, but there were no openings. So, I looked for any opportunity as I had bills to pay. I found a job as a service coordinator with Bytown Communications and was there for two months when the company laid off staff. I hit the pavement yet again and was hired by Colonial Furniture in October 1983 in the service department. I learned a great deal about appliances and furniture and had to think on my feet with customers requesting service or lodging complaints. After a few months, there was an opening in the advertising department. Here I would be able to leverage my copywriting skills. That fell through when they decided to use an advertising agency. After eight months on the job, they hired another service coordinator who reported to me. He was on the job for two weeks, and when I went to his desk to look for reports I saw his paycheque and photocopied it. Why? He was making $200 more a week than I was. I sought advice from the employment office to find out what my options were. The response? "You could complain but we recommend you don't if you have any hope of being employed elsewhere," said a representative of Service

Canada (formerly Employment Insurance). So, I kept silent and hoped for the right moment to come along.

Karma came through. I received a job offer for a three-month term position at Canada Post and they wanted me there the following Monday. "No problem," I said. After that, I typed my letter of resignation and provided it to my Manager. He said, "You have to give me two weeks' notice." "No, I don't," I replied. Then I showed him the photocopy of my colleague's cheque and asked, "Why is he being paid more than I am?" His answer, "Well he's married and has children to support!" I laughed, "So if I have kids you will pay me more?" He conceded that that wouldn't happen and admitted that they had handled this badly. They did give me a letter of recommendation and the owners, Mr. Sid, and Mr. Ed, (the Cohen brothers), gave me a bonus to my paycheque before I left. My sense of justice was evolving nicely.

This was not the first time I was underpaid because of my gender. I learned early on when I worked for CIGM-FM that men were paid more. My brother Mike went into the same field of work but as a cameraman, not on-air talent. When he started at CKSO-TV, also with United Broadcasting, he was making $18K a year, while I, who had been on the job for three years was making $12K. Canada Post also paid women less than men for the same job. In 2011, PSAC won a thirty-year pay equity case at the Supreme Court of Canada to compensate female employees. I received a cheque to cover the time I spent in a unionized (PSAC) position. Unfortunately, inequality still exists today. Stats Canada reported that from 1998-2018, women continue to earn 13.3% less an hour than men.

December 3rd, 1984 was my first day on the job at Canada Post. I had no idea of what was in store for this nickel miner's daughter, at this crown corporation. Growing up in Sudbury, I had never known anyone who worked for either the provincial or federal government. My summer job at the high school reported to the municipal government but that was the little leagues compared to the Nation's Capital. My first month at the job was a calamity. I was hired as an administrative support clerk. After two weeks on the job, I found out that my manager had hired me during a hiring freeze, which technically he was not allowed to do as this was against Human Resources rules. Since I had a letter of offer that they had to honour that, it meant they would have to find me another job, as I couldn't stay in that job they hired me for. There was an immediate vacancy and since I was an extra PY (person-year) in the Finance Department, I was told to report to Mr. Craig, the Vice-President of Finance. I had heard rumours about him from some of the clerical staff and they weren't good. Most secretaries refused to work for him. The job was vacant because his executive secretary had left. There I was with no secretarial experience and skipping several levels into a management job. Mr. Craig was tough and fair most of the time. My Manager had not completed my payroll forms, which meant I was yet to be paid. So, Mr. Craig paid me with travellers' cheques. I was paid with travellers' cheques for eight months. Despite the hiring freeze, my term was extended and I was hired on full-time. Eventually, I was promoted into an officer position, which morphed into a variety of other positions for various projects between 1987 and 1999.

The highlight during this timeframe happened when I became a member of the Commercial Development and then Small Business Marketing team. The team was responsible for implementing the Commercial Dealers and the Business Access programs. These Commercial Dealers operated local package delivery businesses and they became a delivery agent for CPC. Essentially, I found myself within a unique group of small business marketing mavericks. We were at the forefront of marketing to this customer segment. It was considered risky and many companies didn't trust the viability of small businesses yet. After the first two weeks on the job, I feared that I was out of my league. I walked into

Lynn Palmer's office and said, "I think you made a mistake hiring me!" It was then that I saw what real leadership and mentoring looked like. She listened. She encouraged. She believed in me. After all these years, I am most grateful for the gift Lynn gave me. What a team we had and to this day we rekindle that unique spirit when we get together as a 'kindred family'.

If I were to pick my biggest achievement at Canada Post it would be the VentureOne Loyalty Program, now known as Small Business Services. From 1999 until 2008 this program was planned and launched in phases across the country. I was promoted to Manager, Small Business Marketing and reported to Paul Tomascik, a new Director and employee with CPC. We were a great team and fought an internal battle to get this program approved as a pilot in Halifax and Calgary. Eventually, it was launched and small business customers loved the program. I became known as *Ms. VentureOne,* the advocate and voice for small businesses. Recently, I was at a Shopper's Drug Mart and I overheard the clerk promoting the benefits of this program to a customer, while I was waiting in line. When it was my turn, I told her she did a great job explaining it. I mentioned I was one of the innovators who launched this program. She responded that it was the best thing CPC had ever done for small businesses. I felt so proud.

I and many of my colleagues felt that we would end our career at Canada Post but that was not to be. Canada Post had a new President in 2005 and a year later based on the new Federal Government had a darker mandate to reduce costs. They targeted non-unionized employees between the ages of 40 and 50, with more than 20-years' service, and were considered a strain because of their financial benefits. I was a perfect candidate. On August 18th, 2008 I was fired! Nine months from my 50th birthday, 15-months from my 25-years' service mark, and with over $50K in yearly medical expenses. When the Human Resources (HR) representative told me I was fired, all I could think about was Rick. How would I pay for his medical bills? At that time, it cost $6,600 a month for his care at Saint Vincent's under the Sisters of Charity Organization. Rick had no benefits. HR representative presented me with a 'package' that they expected me to sign, on the dotted line, right then and there! I did not. They told me I had to leave and that I would not be allowed to get my personal items. Someone would get my purse and car keys. They did agree that I could call Judy Follet, my colleague and friend, to drive me home as I wasn't able to. This was the start of another dark period in my life. Now I had no job, no way to support Rick and an uncertain future. I was scared. I was disgraced. I was shattered. I was angry.

I don't know if it was denial or stubbornness but I undertook my first 3 km run that day. I had managed to lose weight and to take care of myself after Rick had his stroke. So, I intended to run. I wasn't going to let CPC take that away. I picked up my Mom and then Rick at Saint Vincent's and we walked towards Dow's Lake where we would meet Brian Crook. Halfway up Booth Street, a wheel fell off Rick's wheelchair. I lost it. I was crying when I told Rick that I'd lost my job. He responded, "Don't worry I will find a job soon!" Bless his heart, for you see he still thought it was 2005. I never made it to the race. My brother-in-law and nephew, Norm and Nick Gagne happened to be driving by. They picked us up and brought us back to Saint Vincent's and brought Mom home. I stayed with Rick that night laying in his single bed, wrapped in his arms as he consoled me while I sobbed and trembled. Rick was my anchor in my dark, stormy, unchartered waters.

The next day I hired Peter Bishop as my lawyer and called Mary Ford, my financial planner. They both arrived at my home and gave me hope. I was also grateful to my Dad because he kept me focused on the legal journey. He, along with my lawyer, was there for the final two meetings with the Adjudicator and CPC's three lawyers, my former boss, and two human resources representatives. Finally, in June 2010 Goliath went down in shame. This time I cried tears of joy after a two-year battle.

Like Rick, I too had my self-confidence tattered, so I set out to find a new job but not a career. I did so during the legal battle and latched on to any part-time, term or contract opportunities. From 2009 onward, I worked at the National Research Council – Industrial Research Assistance Program (NRC IRAP), Hewlett Packard, the Canadian Transportation Agency, CTV National News and Industry Canada. I also dabbled into Voice Acting and did a few paid recordings. I plan to reconnect with this profession. With each position, I reconnected with the skills and the passion for things I enjoyed. It wasn't an easy road. I had to prove myself to others and more importantly, to myself.

It's 2019 and I am 60-years old. I've updated my résumé and reflected on the path taken. Ten years ago, I would not have had the strength to write this chapter. I had to find my way back and restore my self-esteem one memory at a time. I can proudly say that my career path had shining moments that far outweighed the bad. I needed to remind myself of that. I still do. As for my future path, ideas continue to percolate. But until I know for sure, I will stand my ground and trust my instincts–and my well-honed sense of justice.

JAVA INFUSED DAYS

In our kitchen, the glass cabinet shelves are dedicated to special dishes including four earthenware mugs, tall and narrow, partially glazed with a simple wheat-like motif, made on a production line somewhere in Japan as the stamp on the bottom states. This quartet of mugs represents precious memories of 'my #1 fan' and our java infused days.

When I worked at CIGM-FM Rick was 'my #1 fan'. He would often drop by the studio to keep me company. When I look at the mugs, I smile and remember his first surprise visit. I could see him through the studio window as I talked to my audience live on-air. He sat and watched me in action while at the same time checking out the latest albums in the music studio. Once I was off-the-air, we greeted each other with a double big hug. I noticed he was wincing. "Are you okay?" I asked. Apparently, he had intended to hitch-hike from Chelmsford to Sudbury but then gave up on his thumb and walked instead. I couldn't believe it. He'd walked 20 kilometres along the gravel shoulder of Highway 144. When he sat down and took off his shoes and socks, he exposed a nasty blood blister on one foot. He wasn't concerned but I quickly went in search of a first aid kit. When my radio shift was done, Rick had another surprise—food, wine, dessert, and coffee.

Our coffee drinking journey—let me rephrase that 'our specialty coffee' drinking journey, started at the Continental Café in Sudbury, Ontario in 1980. Before that time, I had not liked coffee. Now I was the only female radio announcer at CIGM-FM where it was considered a right-of-passage that all radio personalities should smoke like chimneys (second only to INCO's super stack), and drink gallons of coffee loaded with milk and heaps of sugar. A Double-Double paled by comparison. Only drinking Pepsi or Coke 24-hours a day would come second to that. Again, not my cup-of-tea. At the time Hot Chocolate was my beverage of choice made with Fry's Cocoa and brown sugar, the real deal. Not like that Carnation hot chocolate powdered concoction.

Rick changed my mind when he introduced me to coffee mixed with Brandy, Grand Marnier and a hint of Bailey's. That was 'Clara's Coffee' recipe at the Continental Café. To further enhance the experience, the rim of the cup was dipped in a honey-sugar blend topped off with a healthy dollop of fresh whipping cream. As a side was a generous slice of Clara's best Black Forest Cake, made with fresh ingredients in each layer, including dark cherries that were lovingly immersed with a lavish measure of Kirsch. Did I mention layers upon layers of fresh cream and sublime dark chocolate? No calories there! Right?

The Continental Café was known for Clara's Coffee and Black Forest Cake. When Rick and I moved to Ottawa, despite several attempts, we found no restaurant or bakery that could come close to recreating the taste of 'home'. Eventually, we were able to replicate Clara's Coffee, taking care to brew a full-bodied dark roast, whipping up fresh cream, not that oil-based stuff from a can–yuk!

We became pros at making specialty coffee and our friends insisted we be responsible for the after-supper or après-ski pick-me-ups. This meant bringing along our Melitta Pour Over 6-Cup Coffee Maker with Glass Carafe. This was well before the fancy barista equipment of today.

Our four earthenware mugs are silent witnesses to those soirées, particularly those held during the winter months. They had an elixir of flavours that went hand in hand with the conversations and laughter with old friends. Though our social circumstances have changed, those mugs still evoke the heady memories of those Java infused days. I think it's time to reincarnate our Java tradition and create some brand-new specialty coffees and maybe try again to find the ultimate Black Forest Cake, one that can equal that of the now long-gone Continental Café. Rick is still my #1 fan and I am his and together we will continue to savour our special 'Java with Love' filled with infused memories.

CANADIAN SIGHTSEERS — WESTBOUND

We love Canada! Plain and simple. Rick and I have never needed anyone to cajole us into making the effort to explore '*our home and native land*'. We are proud Canadian sightseers who are grateful to have been able to visit all the provinces. The Northwest Territories, Yukon, and Nunavut are waiting on our sightseeing wish list.

Our first foray as Canadian sightseers began on Friday, July 10, 1981, and we were travelling in Rick's 1980 Subaru GL5 sedan. The Subaru was packed with camping gear and Rick's guitar. Rick and I were on our first vacation as a couple since we'd started dating on June 6, 1980. We were heading West toward Peace River, Alberta to visit Rick's friend Jack Balez. I had decided to keep a Travel Journal to record our inaugural trip. We left Chelmsford, Ontario in the morning and arrived at Lake Superior Provincial Park at 10:30 p.m. My first entry read: "We were greeted by friendly park staff and hungry mosquitos!" This was the furthest west we had ever been. A milestone. We regularly shared driving on this trip and many thereafter.

I had a lot of experience with camping because my parents had taught my brother, sister, and I everything they knew. My Girl Guide camping badge had proved that I had the necessary training to rough it in the great outdoors. Mom and Dad had planned vacations to both Canadian and US destinations. They never failed to buy pennants from all the places we visited and these were prominently displayed on the family's rec room panelled walls. Dad was the driver and Mom was the navigator. The Tag-A-Long-tent trailer was hitched to the car and travelled the highways and gravel roads to campgrounds. Our family had visited Québec, New Brunswick, Nova Scotia, and Prince Edward Island. In the US we had visited Michigan, New York, Wisconsin, New Hampshire, Vermont, and

Maine. On weekends we spent time on Manitoulin Island, Ontario and stayed either at Mindemoya or Providence Bay campgrounds.

Rick had limited camping experience. His family had camped twice at Lake Nosbonsing, near North Bay, Ontario, only two hours away from Chelmsford, Ontario. There they would pitch a tent next to his Uncle Fern and Aunt Fernande Cousineau's cottage. Rick's family were not frequent vacationers, preferring to stay close to their Northern Ontario home.

I set about tutoring Rick on the fundamentals of camping. First, I insisted on pitching our new tent a week before our trip so we knew what we were dealing with. We needed to make sure we had all the tent pins, poles, guy ropes, a flysheet, and a groundsheet. We conducted our practice run in the daylight. A tent put up in the dark might have sorely tested our newly minted relationship. Our first night by the shoreline of Lake Superior was breathtaking. The sky was so clear it seemed that we might touch the stars. But it was cold. Thankfully our sleeping bag had room for two, or Rick would have frozen to death. I am the heat-source in our relationship. When I had to go to the bathroom in the early morning Rick was not too willing to let his human-furnace leave. It's nice to be needed!

We continued our road trip following the shores of Lake Gichi-Gami, the Ojibwe name, for Lake Superior. While doing so we listened to Gordon Lightfoot's the 'Wreck of the Edmond Fitzgerald' and thought about the men who had lost their lives in the cold freshwater of Gichi-Gami. When it was my turn to drive, Rick would play his guitar sitting in the back seat because if he'd stayed in the front the neck and headstock of the guitar would have been in my face. Now that's my definition of distracted driving. Rick noted in the journal *I played Walk-on (by Neil Young) but I had to use the music book. Again!* The *Monique & Rick* musical duo was born on the open road.

Soon we saw welcome signs for Kenora Ontario, Saskatoon, Saskatchewan, Lloydminster then Edmonton, Alberta. The big surprise was Saskatchewan. Everyone we spoke to had warned us that we would be bored by all the flat land with nothing to see. My reaction was more empathetic. I found myself connecting to the pioneer spirit that oozed from the vast and enchanting sweeps of the prairie. This province truly lives up to its licence plate tagline 'Land of the Living Skies!' After a long drive of 2,500 km, we arrived at Peace River, Alberta on July 13th. I wrote, "We finally reached the Peace River. Peaceful is a good way to describe the beauty of this area. The town is nestled amongst rolling green hills, and I mean hills." We stayed a few days with Jack and his brother Paul and their girlfriends Llynne and Liz.

Rick and I were quite surprised when Jack and Llynne decided to join us for the rest of our westbound trip. That meant we had to streamline our luggage and regrettably Rick had to leave his guitar behind. Now that's roughing it for a musician. The four Chemmy travellers saw the W.A.C. Bennett dam then we headed to Prince George and eventually camped at Golden Ears Provincial Park, one of the largest parks in British Columbia. It was another late-night arrival but we were now pros at putting up tents in the dark. Our flashlights weren't working but we were able to start a fire and cook supper. Without a Coleman stove, we truly had to rough it by cooking over a fire pit. Llynne used a black cast-iron pan making it hard to see if the bacon was cooked. Rick bravely offered to test the first strip to see if it was done. His first crunch resembled the sound of a brittle branch cracking off a tree. He grabbed a beer to wash down the charred remains.

On July 19th, after a ferry ride on the S.S. Coquitlam at Nanaimo, we drove to the west most point of Canada–Tofino, British Columbia. Here, Rick and I saw the Pacific Ocean for the first time. Of course, we had to roll up our jeans and walk into the cold saltwater to baptize the moment. That was the last entry in the journal but that wasn't the end of the trip. We had to head back to Peace River and drop off Jack and Llynne, pick-up our stuff, especially Rick's guitar, and head back to Chelmsford. We only had five days left before we had to be back at work on July 25th. Of course, the trip was just as spectacular on the way back. Rick played his guitar again; we sang our favourite songs and we created the soundtrack for our first vacation together.

It wasn't until 1999, that Rick and I were able to take another vacation to and through the western provinces. We had three weeks off and were able to appreciate places we hadn't had time to see on the first westbound trip. The Rockies between Banff and Jasper and the Columbia Icefield were the highlights of that trip. We have wonderful pictures to remind us of their beauty. We saw incredible panoramas of Mother Nature's beauty both in her landscapes and the animals that make their homes on these slopes, Mountain Goats, Elk, Moose, Grizzly, Fox, and Wolf were some of the most impressive animals we were able to see, albeit from a safe distance. Most times. I did have a face-to-face encounter with an Elk who was eating flowers from a planter hanging from a light post in downtown Banff. I had turned the corner to walk to our car and then stopped dead in my tracks. My brown eyes stared into the Elk's brown eyes. Rick was right behind me. We were skittish. The Elk was cool and simply sauntered across the street to graze on more pansies. On another occasion, there was Rick's close encounter. He needed to go to the bathroom and left the warmth of the tent. When he returned, he noticed something moving in front of the tent opening. It was an Elk and her two calves grazing on grass, and although they'd noticed Rick they didn't move. While they were foraging Rick was freezing and I was fast asleep. I had no idea what happened until an icy body snuggled up to me in our sleeping bag and I was instantly awake and somewhat terrified. Then through chattering teeth, Rick told me what happened. As for his quivering body, his heat-source came to the rescue.

The weather out west was unpredictable. Some days it would rain others snow–even in July. The ever-present Chinook's may have had a hand in that. We made do with whatever Mother Nature threw at us. We decided to leave our tent at the Banff provincial park for a drive to Jasper and the Columbia Icefield for the day. We brought an overnight bag, the guitar, and the mandolin with us just in case we needed to stay overnight. This was a wise decision. Our visit had taken longer than planned and it was getting late. Rick had heard that the highway back to Banff was closed. We and a lot of other tourists were now stranded in Jasper. All the hotels were booked but a Gas Station attendant told us that many people open up their homes as Bed & Breakfasts for these situations. We went in search of a place to stay overnight. Rick found one, but the Italian homeowner said in broken English, "Bed no breakfast!" We were fine with that. The spotless room was decorated with religious pictures and statues. A double mirrored door compounded the impact of these artistic visions. I had trouble sleeping because I swear the eyes on the statues were watching me. I was glad that we were now married because I'm not sure if devout Italian Catholics would have appreciated common-law sinners sleeping under their roof.

As soon as possible we left Jasper and returned to our tent which was now nestled under a blanket of snow at Banff National Park. Rick wished he had packed his long-johns but not for long. That day we set out to see the Calgary Stampede moving from -2 degrees in Banff to 22 degrees Celsius in Calgary. What a shift! I was melting in a long-sleeve shirt, jeans, and Boulet boots. I bought an official Calgary Stetson white hat to help keep me cool. We scored two tickets, at half-price for the sold-out event from a US tourist whose friends couldn't make it. What an incredible event to watch, except when I closed my eyes during bull riding.

We decided you have to be very brave and wild to be a rodeo cowboy or cowgirl.

As with every vacation, it was time to head back to our home in Ottawa. We said goodbye to the Rockies and headed home via Drumheller, Alberta to the Royal Tyrrell Museum, Canada's only museum dedicated exclusively to the science of paleontology. Rick opted to take a less travelled highway to Drumheller and it soon looked like we were heading nowhere. No civilization in sight. Then I spotted a herd of Buffalo. We stopped and watched these massive beasts. As we drove again, I was concerned about getting lost while Rick was steadfast that we were still on track. We had been driving in the mountains for so long we were conditioned to looking up and not down. Looking down I spotted ditches with deep crevices. Then the road turned and we saw Drumheller directly below us. It was like a big lake minus water. Not minus an eerie landscape though–one reminiscent of a long-ago time and now the resting place of Dinosaurs. The exhibits of these creatures and the work involved in discovering them were truly inspiring. When I was in high school, I had an interest in archeology and digging up artifacts fascinated me. It was very hot that day—much hotter than in Calgary. We had planned to pitch our tent near Drumheller but the heat, the mosquitos, the black widow spiders, and scorpions held no appeal. Perhaps they were the reason why I chose not to pursue an archeological career. Though it would have been magical to camp near the Hoodoos and imagine the stories they could tell.

On July 14th, we rented a cabin at the Trails' End Resort near the Lake Superior Provincial Park. There was a big storm and the park rangers said it wasn't safe to put up a tent and we agreed. This was the last night of our trip and putting up a tent in gale-force winds and getting drenched didn't sound like a nice way to end our vacation. Rick and I walked around the resort and hearing live music, we followed our ears. Tourists and staff had decided to have an impromptu jam session. Rick ran back to our cabin and got his guitar like a kid going to an amusement park. We played until midnight. In our travel diary, Rick wrote: *The session ended when Monique sang 'Crazy' and the folks were quite impressed.* The music and the camaraderie were a great finale for our lengthy trip, a perfect way to end our western adventures.

CANADIAN SIGHTSEERS — EASTBOUND

When we moved to Ottawa in 1982, we didn't truly appreciate how close we were to the east coast until we were planning our next adventure. Rick's employer always shutdown the office during the first two weeks of July and that meant our summer vacation schedule was set for years. Consequently, each year we were in a different Canadian city to celebrate Canada Day—a unique circumstance. Although we didn't keep track of our trips in a diary our photo albums and videos do a good job of documenting our East Coast Adventures.

Adventures abound and one of the most memorable was Newfoundland. Our first time on The Rock was pure happenstance. Rick and I were in North Sydney, Nova Scotia staring at the ferry heading for Port-aux-Basques, Newfoundland. We were drawn to it and decided to try our luck and add our name to the waiting list to get on. We don't usually book in advance and are usually happy to take our chances with no reservations for anything. Here we were again—winging-it! We waited as we watched cars, trucks, motorcycles, and camper trailers drive up the ramp into the ferry. Then the other stand-by cars ahead of us began to drive in. Finally, a crewman came to our car and gave us the green light to drive up the ramp. My 1980 Chevette was the last car on before the ramp was raised sealing off the ferry.

It was 11 p.m. and Rick and I were a little road weary. We needed some sleep but found out that sleeping in our car was not allowed. All the sleeping cabins were booked. All the cafeteria benches and lazy boy chairs had lucky first-come-first-serve passengers occupying them. We would have to sleep outside on the upper deck in our sleeping bag with our clothes on. With the rolling motion of the ferry lulling us we fell asleep quite quickly. In the morning our sleeping was cut short by a loud blast of the foghorn. We were right beneath it. I was shaking and desperate. Where are the lifeboats I thought? Everything was shrouded in fog. Later I learned that the islanders affectionately called this the Newfoundland Fog machine. Then we noticed that there were other passengers peacefully napping on the upper deck. Only a few of us had been traumatized by the horn. We were the tourists; the others were Newfoundlanders and a fog horn to them was simply their alarm clock.

After we calmed down, we were drawn into the magical, surreal beauty of Port-Aux-Basques. Each building was painted in bright colours of fuchsia, lime green, purple and turquoise. The fog blanketed the townscape with just the right amount of artistry. Mother Nature was painting a picture just for Rick and I. When we drove off the ferry and onto terra nova the car was sluggish. I complained to Rick, "my Chevette must be seasick." We drove to the nearest garage and mechanics sauntered over to us. They popped the hood, spoke a strange language, tinkered a bit and before you know it the Chevette was humming along to a local jig. When we wanted to settle the bill, the owner said, "shag it." What? Then one of the mechanics translated that to "forget it." They gave us directions to Green Point campground but since I understood less than 50% of what they had said we would have to use our map. They waved us off saying, "May the wind always blow in your back." That we understood and the wind was with us for the rest of our trip.

We had our second adventure in Newfoundland thirteen years later in July 1995. This time we had two whole weeks' vacation. We booked our tickets for the ferry to Port-Aux-Basques and departed from Argentia, Newfoundland. We made sure our voyage was during the day to avoid the need to book a room. We didn't want another night beside the fog horn. That plan was fine for the 5-hour trip but the 16-hour voyage was pushing it and we could have used a nap. Our other option was a bar that featured local entertainment. The bar was located in the center of the ferry where the swells and waves of the ocean didn't affect us nearly as much. There we could at least relax.

Rick and I decided to go back to Green Point the site of our first camping site in Newfoundland. This time we were in a Mazda MPV van that we had modified for camping. On our first night, we were the only campers at the campground. The next day we had company with campers from Saint John's, Newfoundland. Before we knew it, we were invited to a Capelin BBQ. Capelin are similar to freshwater smelts but larger. I love smelts! This was a treat compared to our standard camping meals.

The next day we left for Gros Morne National Park. We wanted to see Western Brook Pond, the only freshwater fjord formed by glaciers that created the impressive cliffs and waterfalls, including Pissing Mare Falls. Yes, that's its name. I'm not making it up – truly. When you hear 'Pond' what are you picturing? Something small suitable for a rowboat but not a tour boat – right? When I asked the tour guide why they called it Western Brook Pond versus Lake, the matter of fact response was "well a lake (pronounced leak) is a hole in your boot!" Go figure.

We drove on, stopping at various little towns and were amused by the whirly-jigs that decorated most lawns. Other times we sort of channelled the first explorers as they would have ventured through the glorious vistas of the untouched landscape of the Terra Nova National Park. Along the way, we met more Newfoundlanders and shared a 'fine mug up or two' and enjoyed a few 'scoff n' scuffs'. Eventually, we arrived in Saint John's, Newfoundland and George Street, the mecca for traditional music. It seemed like everyone could sing, play guitars, keep the beat with bodhrans and spoons. The Rock has no shortage of natural storytellers. The 2019 TV commercials about Newfoundland say it all, "Around here you'll hear stories. And they are all true. Especially the bits they make up!" Rick and I smile every time we hear that.

The story of our Newfoundland adventures would not be complete if we didn't mention music. We lapped it up. Every note, every word, and every song. We discovered Ron Hynes, Newfoundland's 'Man of a Thousand Songs', a popular folk singer-songwriter and winner of many awards. The most notable song was 'Sonny's Dream' a song any folk-singer would proudly have in their repertoire. Rick and I soon discovered other musicians from The Rock – Figgy Duff, Dick Dolan, Eddie Eastman, Great Big Sea, and later Alan Doyle. In my humble opinion, you are not fully Canadian until you've discovered East Coast music especially the music from Newfoundland.

It is during this trip that Rick and I became whale watchers. Off we were to Bay Bulls on the O'Brien's tour boat – a modified lobster fishing trolley that was not designed for passenger comfort. It started as a 'good day on clothes' (translation: Nice Day) until we left the harbour for the open sea. The waves were five feet high and swells six feet. That made it quite a rough trip under skies that grew ever darker. Rick asked the Tour boat captain when they would cancel a trip? The response, "When no one comes on the boat," and added, "I've seen bigger waves in my bathtub." To calm my nerves, I jumped at the chance to be 'Screeched In'. I wore the Sou'wester, read the Newfoundlander pledge and since there was a moratorium on cod, I had to kiss the arse of a Puffin. Then I drank a shot of Screech

Newfoundland's golden elixir and received my certificate on July 9th, 1995. Rick didn't 'Screech in'. He never did. He is, however, an official member of the Order of The Sou'wester. I bought this oilskin rain hat from Signal Hill Newfoundland during a business trip as a Christmas gift in 1995. Turns out we both had a case of the 'loppies' or so the waitress told us. Rick and I felt like we were constantly moving up and down like the rolling sea even as we sat or stood. It took several hours before that feeling faded. While in Bay Bulls we stopped at a gift shop and Rick bought Ron Hynes's CD *Face to the Gale*, featuring 'Sonny's Dream'. The store owner Chris gave us a warm welcome. When he found out we were musicians he mentioned that there was a CD release party for buddies of his at a pub in St. John's. That night we checked this out. I don't remember the name of the band but I do remember what happened that night. When we got to the pub, we were told they had sold out. No entry. We were about to leave when we heard, "Don't let those Tremblay's in by's!" We turned and saw it was Chris from Bay Bulls – beaming, grinning, and dragging us in as if we were long lost, friends. That night we were adopted even though we were the only non-Newfoundlanders in this pub.

The East Coast would draw Rick and me back time and time again. The connection had become deep and emotional. If Rick and I were to choose between West and East, the choice is certain. East wins. The wonder of the Maritimes from Nova Scotia, New Brunswick, Prince Edward Island and Newfoundland have been imprinted in our memories and our hearts. It would need a separate book to share all of our adventures. Whenever we eat scallops we think of Digby, Nova Scotia. Whenever we see the ocean, I remember Rick sailing Brian and Anne-Marie Bonia's 26-foot sailboat the 'Capella' in Nova Scotia's harbour. Whenever we see the red flat rock in our garden, I remember the peculiar coloured shoreline of PEI. Rick and I became 'Kindred Spirits' with everyone we met along the way. That East Coast connection will last a lifetime.

CANADIAN SIGHTSEERS — SOUTHBOUND

'Ontario, Ours to Discover!'. We live in an incredible, massive, and multifaceted province. There is so much variety in our province, in its landscapes and its people. Ontario has a heart and a soul that Rick and I are a part of. Although we are proud Northern Ontarians with deep roots, we still wanted to explore other parts of Canada's largest province, to revel in its beauty and to mingle with ever more of its varied inhabitants.

I was fortunate that my family had gone camping regularly. All of us learned early on to appreciate the beauty of our country and our province. I wanted Rick to experience some of my family's favourite places. We started with Manitoulin Island situated in beautiful Lake Huron. It's a two-hour drive from Chelmsford to the Little Current Swing Bridge. We could never predict what awaited us at the bridge. It could have been swinging on its pivot to let tall boats travel through the North Channel or we might have to wait our turn to cross while cars leaving the island were given the right-of-way. Soon after crossing this single-lane bridge our adventure began with pitching our tent at the Mindemoya Campground. Then off we went to the 'Cup and Saucer Trail', which climbs the escarpment and provides a panoramic view of the island. Every time I've walked this trail I have experienced something divine, even as a young girl. Rick sensed it too. It was special for both of us. The modern Odawa name for Manitoulin Island is *Mnidoo Mnis*, meaning 'Spirit Island' and this is an apt name.

Our next favourite spot was the Providence Bay Tent and Trailer park. Here the beach is a spectacular place where we could sit for hours looking out over the vast beauty of Lake Huron. We have beautiful photos that capture the sunsets we were fortunate to witness. Rick and I took another ferry ride on the

MS Chi-Cheemaun is the Ojibwe name meaning 'Big Canoe'. We drove our car including our canoe, onto the Big Canoe. The one-hour voyage took us across Lake Huron between South Baymouth and Tobermory that is at the tip of the Bruce Peninsula. When we arrived in Tobermory the weather took a turn for the worse so there was no point putting up our tent. All the motels were booked. What were we to do? Off we went to the local Irish pub to have a bite to eat and decide our next move. We placed our order and the waitress asked if we needed anything else. "We could use a place to stay," Rick said with a big smile on his face. Within a few minutes, she was back saying that her Aunt and Uncle had opened up a Bed & Breakfast that very day. We booked a room on the spot and we were their very first customers. Rick and I like 'winging-it', something that has often paid off. The next day the weather was perfect for a visit to the Bruce Peninsula National Park and Fathom Five National Marine Park. Here we discovered the Grotto, a hidden emerald lagoon, yet another jewel that Mother Nature's spirit gave us.

There are so many sights to discover in Ontario. It would likely take a lifetime to experience them all. Rick and I set out for Sandbanks Provincial Park, along Lake Ontario. The dunes and white sandy beaches said to be among the best in Canada, are perfect. I suspect that Canadians say that because it reminds them of the white beaches found in exotic places like Navagio Beach, in Zakynthos, Greece. Rick and I have never travelled to such places so if Sandbanks come a close second, we are fine with that.

Rick and I rented a canoe and paddled along the shoreline where the water was warm and clear. We had hoped to stay at Sandbanks for at least four days but that plan changed abruptly after our second night. A major storm whipped through the area and provided us with the worst night we had ever endured. We didn't know if our new larger tent, shaped like an igloo would be able to withstand the wicked winds and pelting rain. We lay in our sleeping bag anxiously watching the tent twisting and bouncing back and forth. Miraculously we fell asleep.

The next morning the winds had died down but it was still raining. When we crawled out of our tent we couldn't believe our eyes. Our silver tent was now plastered with wet sand and broken branches. Yet we were luckier than the folks two campsites away. A fallen pine tree lay across the roof of their motor home. Thankfully, no one was hurt. What if the tree had fallen onto a tent? Because this storm front was forecasted to stick around the Prince Edward County area we decided not to stay for any additional drama. We folded our mucky wet tent into a garbage bag and went on our way.

We decided to drive the seven hours to Pelee Island via Leamington, Ontario, the Tomato Capital of Canada. At the campsite, we were a curiosity. Campers wondered about the tent that emerged from a garbage bag. The muck was slowly morphing into the white sand from the beach at Sandbanks. Soon the tent was up and the sun along with a light breeze returned it to its original silver colour. When we packed up again there was a sandy outline where our tent had rested. Onward, Rick and I travelled on another ferry, the MV Pelee Islander II, via Lake Erie to moor on Pelee Island. More adventure and more discoveries such as prickly pear cacti and other exotic plants, and turtles of all types sunning themselves in the marshlands. A picture of Rick on the boardwalk with his arm raised over his head show cattails towering over him. Monarch butterflies stopover on Pelee Island during their migration. It must be a spectacular sight to witness. While we wouldn't get to see the butterflies, we celebrated Canada Day watching fireworks and drinking wine at the Pelee Island Winery. What better way to celebrate Canada's birthday!

Rick and I treasure the memories of our Canadian adventures. We have been to Canada's easternmost point Cape Spear, in Newfoundland, the southernmost point Pelee Island in Ontario and the westernmost point Tofino in British Columbia. All that's left is Cape Columbia Ellesmere Island in Nunavut or the magical North Pole. We have often said to anyone who cared to listen, "when you travel this country take the time to embrace its beauty and the wonderful people in it." If, during your travels, you need information or need to take a welcome break, go to the nearest Irish Pub or its equivalent, and there you will meet kindred spirits willing to give you great food, great entertainment, and great advice. It has been a long while since Rick and I have been able to travel long distances. With perseverance and good planning, we hope to finish our Canadian Sightseers ambitions with a trip to The Canadian North. Where there's a will there's a way.

SERENE SCENE

Globetrotters would not be a word to describe our travel style. No Rick and I were not enamoured with the common Snowbird destinations, like Florida, Bahamas, Cuba, and other must-see vacation hot spots like many of our friends. We were different though we never truly understood that until later. Most of our vacations were in Canada from coast-to-coast. We have driven to the West Coast three times and the East Coast six times and each time we witnessed Serene Scenes.

There are a dozen or so photo albums that have various pictures of our Canadian vacations. Photos of various landscapes and landmarks and of course pictures of Rick and me. Lots of sunrises and sunsets and my veiled attempts at artsy shots as a wannabe shutterbug! Then the quality of the photos surprised me when I had the film developed. Remember bringing film in for developing? Keeping your fingers crossed that some of your pictures turned out? Most were so-so, some out of focus and then there were the gems – wow look at this!

That's the case with the Peggy's Cove photo. This was taken with a disposable panoramic camera – simply point and click. I remember buying this camera at the tourist shop in Peggy's Cove Lighthouse, as I was curious about panoramic format pictures. I was looking forward to testing it out.

The following day very early in the morning, Rick and I were taking a stroll in town. Along our way, we came upon the wharf. Time stood still. No breeze. No sounds. Not a ripple on the ocean. Only the boats floating in stillness while we looked on lost in the moment. It was perfectly serene!

I took out the panoramic camera and took two pictures to capture the moment. Weeks later, I was rewarded with a perfect photo – a perfect memory. My brother Mike, a cameraman and photographer was impressed by the photo and surprised that it was taken with a disposable camera. I remember Rick and I looking at that picture and said that one day we should have it enlarged.

Years later I followed through on our plans and had this photo enlarged on a canvas format and it is prominently displayed in our living room. When we look at it we remember that day when we captured that serene scene. We appreciate all our Canadian vacations, the adventures we shared and the memories we made.

SIDETRACKED CANADIAN SIGHTSEERS

The majority of our vacations were spent in Canada. However, sometimes we could get sidetracked, especially when the distraction tempting us appealed to our musical spirit, the soundtrack of our lives. That is why, in late June 1990, Rick and I found ourselves deliciously sidetracked and on our way to the *Home of Country Music* and its soulful neighbour *Home of the Blues*. Nashville and Memphis, Tennessee. We had enlisted the help of CAA and had with us a TripTik travel planner that guided us throughout our trip. We soon found out that driving in the US demanded a delicate combination of patience and assertiveness. Courteous drivers, they were not. To merge onto a freeway, you had to aggressively claim enough space to squeeze into the flow without causing multiple crashes. Eventually, we found our groove. We relaxed and moved on along the 754-kilometre Blue Ridge Parkway. This scenic motorway connected the Shenandoah National Park in Virginia and the Great Smoky Mountains National Park in North Carolina and Tennessee. We followed the crest of the famed Blue Ridge mountains that rise from 649 feet to an impressive 6,053 feet, we stopped frequently at the various lookouts. The blue velvet hue of the mountains was breathtaking and we amplified the experience with mood-enhancing ambient traditional country music strumming from our radio.

Finally, the 'Welcome to Nashville!' sign loomed in front of us. Our first order of business was to find the KOA campground. We had no problem getting a campsite. However, we were the only tenters in the place. Everyone else was camping in a motor home. Some had modified Greyhound buses and towed BMWs behind them. All had air conditioning. We 'po-folk' (translation poor folk) were undaunted and happily pitched our humble abode – minus air-conditioner. Rick and I were so used to camping in Canada that it hadn't occurred to us to check weather trends in Tennessee. We learned quickly that 31 degrees Celsius in the hot sun with no sheltering trees was taking 'roughing it' to a whole new level. At night we stayed on top of our sleeping bag and prayed for a breeze to waft its way through our tent. The temperature did drop to 25 degrees Celsius but the humidity was stifling. Minus electricity, we decided to purchase a battery-operated fan for the rest of our stay. We used public facilities to shower and to enjoy the comfort of temporary air conditioning. Our Subaru DL 1988 red station wagon also lacked air conditioning. Rick was comfortable with the heat. I melted, wore hats, and carried a fan.

The challenges of weather were soon forgotten when Rick and I walked into the Ryman Theatre–the original Grand Ole Opry. Much history had been made in this sacred location since its beginning in 1892. Rick and I were surprised to learn that it wasn't until 1943 that the Opry had moved in officially. The venue had been a hall for Operas, Plays and Political events. So much talent had graced this hall. Mother Mabel and the Carter Sisters, Johnny Cash, Patsy Cline, Mae West, Lorretta Lynn, Kitty Wells, Hank Williams, George Jones, Merle Haggard, Willie Nelson, and Elvis Presley just to name a few. When I walked on the stage and looked out at a crowd of fellow tourists, I tried to imagine what it would feel like to perform here with an official audience sitting on wooden church pews lit by brilliant light pouring through stained glass windows. If the room hadn't been filled with tourists lead by an impatient Tour Guide, Rick and I would have been tempted to belt out one of our songs. After the tour, we went next door to Tootsies Bar where famous musicians had hung out. We gazed at faded photos, old programmes, unplayable musical instruments, and even Patsy Cline's big girl panties—somewhat unexpected but definitely in keeping with her bodacious character.

We continued our adventure to Opryland. There we paid homage to THE CIRCLE! A six-foot circle of wood sitting on the center stage at the Grand Ole Opry House, removed from the Ryman Auditorium stage when the show moved to the Opry House in 1974. The Circle has ringed every performer throughout Opry history. We had seen Brenda Lee and Lee Greenwood performing at the main stage and both told stories about their first time performing at the Opry. So much talent everywhere. Everyone there was a musician, a songwriter, or a singer. This left Rick feeling second-rate, "I can only play guitar, these guys play everything!" Rick noticed guitar players using an unusual capo, one that was easier to clamp on the neck of the guitar to raise the tuning. We searched for a music store, found none, and were advised to go to a Pawn Shop. They were everywhere and sold everything, instruments, wedding rings both new or used, and capos. Then we made our way along 16th Avenue–Music Row. Every record label, publishing house, music licensing firm, recording studio and radio station were there. A song that I loved to sing was Lacy J. Dalton's song about Music Row and her lyric was in my mind: *They walked away from everything just to make a dream come true. So, God bless the boys who make the noise on 16th Avenue.*[21] Yes, dreams did come true on Music Row for the lucky ones.

On June 30th, we went to The Captain's Table in Nashville for supper and to listen to local entertainment. The band was slick and knew every riff and every song. When they finished their set, they mingled with the members of the audience. The leader of the band, Alan Stroud, joined us at our table. When we casually mentioned that we were musicians from Ottawa, Canada he insisted we play a song with the band. On a Captain's Table matchbook, I wrote: "At 12:30 a.m. we sang at The Captain's Table." Rick got to play Allen Stroud's electric Strat guitar. I sang 'Crazy'. I was nervous and Rick too, but the crowd liked us. The bass player and drummer accompanied us. This was a dream come true, our five minutes of fame—a perfect way to end our last night in Nashville.

Well almost perfect. We got back to our campsite at 1:30 a.m. only to find that someone had pitched their tent three feet directly in front of ours. We couldn't believe it. Worse, the guy in the intruding tent was snoring so loud there was no chance we could sleep. Rick and I packed up our tent not caring if we made noise. Our unwelcome 'neighbour' snored on. We had planned to leave for Memphis mid-morning. Instead, we hit the road for Memphis at 2:00 a.m. A three-hour drive is no big deal under normal circumstances but we were tired. We stopped in Hurricane Mills an hour later at Loretta Lynn's Family Campground. Our tent was pitched in the late arrival section and we fell asleep to the sound of crickets and the caress of a comforting cooling breeze. In the morning, we feasted on grits, bacon, eggs and homemade jams and several slices of bread at the campground restaurant. Lorretta wasn't there but her music was streaming from an excellent sound system.

Rested and fed we drove to Memphis– the *Home of the Blues!* As the usual first order of business was to find a place to stay. Camping was not an option. It was 38 degrees Celsius, with no breeze and lots of bugs, particularly cockroaches strolling in broad daylight. Yikes. We found a good hotel within a few blocks of Beale Street and booked for two nights. This was a perfect choice. Music was everywhere on every corner. Buskers were unbelievable and we were mesmerized. Rick was thirsty and stopped at a lemonade stand where he placed our order. Then he noticed they were selling Jack Daniels (JD) on ice. I got lemonade in a standard cup and Rick's JD was in the same sized cup. "Was drinking alcohol on the street okay?" Rick wanted to know. The server looked at Rick as if he had two heads and said: "Why not?" We sipped and listened to music for hours and tipped the buskers each time and more generously as the night wore on.

Our next day was devoted to Elvis. Driving down Elvis Presley boulevard towards Graceland was a feast for the eyes. Elvis is revered on every corner, on every door of every home. He was everywhere. When we walked through the gates of Graceland it was surreal. As we approached Elvis's gravesite we were surprised by the open weeping and wailing of some of the visitors. You would think he had died only recently—not 13-years ago. We quietly paid our respects to the King of Rock & Roll and we certainly remembered where we were August 16th, 1977 when we heard the news the 'King was dead.'

Rick and I could have spent weeks, versus hours at Graceland to view the hundreds of artifacts and photos from significant events in his life. Elvis' amazing collection of gold and platinum records, his stunning jumpsuits, rings, sunglasses, and other memorabilia from his movies were mind-boggling. We also stepped on board the *Lisa Marie*, his customized plane. It was like stepping into another world that included a living room, conference room, and a private bedroom complete with a King Size bed with a gold-plated seatbelt across its width. The FAA (Federal Aviation Administration) insisted that it be installed. I doubt it was used. The King of Rock and Roll lived large! Rick and I left in a state of shock and awe by the ongoing impact this young man from Tupelo, Mississippi had on the music world of his time.

It was time to head back to Canada and we hit the road again driving through Kentucky, Ohio, and Michigan. We saw amazing countrysides. A blur perhaps, as we drove anywhere between 8 to 10 hours a day. Late in the day, as we pushed our luck in Ohio with me driving, Rick asleep and dark was setting in. We were now on a side road following campground signs. I turned the next corner and was face to face with a massive well-lit white billboard with black lettering that read: "Prepare to meet thy God!" My head flooded with negative vibes–biblical warnings, from Bette Davis's performance in the 'Harvest Home' television series and her twisted version of that saying. I did a gravel spewing U-turn worthy of Bo and Luke Duke, from the *Dukes of Hazzard*, high-tailing it in the General Lee and headed back to the main road. Rick was now awake and admired my move. "Good plan," said he. We soon spied a Super 8 hotel close to the main highway. We checked in but brought in our sleeping bag as their housekeeping was not up to our standards. My knuckles were no longer white and I was breathing normally halfway to dreamland when Rick spoke up, "Ohio is a strange state." Staring out the window he noted: "On the one hand they say prepare to meet thy maker. Then, on the other hand, they promote X-rated adult entertainment." I got out of bed to see what he was talking about. There in a dark field was a brightly lit fort-like structure promoting an alternative way in which to prepare to meet your maker. I rolled my eyes, went back to bed and was looking forward to driving out of Ohio.

Finally, having entered the state of Michigan, I now felt safer. I had been here before with my parents and relaxed a bit until we got to the Canada-US border crossing. The relaxation bit did not last long. The customs officials must have thought we were suspicious or maybe they had a quota to complete for Canadians going back home. There we were, emptying our car as they instructed. Then they needed to see the receipt for Rick's guitar and my camera as we hadn't claimed it as a purchase. Fortunately, I had paperwork that proved we had owned these items before entering the States. Finally, they let us continue home to Canada. We were one day behind schedule and needed to get to Sudbury to attend Wayne and Carol Golder's wedding on July 7th, 1990. Luckily, we were less than a day's drive away on familiar highways.

We had so much to share with family and friends about our unique vacation–both the ups and the downs. Family and friends may have wondered if we had been exposed to some magic mushroom or one of its relatives as they listened to our enthusiastic stories. We had fallen in love with the warmth and welcome of down-home country, the western wholesomeness of Nashville and our souls rocked with the blues Memphis-style. We had allowed ourselves to veer away from some of our usual haunts in Canada. Our reward was a trip that continues to rewind and playback the wonderful music and camaraderie that we had experienced down South in the good old USA. Rick's Nashville capo is securely clamped to the headstock of his guitar and it is a touchstone to a special time when we were sidetracked by our musical spirit.

IRISH CRAIC

After 1980 Rick and I travelled together and often with friends or family. The times we travelled solo were work-related. That was frequently the case when I worked with Canada Post. In May 1994 a new opportunity came knocking in the form of an Irish Craic.

We received a wedding invitation from Mary-Ellen Lanteigne, my CVDCS classmate, who was getting married in Dublin, Ireland. Only one of us could go. Rick insisted that I make the 10-day trip. I was accompanied by a classmate and long-time friend, Debbie Williamson, from Azilda, Ontario. Since we had been on a few trips together before, one for an Anne Murray concert in Toronto and another to the Stratford Festival, we had first-hand knowledge of each other's quirks. Rick was concerned when he heard that Debbie and I would be sharing a room. I have a unique quirk. Rick called Debbie and gave her some tips on how to handle me if I start talking, singing, or screaming in my sleep. I am quite the performer when in a dream state. I've been known to pick up the phone while sleeping and even answer simple questions without knowing it. Debbie couldn't stop laughing while Rick told her what she might have to deal with in our nine nights together. I rolled my eyes and listened to him explain the problem. "If she starts talking, quietly ask her complicated questions that require some thinking and then she'll stop." He continued, "If that doesn't work, turn the light on and shake her. She might get annoyed but she'll wake up." Now Debbie had inside knowledge just in case.

I planned to meet Debbie at the Toronto Pearson Airport and together we would fly to the London Heathrow Airport followed by a quick flight to Dublin via Aer Lingus. I was excited. This was my first International flight. Everything was going fine as we waited on the plane for our British Airways flight to depart, it was running late. Turns out a 'Mrs. Rodriguez' was the problem.

Her luggage was on the plane but she was not. When she finally arrived, we were 40-minutes behind schedule and that meant anyone who had a connecting flight in London might miss it. A host of cold and angry stares greeted her, mine included. I don't know why they didn't just take her luggage off the plane.

We landed in London in a thick fog. London was all but invisible from the sky and when we hit the tarmac we couldn't see past the airport terminal. We raced to catch an alternate flight to Dublin and were an hour late arriving. Here we picked up a message to take a cab to the Leinster Pub to meet Mary-Ellen. Initially, Debbie and I had considered renting a car, but after our 20-minute cab ride to the pub, we quickly changed our minds. Driving on the wrong side of the road was not for us. It was around 10:30 a.m., or half-10 as Mary-Ellen would tell the time. She was picking up the lingo of her new home. English is spoken everywhere but Gaeilge (Irish) is the official and national language. I heard many dialects during my stay. Mary-Ellen explained that accents varied depending on what part of Ireland people were from. County Galway versus County Cork would be dramatically different to my untrained ear. I was seated next to someone from County Cork and only understood about 20% of their English, but could understand 80% of the English from someone from Galway. Eventually, Debbie and I 'got the drift' if not Mary-Ellen would translate.

The pub on a Saturday morning was a hub of activity. Debbie and I found this most unusual. We soon realized that Irish pubs in Ireland were more like The Legion in Canada. They were community meeting places. People didn't drink at home they went to the pub. Their local pub was like going to their church or their school. Everyone could go regardless of age. I sensed a direct connection to Newfoundlanders and felt at home. Perhaps this is due to my 15% Irish DNA. We met Mary's fiancé Arthur Timmins and friends Gussie and Angela McNamara. Gussie insisted that Debbie and I have a Guinness. It was morning and we hadn't eaten very much but that wasn't a good enough excuse. "Thanks, but I don't like warm beer!" said I. This was true because Rick and I experienced our first Guinness in Ottawa and it had been served warm and we didn't like it. Gussie responded with a few colourful swearwords including a wry comment, "Must have been a goddam Brit that served you." Then he proceeded to give us a lesson on the art of drinking a Guinness. I paid careful attention because I wanted to share this critically important wisdom with Rick when I returned. Debbie and I drank 'The Guinness' with Irish commitment. We may have practiced it a bit more just to make sure we had the process down pat before heading back home to share it with others.

During our brief stay, Debbie and I visited various places and praised each other on our decision not to drive. We took double-decker buses and struggled with the currency to pay our fares and usually figured it out on our own or with the help of a sympathetic conductor when our Canadian accents gave us away. We also travelled by train to Galway on the west coast of Ireland, only a 2-hour trip. The most memorable experience was a bus tour to Newgrange County Meath. I just had to send a postcard to Rick from this place:

> *Dear Rick, sure miss having you with me and I know you would have liked to see the Newgrange. This place was built before the pyramids and no one knows how they managed to do this. I went in and it was a bit scary, but luckily, I was short enough to fit in. Except once I had to duck. We won't rent a car because the chance of surviving is minimal. We are trying to see several places before Friday's wedding. Monday I'll be back in Canada to see you. Going yet again to another pub to check out a session with Noel Hill at the Harcourt Pub.*

*He's one of Ireland's best. I often brag about you
and the men here ask why you didn't come with
me? Love Monique*

My presence in Ireland without my husband was quite an oddity for the Irishmen. Gussie queried: "Your husband allowed you to go on your own? I would not let my Angela do that!" Most bizarre. I was to learn that women in Ireland had less freedom than Canadian women. It wasn't until the 1970's that women were allowed to attend College or University. The women of Ireland had a lot of barriers to overcome. It increased my appreciation of the opportunities I'd had as a woman in Canada.

In honour of their Canadian guests, Mary-Ellen and Arthur decided to have a BBQ. Someone managed to purchase a Hibachi for the event. So here were a bunch of Irishmen hanging around the BBQ trying to figure out where the briquettes should go. When I walked over to offer my assistance I was told that only men BBQ. Undaunted I went ahead and showed them how it was done. After all, it's a Canadian rite of passage regardless of gender to learn how to BBQ.

Spending time with Mary-Ellen in her new home and meeting her new friends and family was a special time. She took us to different areas in Dublin and introduced us to Irish Chippers–traditional fish and chips. Of course, we were immersed in the music of the Emerald Isle. It was everywhere, on street corners, pubs, buses, etc. Like Newfoundlanders, everyone had the gift of song and music running through their veins. It was during these musical moments that I missed Rick the most. I treasure a picture of me singing in a pub at a ceilidh for the newlyweds. I don't remember what I sang but allowed myself to imagine Rick at my side playing his guitar.

On Monday, May 29th I returned home to find, on the dining room table, two-dozen red and yellow roses and a beautiful note from Rick. I immediately set off to the LCBO to buy some Guinness to go with Fish & Chips for supper. As soon as I saw the Subaru pull into the driveway, I played Mary Black's *Collection* CD to add to the temporary Irish scene I'd set up. Rick enjoyed all of my stories and paid particular attention to the lesson on how to pour a perfect Guinness and how to drink it with commitment. We had our own Irish Craic. Sláinte (pronounced slawn cha).

A NEW YORK MINUTE

In March 2004 Rick and I experienced the frenzied and hectic pace of New York City (NYC) first-hand. It was a four-day adventure planned on the spur-of-the-moment. The lure for Rick was an Ian Hunter concert. Rick was a big fan. Within a New York minute, we decided we needed to go despite a few obstacles. Rick was then unemployed and struggling with this unexpected and undeserved status. He needed a diversion from this frustration. When he heard the news of this concert and its location Rick immediately set plans in motion. By the time I got home from work, he had all the plans in place and this on a limited budget. He was excited and he couldn't wait to share the details. He needed this shot-in-the-arm.

On Saturday, February 28th, we drove to the Montreal Central Station and boarded the Amtrak Adirondack and headed for the famous Penn Station in New York. This was a ten-hour train journey, the longest we had ever taken then and since. Rick had decided not to bring his guitar on this trip because he was concerned about losing it. He did bring his songwriting satchel just in case he got inspired to fine-tune a current composition or to create a new one. The train made one stop mid-journey at the Canada-US border. Customs officials came on board and spoke to everyone at their seats, asked the typical questions and that was it. It took less time than airport security or border crossings when we travelled by car.

We saw impressive countrysides along the two-lane iron road. I imagined what the first train travellers must have felt like with the excitement of reaching their final destination. Eventually, landscapes gradually changed into cityscapes. Finally, the announcement we were waiting for came over the loudspeaker, "Arriving at Penn Station. Last Stop!" Rick and I, the enthusiastic Canadian sightseers were ready to explore, but not before we registered at our hotel. It was too far to walk with luggage, so we hailed a New York cab. Cool—until we noticed the extra black-framed contraption attached to the bumper. Other cabs had that too so we assumed it was a standard feature. We thought wrong. Rick and I hopped into the yellow cab and off we went in a New York minute. Or as Johnny Carson once said, "A New York minute is the interval between a Manhattan traffic light turning green and the guy behind you honking his horn."[22] In our case, it was our Taxi driver bumping the car in front of him and there was no horn involved. Rick and I looked at each other. "What had we got ourselves into?" We safely arrived at our hotel, paid the cab driver who then went off in a flash.

I can't remember the name of the hotel other than it was downtown and within walking distance of several NYC attractions. The hotel had been booked by Rick's brother, Gary. He and Janis, his girlfriend, were going to the Hunter concert as well and had been to New York before. They had flown into New York as their budget was in better shape than ours. The hotel décor was reminiscent of the 1970s, panelled walls, macramé wall hangings and a beanbag chair but the room and the hotel were clean. The elevator was the old-style accordion-cage double door system. I hadn't seen an elevator like this since I was a kid shopping at Woolworth's in Sudbury. We couldn't use it, however, as it was broken and being repaired. Luckily our room was only on the second floor so we took the stairs. We enjoyed the energetic give and take between the two Italian repairmen as they shouted at each other in a rapid-fire mix of Italian and broken-English.

We met up with our travel buddies at the hotel and decided to explore the New York City nightlife. Our hotel was near the Ed Sullivan Theatre. Rick thought maybe we could score last-minute tickets for Letterman but no such luck. We continued to walk to Times Square just a seven-minute walk away and easy to find. Then we followed the glow from all the marquee signs. I have seen many movies, news clippings and the New Year's Eve broadcasts from New York and I thought I knew what to expect. I was wrong. I was overwhelmed by the onslaught of sights, sounds and smells surrounding me. And why hadn't we purchased tickets to a Broadway show along with our tickets to see Ian Hunter? I love musicals and here I was in the heart of it. Rick sensed my disappointment and noted that we could catch Broadway on our next trip. That hasn't happened yet but someday it will. The four of us were hungry and we wandered the brightly lit and extremely clean city streets until we found an Irish pub. We shared a table with a few local musicians who were taking a break from their set. Of course, Rick struck up a conversation about the music scene and before I knew it we were asked to sing a three-song set. *Monique & Rick*, an Ottawa folk-based duo, could claim their 15-minute of fame in the 'city that never sleeps'. Eventually, we made it back to our hotel. Though we were exhausted it took a while to fall asleep partly because of the sound of sirens throughout the night.

The next day we aimed to cram in everything we could see of New York. We walked everywhere. Empire State Building, Central Park, SOHO, etc. Rick wanted to go to the Chelsea Hotel all because of Leonard Cohen. Rick longed to see and feel this place that inspired Leonard to write 'Chelsea Hotel #2' about his romantic encounter with Janis Joplin. Rick and I went on our own and when we walked into the lobby, we instantly felt the unique vibes of the place. Rick bought a T-Shirt, and although it is faded and worn, he has it still.

We connected again with Gary and Janice and made our way to Ground Zero where the Twin Towers had once raised themselves 104 floors. Now the skyline was empty. The area was clear of its rubble and fenced off for safety until the Memorial Fountains were opened September 11th, 2011. When we stood by this hallowed ground, I couldn't help but tear up remembering the tragic event. The images of the towers coming down, choking ash, people fleeing in fear and the hopelessness in the voices of the reporters and announcers from New York. It brought things into vivid perspective and gave a new meaning to Don Henley's lyrics *"In a New York Minute, Everything can change."* By now we had decided that we didn't have the energy to walk back to our hotel, considered taking a cab but opted for the subway instead. This was my second time on a subway, the first time was in Toronto. The Toronto experience had not been positive, so I was a bit nervous. We missed our stop and we were heading to Harlem instead. Off we got and doubled back. Rick had followed his gut instincts and we were soon safely back at our hotel.

The main reason for our trip had been to enjoy Ian Hunter and the Rant Band concerts. It was scheduled for Monday, March 1st, 2004 at 8:00 p.m. at the B.B. King Blues Club & Grill at 250 West 43rd Street between 7th & 8th Avenue under the Carter Hotel. How do I remember these details? It helps to have postcards and ticket stubs. This was a dinner show with a ticket price of $23.50 US and the doors opened at 6 p.m. Seating was first-come, first-served. Rick didn't want to take any chances. We wanted a good table with great sightlines and placement for optimum sound. Therefore, we were at the door by 5 p.m. and first in line. A few minutes later the line-up went around the corner. If you don't know who Ian Hunter is chances are you won't know who Mott-the-Hoople is either. They are a Rock-Hard Rock-Glam Rock band that was popular in the '70s. They are best known for the song 'All the Young Dudes', written for them by David Bowie. I didn't know anything about them either until I started dating Rick. Whenever we went to concerts, Rick always had a pocket-sized pen and notepad so he could write down the songs played by the artist. I came across his list from the Ian Hunter concert where nineteen songs were played including our favourites 'Once Bitten Twice Shy', 'Standing in My Light' and 'All the Way from Memphis'. Also playing with Ian was his youngest son Jesse and Mick Ronson's daughter Lisa Ronson. Mick, who died in 1993, was the lead guitar player and Ian's best friend. Singing and dancing that night with Rick was like a trip into the past. I think he was channelling his teenage carefree self.

Grudgingly, we had to leave New York City early the next morning and head back on the Amtrak train to Montreal. We were tired, it was raining and now we had a 10-hour trip ahead of us. I fell asleep while Rick pulled out his satchel and began writing a song. Later he woke me up to add a few verses. The song was entitled 'From the Viewpoint of a Train'.[23]

> *The Whizz Kid's still on the beat.*
> *(reference to Mott the Hoople's Whizz Kid written by*
> *Ian Hunter)*
>
> *The cash flow comes off the street*
> *Something ventured, something to gain*
> *From the viewpoint of a train*
> *And my verse:*
> *From the viewpoint of a train*
> *It's a rockin' rollin' lullaby*
> *With a heartbeat rhythm and an endless rhyme*
> *Taking over your brain*
> *From the viewpoint of a train.*

The frenzied and hectic pace of New York City was now behind us. It was back to work for me and back on the job hunt for Rick, now equipped with renewed optimism fuelled by the energy from the Big Apple and the music from *All the Young Dudes*.

CANADIAN SIGHTSEERS — BUMPS IN THE ROAD

Vacations are a great training ground for any relationship. As Canadian Sightseers, Rick and I learned a great deal about each other. Yes, there were bumps in the road and touchy tests of each other's patience.

Whenever we travelled we always looked at a map to plan our trip for the day. GPS didn't exist then. Even if it had I would still have used maps as I do today. Rick was more of a risk-taker. If something couldn't be found on the map, he clicked on instincts. "I think we are lost" I wrote several times in our travel journal. Later I would notice that Rick had penned in: "We were not lost – just took an inconvenient exit." How could I argue with that logic? Most of the time I trusted Rick's instincts—except when I noticed the gas needle heading for empty. When the warning light came on, my panic increased. I have a video of the gauge with my comment, "Rick is pushing the needle too far." About then a miracle gas station would appear out of nowhere. How did he do it?

There would be communication breakdowns over different issues. What did I mean when I wrote: "We are giving each other the silent treatment about stupid coffee mugs"? I do know that when we travelled with others, we sometimes got out-of-whack with each other, such as when we travelled with Rick's cousin Marcel Bouchard and his wife Wendy. While in Halifax and checking out the music scene, Rick and Marcel took too much advantage of the free rum offered by Captain Morgan and his Morganettes. Unfortunately, they behaved like Barrett's Privateers complete with slurred speech and distorted intelligence. The next day they were in the shackles of a hangover. I didn't feel sorry for them at all. Rick videotaped our walk along the beach that afternoon, and as he zoomed in on me he said to the camera: "There's my wife Monique and she is not talking to me. Need to fix that somehow". I don't recall how he fixed it, but fix it he did. We probably used our now well practiced-way of working out our disagreements. Talking and listening with a balance of emotional outbursts from me and philosophical interpretations from Rick and in the end, a détente would be reached. Always sealed with a kiss.

Yes, our travel adventures in camaraderie would get sidetracked now and again. Then we would work things out and go back to enjoying our trip and learning more about the places we were exploring, and more importantly, learning about each other and ourselves. Life is the ultimate vacation, bumps, and all.

REFLECTING UPON IMPULSE

I am an impulse buyer. Eighty percent of the time my instincts have managed to steer me in the right direction, the right opportunity, and the right choices. The other 20% reflects my valiant efforts through trial and error.

Through 1980 I worked as a radio announcer and music programmer with CIGM-FM, in Sudbury. When I couldn't afford an apartment, I went home to Chelmsford, Ontario. I was up to my neck with college debt. Moving back home meant letting go of the two-years of the independent lifestyle I'd enjoyed at Canadore College in North Bay. I was back in my old room and paying a modest room and board fee to my parents. Mom and Dad still expected me to follow house rules as if I was still a student at Chemmy High. This was very constraining to say the least. There were, however, adjustments we all had to make along the way as well as a few rough edges to smooth out. Returning home after college was my short-term plan. I kept exploring my options based on my budget and my goals toward recovering my independence.

Usually, I am level headed and somewhat cautious. From time to time, however, my impulsive side takes me by surprise. Could it be my Gemini nature taking over? Gemini's are described, as being responsible, disciplined, drastic and hasty in equal measure. That's me! It was that side of me that stepped into an antique shop on Lisgar, Street in Sudbury just a few blocks away from CIGM-FM. It was an old two-story house that had been converted into a store. Their inventory was eclectic and traditional featuring unusual furniture, accessories, and other knick-knacks. Eventually, I meandered into a section of the house that was off-limits to customers. Further inspection revealed, tucked in a corner full of dust and partially wrapped in a tarp, a small bedroom set. The set included a highboy dresser on wooden wheels, an armoire, headboard, and footboard. I also spied an unusual looking mirror. I started visualizing how all these dusty treasures would look in my yet-to-be-realized apartment. Then I heard someone behind me say "Can I help you?"

I went quickly from a dream state into reality. It was the store owner. I explained that I'd like to know more about this bedroom set and what it would cost me. She hadn't decided that yet as it needed repair. The bed frame was a non-standard narrow double. It was designed to hold a mattress on top of wooden slats. No box springs. Slats were missing and the hardware could not be found. She pointed out that the mirror needed to be re-silvered.

I looked at my reflection in the mirror and understood what she meant. My reflection was distorted as if there were different layers of clarity; a clear past, a mysterious present and yet-to-be-revealed future. I just knew this bedroom set and I had a future. 'We' were the perfect balance of instinct and impulse. The set would need some TLC, but luckily my Dad, a miner by day and furniture maker by night, would make the necessary repairs including adjustments to accommodate a standard double mattress with box spring. This would be a nice project to work on with my Dad, the first of many.

I negotiated and was able to convince the owner to sell the bedroom set 'As is' with its odd sized bed, a mirror that needed re-silvering and the dressers that displayed scratches, gouges, and perfume stains. The deal was done for $500 including delivery. I was excited and nervous. I was having doubts about my impulsiveness. Psychologists call that feeling of stress by having two (or more) ideas or values that seemingly contradict each other as 'cognitive dissonance' I was a textbook case. The set was delivered and stored in Dad's workshop. Unfortunately, the mirror with all its imperfections was broken during the delivery. The owner covered the replacement cost of the mirror.

My rejuvenated bedroom set travelled from Chelmsford to Ottawa in 1983. There it would serve in two apartments and two houses through the early stages and adventures of a young vibrant twosome and later on to a wise married couple. In 2014, the set was given yet another makeover to accommodate a Queen size bed. Henderson's Refinishing Company did a wonderful job and brought the set back to its original beauty. They took special care not to raise the profile of the bedframe. Keeping the same height from the floor was important because it made it easier for me to safely transfer Rick in and out of bed.

The restoration was five times as expensive than what I had paid for the set all those years ago. But nothing new could come close to my enduring find. This solid walnut bedroom set, made in the 1940s, is priceless. Of all the furniture pieces Rick and I have owned, this bedroom set is the only piece we have kept permanently.

If they could, I wish the tongue and groove joints could come alive to tell the life story of their previous owners. I don't have to wonder about Rick's and my story. My memory is a mirror and like my bedroom mirror, it holds the reflections of the past, the present and will surely capture the future with a balanced measure of impulsive and reflective adventures.

PENDULUM OF TIME

To the average observer, it is an antique clock made of wood, glass, and brass. Some may see it as a useless relic, relentlessly annoying whenever it chimes on the hour and the half-hour. Throughout the years, Rick and I have had various houseguests who have asked us, "Can you turn it off? or "Do you need to wind it? Yet some were curious about it. When the clock would chime, they would recall a personal memory they had about clocks owned by their grandparents. Like the clocks of their grandparents, Canada's Peace Tower, or the Tremblay Mantel Clock, they all are harbingers of the pendulum of time—historians, observers, timekeepers.

In 1990, the Tremblay Mantel Clock was given to Rick by his parents Ernie and Joan. I remembered seeing this clock at his parent's home in Chelmsford, Ontario where it sat on top of the television set. It hadn't worked for a long time. Ernie wanted Rick, his eldest son, to have it because it was a family heirloom. Rick's Grandfather, Wilfred Tremblay bought this clock in August 1933 as a gift to Rick's Grandmother Ida (*nee* Ramsey) Tremblay. This chiming clock, distributed by the Black Forest Clock Company in Toronto was likely purchased in Kirkland Lake, Ontario where Rick's paternal grandparents lived. The reason Wilfred bought this clock for Ida was that she had finally given birth to a son—Ernest Tremblay born on August 23rd, 1934. I remember asking Ernie if his father had purchased special gifts when his two older sisters, Carmel Robitaille and Lorraine Bouchard were born. His answer? "No, it wasn't done back then because only a son could carry on the family legacy." I would suspect that Rick's Aunt Carmel and Aunt Lorraine would have challenged their then 57-year-old baby brother's viewpoint. They were both very outspoken women.

I remember how Rick and I examined staring at this clock once we got it home. Rick looked inside the clock and tried to see if there was something that might be jamming up the gears, cranks, and other mechanical mysteries. I was focused on the wood and brass. The clock was sticky to the touch. I wasted no time before getting it clean with Mrs. Murphy's oil wood soap. It took me several hours to clean it. For a thorough job, Rick helped me remove the brass numbers that were connected to the overall clock face. Even after removing the screws, the face wouldn't budge. It was glued tight from years of nicotine and dust and sealed with Pledge furniture polish. If the clock had had lungs it would have died of lung cancer!

We decided to take the clock to the Watch Clinic Jewelers on Bank Street. The Horologist looked at the clock with mild curiosity laced with condescension. His beady eyes peering over odd-looking magnifying eyeglasses glared at Rick and me. Were we being unfairly judged for the ill-treatment of a beautiful masterpiece? We waited in suspense, only relieved when he said he could fix the clock. Two months later, when it was ready to be picked up. Rick and I walked into the shop we heard a beautiful melodic chime precisely at the half-hour.

Bong Bong Bong Bong! It was the Tremblay Mantel clock—sound Rick had never heard before! The Horologist – clock saver as far as I'm concerned—gave us lessons on how to maintain and care for the clock and we drove home ever so carefully not to damage our precious family treasure.

When Ernie and Joan came back to Ottawa for a visit, they were quite surprised at the sound and the look of the clock. They couldn't believe that all it took to get it going again was a thorough cleaning of its gears and cranks.

It took us time to get used to hearing the clock chime on the hour and the half-hour every day. Eventually, we couldn't bear the silence because we forgot to wind the clock. If we were lucky enough to hear the sluggish, slow, offbeat chime we would rush to quickly wind the clock with the big brass key before it stopped.

While the Peace Tower marked Canada's 150th birthday in July 2017 the Mantel Clock will have chimed on its 84th birthday in the Tremblay family in August 2017. Eventually, this heirloom will be passed on to Taddrick Wilfred Tremblay, Rick's nephew. Tadd did not think he would need such a timekeeper but once he heard the backstory of the Tremblay Mantel Clock, he has accepted to become the next curator of this pendulum of time—historians, observers, and timekeepers.

TIME FLIES — LOVE LASTS

Funny how a memory can pop into your head when you find something you've overlooked tucked away in a dresser drawer. That was the case with two unique Wearable Sundials, one of my many impulse purchases. I had spotted the sundials on display at Lee Valley close to where I waited to pay for some Christmas gifts. When I saw them, I immediately thought of Rick!

Rick would not wear a watch. He found wearing a watch uncomfortable. He also admitted that he usually preferred not knowing the time. Rick 'lived in the moment', very laid back—even back then. When he needed to know the time, he would either:

- go to a convenience store and buy a small item so he could see the time printed on the receipt. He wouldn't ask the clerk for the time so as not to be a bother;
- listen to the radio and wait for the announcer to mention the time;
- estimate the time based on the last time he saw a clock;
- ask whoever he was with if they had 'the time' or
- look at the sun's placement in the sky.

I would be quite annoyed by Rick's laid-back style, particularly when we were expected to arrive somewhere at a specific time. When he was playing guitar with the boys, particularly with his cousin Marcel Bouchard, Rick would lose track of time. Add a few beers and a few bars of music and time stood still. Musicians are notorious for losing track of time when they are creating music. Then they are in a state of suspended animation. How often did this test my patience? How often did I look at my watch? How often did I peer out the window at the same time standing by the phone willing it to ring? Cellphones didn't come on the scene until the '90s so standing by the phone waiting for a call was a common pastime. Funny word 'pastime'—Rick's pastime is music which could also mean he was 'past *the* time' to arrive for our date.

As soon as I had seen it, I knew I had to buy the pocket watch-style compass sundial. I knew Rick would be intrigued by this timepiece. Rick has always had a sense of wonder about how or why something was created.

According to the brochure, this Compass Sundial was in demand during the early exploration of North America. It can tell time and provide direction. To use it is quite simple. Hold the sundial level and raise the gnomon (pronounced no-man) which is a small pin. Then align the North pointer of the compass with the gnomon. The shadow will fall on the time of day.

The Aquitaine Dial was made for me. History says Eleanor of Aquitaine, Queen of England, had a dial made for King Henry II so that he would know when to leave off hunting and come home to his beloved wife—the time for love. Engraved with the words 'Carpe Diem' which means 'Seize the Day'. Later I would see the parallel between Lady Aquitaine and myself both needing to remind our husbands to come home. Henry lost track of time while hunting and Rick while playing guitar.

To use this requires a bit more effort. Turn the inner dial until the small hole aligns with the current month. Suspend the dial by the chain and turn it so that the small hole faces the sun. The pinhole light will shine on the number inside the ring to identify the time. During daylight savings time, add an hour. Both Compass and Aquitaine dials had their drawbacks. No sun. No telling of time.

From time to time Rick and I went cross-country skiing. This was the only sport Rick participated in. For him, it wasn't a sport but rather a mode of transportation, similar to cycling. It was a way to get from point A to point B in a leisurely fashion. He enjoyed it, especially when breaking trail. Could he have been channelling a *coureur-de-bois ancestor* exploring Canada—the unknown frontier?

I understood Rick's leisurely viewpoint to cross-country skiing. But I also enjoyed improving my technique and increasing my speed on the trails. The competitor in me would imagine I was racing. Often, I would be far ahead of Rick when we went skiing. We always hoped for powdery snow. We would pack up our skis, poles, wax, coffee with Baileys and our headlamps.

If the snow fell during the workweek, we would go after work. If it fell during the weekend, we would be up by 6 a.m. Our goal, to be the first skiers to break the trail. Our favourite—Stoney Swamp Trail in the National Capital Commission Greenbelt, a 20-minute drive from our Nepean Ontario home.

On one particularly wintery, powdered snowy Saturday morning, Rick and I headed for Stoney Swamp trail. It was a partly sunny and partly cloudy day with fresh snow crunching under our skis. As usual, I would be ahead of Rick but I tried not to get too far ahead. I would stop occasionally and look behind me. If I saw a bright blue coat and red cross-country ski socks that meant Rick was nearby. I bought that jacket so I could spot him in the snow. While he preferred brown or black jackets, I chose this colour for safety reasons so he wouldn't blend in with the trees. But on this day when I stopped and turned, I couldn't see him. Maybe I had increased my speed more than I had realized. I waited. I took off my gloves and put on some lip balm. A Chickadee landed on my hand, hoping for food. I normally pack birdseed but that day I was empty-handed. Still no sign of the blue and red *coureur-de-bois*. Silence. No swishing sounds of skis massaging the snow. I stopped waiting. I turned and skied with resolute speed. Goal? Find Rick!

I'm not sure how far I travelled. Time sped up based on my heart rate. Then I spotted him. He was standing still. Mitts off. Facing North. Head down. Oblivious that I was heading toward him. Winded, I stopped next to Rick and said, "What are you doing? Are you okay?" He looked up and calmly said, "I'm waiting to find out what time it is." He was holding the Compass Sundial I had given him. The North pointer of the compass with the gnomon was in position and he was waiting for the shadow to fall on the time of day. Rick was patiently waiting, in his laid-back fashion for a cloud to move past the sun so he could see the shadow on the dial. I couldn't believe it. I was speechless. I wished I had never bought the sundial. A Joni Mitchell lyric from 'Both Sides Now' came to mind: *'So many things I would have done, But clouds got in my way'*.[24] I doubt she thought about sundials when she wrote it. Clouds were in the way of Rick telling time, but here he was, beaming with excitement like a little kid anticipating magic to unfold. So, I waited too. Finally, the shadow of the gnomon appeared and indicated the time which I compared to my watch. Timepieces were synchronized. Mission accomplished. Rick was thrilled. I was laughing at the irony of this scene.

To this day when I see freshly fallen snow, I think of that cross-country skiing adventure and the boyish grin on Rick's face. I wonder if Lady Aquitaine witnessed the same look on King Henry II's face and chuckled inwardly to herself as I did. The inscription on the Compass Sundial reads 'Time Flies—Love Lasts' the inscription on the Aquitaine Dial reads 'Carpe Diem'. These sayings complement each other much like Rick and I do. How uncanny is that? A magical day remembered when I was looking for something else. What a beautiful metaphor for *Monique & Rick*.

KEEPER OF MEMENTOS

Lost Items? I surely have. Found items? Sometimes, if I'm lucky. Thrown some items away? Guilty, but I eventually got over it. What I didn't get over, for the first few years at least, was being robbed.

I'm reminded of it every year on Remembrance Day, specifically Thursday, November 11th, 1999. Rick and I were working that day and other than taking time to observe a few moments of silence for those who had lost their lives to give us freedom, it was a typical workday.

Typical that is until we pulled into our driveway and noticed that something was wrong. Our front door was open. For a second, we thought that maybe Rick's brother Tim was home but then we remembered he was out of town. We quickly got out of the car, ran up the sidewalk and then hesitated before peering inside the doorway. Rick was the first to enter and before I could see what had happened, he said, "We've been robbed!"

We must have been like the Three Bears from the Goldilocks nursery rhyme as we shouted out everything that seemed to be missing. The DVD and CD player; CDs & DVDs and that was at a first glance. Luckily, Rick's Martin cutaway guitar was sitting on its stand next to the fireplace. Untouched the robber had no idea of its value. Rick got a look of panic that flashed across his face and rushed downstairs to the basement to the recording studio. His equipment still there but more importantly his songwriting satchel that held the lyrics, music, and recordings of his original work. Relief.

What next? The master bedroom and the dresser showed the naked dust-free outline where my keeper-of-mementos lay. The jewellery box was stolen and in the embrace of a heartless robber. Luckily, I had had the foresight a few months earlier to store my valuable jewellery in another place so that only costume pieces had been taken. Only—what a word! The jewellery box itself was incredibly special and unique. It was covered with soft suede in shades of teal pink, blue and green a wedding gift from Rick that he gave me in June 1989. I had my pearl drop bow earrings in the bottom drawer along with other special wedding mementos that while of minimal monetary value were of maximum sentimental value to me. Gone.

Not only were our things gone but we also lost our sense of security in our home. The robber knew what we looked like. After all, there were pictures of us everywhere, including my bodacious boudoir picture. I remember that after that I was leery of any strangers lurking in our neighbourhood. I wondered at how creepy it would be to bump into the robber at the grocery store him knowing who we were but without our realizing it!

The insurance company eventually compensated us for the monetary loss of the stolen items but it took a while before we felt safe in our home again. We updated our security system for additional safety. I now have a mementos keeper, made of wood, that Rick purchased years ago. Still, from time-to-time, I reminisce about its predecessor and the memories it held. It was one of a kind.

PASTIMES & EXPLOITS

Work-life Balance refers to the delicate balance you need to tread the tight rope that separates work and leisure time. I doubt that Rick and I have ever achieved a perfect balance. What I do know with certainty is that we did our best despite the challenges of working full-time and all that that entails. Somehow, we made time for our favourite activities and for discovering new exploits.

One of us, namely me, was a semi-dilettante who revelled in multiple interests and regularly sought out new challenges. Rick, however, was more focused, specifically on anything related to music. This was not a problem. I happily went off to pursue my passions while Rick explored his. But we also recognized the importance of finding things we liked to do together.

Before we got married, we took ballroom dancing lessons at Laurentian High School on Baseline Road in Nepean. When those courses ended, we sought more personalized lessons and signed up with Fred Astaire Dance Studios in the Glebe. Rick and I got to learn to 'cut-up-the-rug' with confidence, but only when I allowed myself to be 'led on the dance floor'. Both instructors had noted that women of the '80s tended to want to lead. I suspected that this might have been because many of us already had. In the '70s when the guys didn't want to dance, we '70s chicks' improvised just as we had when I was in high school and girls outnumbered the guys 5 to 1 putting guy-led dance partners at a premium.

Once I'd learned how to be led on a dance floor, we quickly learned the Foxtrot, Tango, Cha-cha, Viennese Waltz, and

Rhumba. Many of these dances were based on the 'box step' and that proved to be handy later. Our favourite dances were Rhumba and Tango. Both are romantic and sensual dances. There was a structure to these dances and eventually, we found the freedom to let the music move us. I remember a Halloween Party at the Fred Astaire studios when I had seen a reflection in the mirror of Zorro dancing with Cruella Deville. An unlikely pairing but dramatic. I wanted to continue with dance lessons, but Rick felt it was too much of a time commitment and wanted to stay focused on music. I supported his decision.

Years later I decided to take Flamenco dancing lessons as a fitness alternative. I've always been drawn to Spanish culture, particularly the music and the vibrant clothes worn by female Flamenco dancers. Arriving for my first lesson, I remember climbing a steep set of stairs. Ahead of me was an elderly woman who struggled to climb each step. I thought she must be here to watch her granddaughter dance. As soon as I entered the Flamenco dance studio, I saw this same woman again, standing majestically in the middle of the dance floor. She was the instructor! Then I saw her dance. It was spectacular. Her upper body flowed like a delicate flower in the breeze and her hands and fingers caressed the air with fluidity as she danced her story. Her legs and feet moved with staccato speed in a rapid tapping rhythm. I was mesmerized.

After two classes, I knew I needed official flamenco dancing shoes to protect my calves from excessive pounding. I also bought a sheet of plywood for practice at home and the safety of our wood floors. I learned a great deal about the culture and the difference between gypsy and flamenco dancing. It has everything to do with how a senorita raises her skirt as she dances. One is brazen and the other is demure. I liked that because I am a bit both depending on my mood. On one occasion, Rick came along to watch the class. This was the first time that the instructor had brought along a professional male flamenco dancer to teach her female students how to connect with a male dancing partner. Rick walked in just in time to watch me dance the Sevillana with the professional dancer. The Andalusian music was infectious to dance to because of the cante (singing), the toque (guitar playing), and the palmas (handclapping) snapping sounds. After that night, Rick and I bought CD's of the music and went to see a concert at the NAC featuring a Flamenco Dance group with Andalusian musicians. Rick was intrigued by their percussive style of guitar playing and tried to learn how but it proved to be more than challenging. Unfortunately, my Flamenco dancing lessons ended when the instructor became ill and the Dance Studio didn't have a replacement. One day I hope to get into my Flamenco dance shoes again.

Rick and I also enjoyed cycling, cross-country skiing, and canoeing. Cycling was a convenient mode of commuting, but sometimes I did participate in long-distance cycling fundraising events. Rick and I commuted to work at least three times a week. Rick wore jeans, a long sleeve shirt and jacket most days. No helmet. I, on the other hand, wore cycling clothes and a helmet. I had a longer distance to cycle and this made it into a workout that had a healthy balance of safety and speed. Rick had a shorter way to travel and never had to worry about his weight. That has always annoyed me.

Canoeing was another favourite pastime. In 1988 we bought a Subaru DL Wagon. We had a choice of saving $500 on the price of the car or taking home a fibreglass Echo canoe with a Eureka 2-man tent. I wasn't keen about the canoe as I didn't know how to use it and wasn't a confident swimmer. Although I'd had swimming and drown proofing classes, I had heard too many stories about tipping canoes and was apprehensive about getting into one, let alone owning one. Rick decided that we should rent one at Dow's Lake and test it out. I sat at the bow and Rick at the stern, paddling around the lake to the mouth of the canal. We managed to avoid a tour boat and ducks. I was certainly nervous but Rick patiently coached me through it. The result was that we drove home with a new red Subaru, a red canoe, and a green tent.

In the years that followed, Rick and I explored many different lakes and rivers. Canisbay Lake, Algonquin Park, Palmerston Lake, Ompah Ontario, and Mindemoya Lake on Manitoulin Island. Rick and I also explored Lac Long, Québec with Linda Cousineau and Leon Tarasoff. We spent many summer and fall weekends exploring their piece of heaven. Then we got even more adventurous on Providence Bay of Lake Huron also on Manitoulin Island. It was a beautiful sunny July day and the water was mirror smooth and perfectly reflecting the sky with its innocent fluffy white clouds. We followed the shoreline of the bay taking in the beauty so much so that we hadn't noticed the change in the weather. When we did Rick acted and we headed back power-paddling our way back to the main beach. Since the water was rougher by the shoreline, he steered the canoe into the open water and a direct line. The waves got bigger and before we knew it we were canoe surfing. Yes, we were riding the waves and it was exhilarating. I was nervous but as we got closer, I relaxed. When we reached the shore, Rick said, "Let's do that again!" So back we went but not too far, and surfed again until thunder and lightning gave us warning that it was time to get back to shore. This memory will stay with us forever.

After Rick's stroke, I constantly relived that part of our life. Whenever I drove the Subaru into the garage I would see the canoe hanging there seemingly taunting me. It wasn't until July 2011 that we decided to go canoeing again. I had a third seat installed in the centre of the canoe and with help, I got the canoe onto the 2002 Subaru Outback, then Rick, Julie Element and I drove to Brian Crook's home in Sheenboro, Québec. There we got on board with Brian at the stern, Rick at the centre and me at the bow of our bright red canoe. Off we went. The Aurora voyageurs paddled with smiles as bright as the sunbeams dancing on the Ottawa River. Rick did well considering that his right side is weaker making it difficult to control the paddle. What I didn't know, because I don't have eyes at the back of my head, was that Rick was helping Brian steer the canoe by awkwardly switching his paddle from the right to the left side of the canoe. I had felt a strange breeze behind my head, the result of Rick's awkward technique. The paddle was inches from hitting me on the back of the head. For our next trip, I planned to purchase a kayak paddle, safer for me and easier for Rick to use. We never did do the next trip because it was too difficult to orchestrate another one. In the end, we gave the canoe to my brother Mike. Later on, I kayaked for the first time with Susan Jahudka, a member of my Small Business Marketing family, and later more frequently with Diane Laakso and her dog Lewis. Each time I hear the sound of a paddle hitting the water I look around me and treasure the images of our earlier exploits in that beautiful red canoe.

(Left to Right) Brian Crook, Rick and Monique paddling our red canoe. Photographer: Julie Element

Rick barely broke a sweat and never needed to lose weight. He was always slim and rarely participated in formal exercises. His exercise consisted of commuting by bicycle, skiing, skating, canoeing, and swimming. I was in organized sports most of my adolescent life including figure skating, ringette, track & field, and many others. I did my best to keep on top of a fitness regime, but college, work, and life in general continued to eat up my leisure time.

Maintaining my physical health and mental wellbeing became very difficult after Rick had his stroke in 2005. Then in 2008, at 50-years of age, I lost my employment. I also lost the support of some of the friends and family that I thought I could rely on. Somehow, I kept afloat. Was it my competitive spirit, a sense of justice, a combative nature or sheer force of will that somehow kept me from crashing? Each time I have been knocked down, I have been able to claw my way back up one step at a time. Joining the Running Room and eventually running two half-marathons certainly helped. Joining the gym and finding personal trainers to help me regain my physical self, worked wonders. Dakin Drake my Personal Fitness trainer said, "Monique is one of the hardest working most dedicated clients I've ever had. She never backs down from a challenge and gives 100% every session." I must continue working on both my physical strength, my nutrition, and my mental health. I've had ebbs and flows of success and failures over the years, but I am tenacious.

In October 2010, I took a step towards improving my mental health though I didn't know at the time that this new exploit would help me reconnect with my former self. I became a member of the MDPW Toastmasters Club. I remember my first meeting, seeing some of my MDPW Carleton University 2000/01 classmates, Shirley McKey, Janissa Reid, Lynn Burritt and Florence D'Eon who were also charter members who started the club in 2003. They kept tabs on me, especially after Rick's stroke and again after I lost my job. It was here that I regained a sense of community, of belonging again. Meeting-by-meeting, speech-by-speech I was finding my voice again. These ladies became a source of comfort for me. I made new friends with Christine Coulas-O'Connor who came to my rescue with financial planning and Jenny Murphy who inspired me to write this memoir. The MDPW Toastmasters club became the outlet I needed to redirect my focus and reenergize my self-esteem. Ten years and 50 contests later, I have found my stride and then some. Shirley my classmate, Distinguished Toastmaster and friend, had this to say:

> *"I have come to admire Monique's tenacity and the amount of effort she puts into everything she does, especially her contest preparation. When she wants something, she goes for it with all her heart. When she shared the statistics of the number of contests she has competed in and the number of wins she achieved I was impressed. I have competed in a few contests myself, so I know how much work goes into each speech. Monique is passionate about competing and she does the work that counts. She writes, edits, practices, rehearses and delivers winning speeches, evaluations and table topics and she represents our club with pride."*

I can attest that my success was genuinely nurtured by the support of my MDPW Classmates and club members. It was a lifeline I needed during a very insecure time of my life.

Rick is with me on my journey. He has heard every speech and has provided honest feedback both verbal and non-verbal. If his eyebrow rises with a questioning look, it is a good indicator that I need to make some changes. He has attended the odd contest too where I would notice him shaking his head with an "Oh no, there she goes" look. Then he holds his breath hoping I won't let my adlib mind take over too far. Sometimes it worked, sometimes it didn't. What is most important is that I try. Having Rick there to witness it is a bonus.

Our life together has included many adventures, many challenges, and many rewards. Before and after the stroke Rick and I have learned a lot about ourselves and each other and we aren't through yet. There's more to learn and more discoveries waiting for us. We know how to plan and we know how to implement whatever the task may be. We are *Monique & Rick* and we are a class act!

QUIRKS & TRADITIONS

Our story would not be complete if we didn't mention a few factoids about the quirks that we have developed in our 40-years together. There are traditions long gone and new traditions that have been refined to suit our current lifestyle.

Some Like it Hot

Rick is always cold so it was never surprising to see him wear a leather jacket on a hot summer's day along with a pair of jeans and a long sleeve shirt. So, it would be a rare occurrence to see him wearing shorts and a T-shirt. Much like Hailey's comet, Rick may have worn shorts ten times in his life and when he did, they were usually cut-off jean shorts. They were very short, shorts such that the pockets were longer than the bottom hem.

Rick relished heat. When the leaves started falling this meant the thermostat would start rising in our home. It drove me crazy and I wasn't menopausal yet. I would often ask Santa, "All I want for Christmas is a thermostat guard box with a lock for which I would get the only key." That wish never came true. The 'thermostat wars' occurred often in our home and we would eventually compromise. Rick would wear a sweater and I would wear a T-shirt. There were other grievous encounters. Jack Balez, who lived with us for a few years when we had a garden home on Kingston Avenue, in Nepean, occupied the smallest bedroom upstairs. Heat rose directly into it making it a rival to a very hot and dry sauna. It was common for me to hear Jack stomping out of his room and down the stairs in the middle of night cursing, "F*#... Tremblay!" Since I frequently felt the same way I could only chuckle. I knew Jack would turn the thermostat down. Yea! The most frequent casualty was my Mom. This time my Dad and I would witness the comedy unfolding throughout the day. Mom would turn the thermostat down while moments later Rick would turn it up. Neither of them knew that the other had adjusted it. Frankly, I'm surprised the thermostat survived the wrist-workout.

Simple & Complex

In certain aspects, Rick was a minimalist. When the front sidewalk needed shovelling at our Kingston Avenue home, Rick would only scoop the snow the width of the shovel and not the width of the sidewalk. To add artistic flare, he would shovel in a wave pattern and not a straight line. I was merely amused, but Jack was not and would mutter under his breath yet again and try to get Rick to do it in the right way.

When we moved to our Whitehill Avenue home we sometimes had critter problems. When Rick discovered mice were coming through a half-inch hole next to the vacuum vent in the garage, he blocked the hole with a 4-foot-by-4-foot scrap piece of gyprock. On another occasion he noticed a starling fly into a ¼ inch gap in the wooden soffit. He blocked that entrance with a 6-foot strip 4" wide baseboard. I had a fine time years later explaining these repairs when contractors came to replace the wooden soffits with metal ones. A handyman Rick was not. His methods were more akin to Franklin 'Pa' Kettle. Maybe that's why his nickname in high school was 'Slack'.

On the opposite end of his ability spectrum was Rick's meticulous attention to detail. He regularly put his canned goods and spices in alphabetical order in the cupboards. Not a bad idea. I do the same for spices. When he made a large batch of spaghetti sauce, he made sure that the same number of meatballs went into each container and that those amounts were labelled on the lids. Shopping with Rick was always an exercise in extreme patience. Shopping with Rick could be exhausting. He had many criteria for any object he was shopping for and often came home empty-handed. For example, it took over a month for Rick and his brothers to find the ultimate anniversary clock for their parents. Clock criteria included glass globe, self-winding, brand name and size and more.

In our home, the cook does not have to do dishes. Rick did the dishes a lot and he was thorough. This too could drive Jack crazy. Those two were like Ralph Kramden and Ed Norton from the Honeymooners. I recall Jack saying in a Ralph delivery to Rick, "Are you planning on washing the dishes in this century?" Rick's Norton laid-back reply, "I'm taking my time to do the job right!" Listening to them arguing was great entertainment. Rick was also well known for his 'parking lot tours.' He had to find the right spot based on a variety of criteria and only Rick could explain the rationale behind his process. I haven't figured it all out even after all these years.

The Zimmerman Effect

Most Canadian girlfriends and wives have to tolerate their sports-obsessed men when it's hockey season. I understand the plight of 'Hockey Widows'. I am a 'Dylan Widow' and Rick is a Bob Dylan fanatic. I have lost count of how many Albums, CD's, VHS, DVDs, books that Rick has in his collection. I once suggested to Rick that we should charge Dylan rent because his voice was heard as often as our own. Of course, no Monique & Rick set was complete if there wasn't a Bob Dylan song or two, or three if Rick got his way. I still can't get away from Mr. Dylan (aka Robert Allen Zimmerman). He is omnipresent. It could be muzak in the mall, a sound byte in a movie or his name brought up in conversation. Which is worse a 'Hockey Widow' watching eight hockey games in a row or a 'Dylan Widow' going to eight live Bob Dylan concerts? I accept your wishes of condolences for the pain inflicted on my eardrums.

Annie & Me

I too have my share of quirks and usually, they are quite opposite to Rick's. Case in point, I am more spontaneous while Rick is more guarded. I tend to latch onto spur-of-the-moment opportunities while Rick has to think about all the options before deciding on a course of action. My spontaneity has mixed results, outcomes often depend on my combination of determination and good luck. When our family moved to Levack, Ontario my Dad was working at INCO's safety department and was responsible for providing Mine Safety and First Aid Training. Sometimes he brought his training materials home, including Resuscitation Annie. This mannequin was first created in the 1950s by toymaker Asmund Laerdal. It is not surprising that a 10-year-old Monique thought this was the best doll ever. None of my friends had such a doll. You could blow air in Annie's mouth and her chest would rise. I wanted to show her off. Somehow, I managed to lift her and climb up the basement stairs and into my doll carriage, a carriage that was made of metal and had decent shock-absorbing wheels. I covered her up in a doll blanket and off I went. Picture this—a 4-foot little girl with a 5-foot doll shoved into too small a carriage with arms and legs hanging over the edge nearly dragging on the pavement. My friends thought this was the neatest doll ever. Everyone took turns blowing Annie up. Then one of my Dad's first aid students, and a parent to one of the girls, called my Dad. He went looking for me and Annie and escorted us back home. He couldn't figure out how I had managed to get Annie out of the basement but he emphasized that I should not do this again. Annie was not a toy and she was expensive and it was INCO property. Did Dad appreciate that I was instrumental in teaching basic resuscitation to my friends and cleverly testing Annie to make sure she worked? I hope so!

Vertically Challenged

We weren't very tall in our family. My Dad was the tallest at 5 foot 7 inches. Who's next tallest has always been in contention between my brother Mike and myself. Every year since high school, and well into adulthood, there was always the 'official' measurement. This took some doing. Mike insisted that a book be placed on my head because my thick voluminous hair gave me an unfair advantage. I, on the other hand, insisted that my brother keep his heels on the floor. Why? When we were back to back, he would shimmy his butt upward to add an extra half-inch. So, who is tallest now? I think my 5-foot 2-inch stature has the second tallest distinction. Unfortunately, we haven't had an 'official' measurement by Dad since he passed away on November 29th, 2011. We could get our measurements done by someone else but it wouldn't be the same without Dad there to referee the accompanying sibling disputes.

The Frog Jumper

My vertical challenges have never stopped me from playing sports like basketball and volleyball. I was a 'little scrapper' always doing my best to get the ball for the team. On one rare occasion, I had a jump ball (like a face-off in hockey) against a girl who was 5 foot 8 inches tall. One look at her daddy-long-legs and I knew I had no chance of winning. So, I made it look good and jumped as high as I could and mistakenly hit her arm and not the ball. She missed and I got the ball and passed it to my teammate. After the game, I was told I jumped like a frog. That's when my frog collecting began, thanks in part to Diane Ramarr, the 'bunny collector' and Ruby Matthews, the 'lion collector' who started this tradition. Today, I've stopped collecting, but have kept a few treasured frogs.

Gadgets & Guts

I have however accumulated various kitchen gadgets, marvels to those who have rifled through the drawers wondering about the purpose of each. This includes a pickle-picker-upper, corn-on-the-cob butter dispenser and various jar opening contraptions. I've never had a large kitchen but that didn't stop me from experimenting with new entrées, side dishes, and desserts. This annoyed Rick because I often tested these new meal ideas when we were having company for supper. He would shake his head and say "How do you know it will taste good?" or "What happens if it doesn't turn out?" I understood his apprehension. His Mom never veered from standard meals. Even as a bachelor, Rick ate the same thing day-in-day-out and was fine with that. That would bore me. Happily, most of my foodie experiments were a success—Pumpkin Soup served in the pumpkin, Perogies with my trusty Hunky-Bill Perogy maker (yes, another gadget), Maple Syrup Mousse, Maple Syrup pie, and Grand Marnier chocolate truffles. I've also cooked Duck-a-l'orange, and a stuffed Turkey in the microwave which turned out to be an entertaining event. The microwave was in the dining room, as the kitchen was too small at our Kingston Avenue home. Dad and Rick watched the turkey cooking in its microwave bag. Every so often they adjusted the bird when it wasn't turning on the turntable. It was the juiciest turkey ever. Spontaneity and determination won out on that occasion and Rick breathed a sigh of relief.

Monikers

I too have acquired various nicknames over the years. In high school, it was 'Peanut' given to me by Mrs. Salisbury because of my petite yet determined character. There is a silver Peanut charm on my 70's charm bracelet, which I still have. Other nicknames 'Monique-la-bibitte', which my brother used often to annoy me, but at least he pronounced my name correctly. My biggest pet peeve is when someone pronounced my name as *Mow-neek* rather than *Mon-nick*. I noticed Americans, and not Canadians, tend to use the anglicized version of my French name. However, I do like a nickname, that our Woomie Kevin came up with, that is an engaging play on my name and that's 'Mon-Eee-Q'. I still hear it to this day. What warms my heart most are the nicknames Rick has given me depending on the situation. 'Mrs. Dollies', 'Ms. Minou' and 'Mrs. Bratties'. 'Brat' is a term we use for each other but we are both in denial of that or so we let on. It's our endearing quirk!

Vivid Traditions

Traditions have come, gone, or been altered over the years. Yet they remain vivid and have contributed to our growth as individuals and as a couple. During our early years, Rick and I often spent time with Chris and Ed Poisson. One key activity was cross-country skiing in the backcountry of Morgan, Ontario just on the outskirts of Chelmsford. Ed was very familiar with the area and preferred to cut cross country ski trails versus skiing on groomed trails. Ed led the pack, followed by Rick, Chris, and me. When we reached the top of the hill and the halfway point, we would set up a campfire and treat ourselves to sausages on a bun with other fixings. We had wine skins loaded to finish off the mid-day meal. Then we would ski back down the trail we had groomed ourselves. One hill had a blind corner where we each took our turn going down and when we had safely made it to the bottom we were to shout out "Okay to go!" When I heard Chris shout out "Okay to go" off I went. I love speed and going downhill was a great thrill. As I picked up speed with snow swooshing about my skis, I heard another shout "Oh no!" When I turned the blind corner, there was Chris somewhat spread-eagled on the trail. I had to think fast. I avoided colliding and detoured into the deeper ungroomed snow. It was so deep that my skis sank and became stuck. Down I went into deep snow. Rick began shouting "Where are you?" as all he could see was a trail with no skier. I remember my bright pink ski gloved hand punching through the snow until I managed to clear it from my face so I could breathe. After that Ed and Rick dug me out unharmed while Chris and I couldn't stop giggling.

Another tradition was the Poisson Boxing Day supper. The whole gang would be there and we would enjoy great food, music, and hilarious conversations. Their two young boys Ryan and Nathan would witness the shenanigans of these so-called-adults as they went on well past midnight. Ryan and Nathan, to this day and now young fathers, fondly remember those parties of long ago. Hopefully, we imprinted on them the value of enduring friendship. I know that Rick and I are extremely grateful that we are still an important part of the Poisson family tradition. Though the Boxing Day suppers of the past are simply a memory, Ed and Chris continue to invite us to their home whenever we visit Sudbury. Some friends are forever.

From 1983 until Christmas 2005, Rick and I travelled to North Bay, Chelmsford, and Sudbury for most holidays. Christmas was always a frenzy of tight deadlines, commitments, and limited sleep. Our normal schedule was Christmas Eve gift opening at the Tremblay's in North Bay that would start at the stroke of midnight accompanied by appetizers and champagne. Then off to Chelmsford where we would arrive by 5 a.m. at my parents' house so we could see our niece and nephews open up their Christmas gifts. These Christmas's were simple, innocent, joyful but unknown to all these would be fleeting family traditions.

Christmas took a dark detour on December 22nd, 2005. Rick was in the hospital. For a few years after that our Christmas's were low key though we were able at Lupé Brixhe's insistence to get Tim (Rick's brother, her boyfriend and then later husband) to help me bring Rick to North Bay to visit his Mom as she would not come to Ottawa. These were stressful Christmas's for me but I endured them because I wanted Rick to spend the holidays with his family. Christmas eventually was celebrated in our own home and we shared it with those who still wanted to be a part of our lives. There is one tradition that remains. I am beyond thankful that Rick and I can still celebrate Christmas together where we can gaze upon our tree, embrace in front of a warm fire, snuggled under a blanket and where we can reminisce about our varied quirks and traditions.

HOPE IS THE LYRICS

HOPE IS THE LYRICS focuses on our story after Rick's brain-stem stroke changed the course of our lives. It is a collection of stories about latching onto hope, finding a new normal and simply trying to do our best despite life's challenges.

WHERE LOVE RESIDES

Over the last several years I find myself more aware of messages that I hear, that I read or that I see. It could be a billboard ad on the side of a bus, a lyric from a song or dialogue from a movie. Most times I write it down in my journal, my dream board, or in my speech writing ideas list. However, there was one message that hit me so hard that I dropped what I was doing and I walked towards the sound of a voice saying "the theme of our quilt, ladies, is Where Love Resides!"[25]

It was Maya Angelou's voice in the movie *How to Make an American Quilt* which also starred Anne Bancroft, Wynona Ryder, Ellen Burstyn, Jean Simmons, and Lois Smith. As I watched their character's love stories unfolding in the 10' X 10" squares they were creating—I could imagine my square showing my view of where love resides.

It was March 2014. I was inspired. I wanted to make the *Monique & Rick Story Quilt* as part of the Legacy Project that would tell our story based on our love of music, love of travel and love of each other.

I know how to sew. I have made everything from Barbie doll clothes, curtains, suits, and various mending projects. But I have never made a quilt, though I have always been curious to try. To help me put my idea into action I asked Jenny Murphy, an avid quilter, to show me how. With a shopping list in hand, she and I went to the Perth Fabric Store and purchased the fabric, batting, thread, and other notions that I needed. We got everything we needed. Except for one thing—Time! The project was shelved.

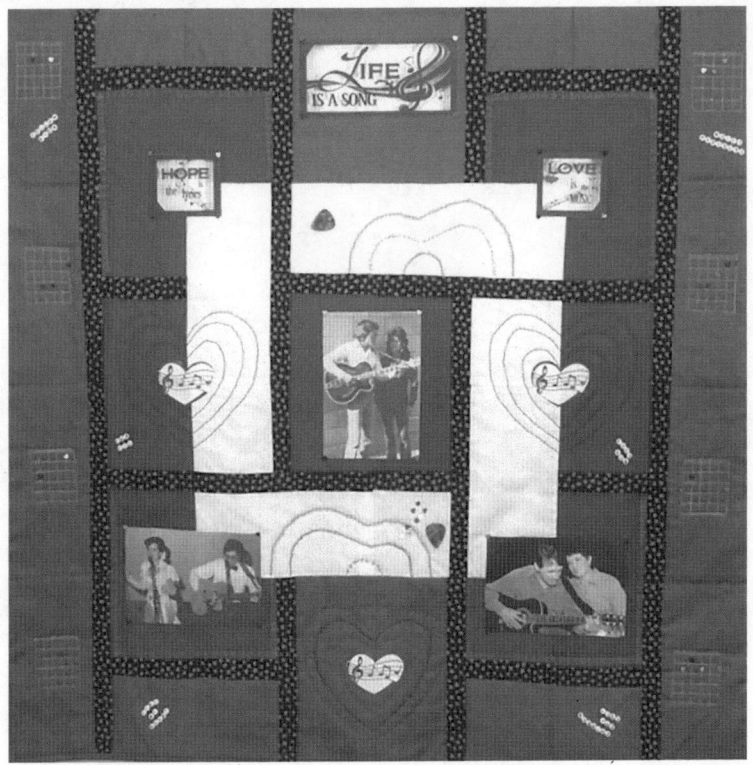

The Story Quilt — Where Love Resides. Quilter: Monique Tremblay

Time was finally on my side in June 2016. I was determined along with Jenny's expertise to complete the 40" X 40" quilt. The design is untraditional, much like the relationship Rick and I share. It features various elements that help tell our story and show where 'Our Love Resides!'

At the top of the quilt are the words 'Life is a song – Hope is the lyrics – Love is the Music.' Pictures where carefully selected and printed on fabric that shows three phases of our relationship the 1983 Music Promo Shot; our 1989 Wedding photo; and the 2010 professional photoshoot. This story quilt also inspired the sections of this memoir and all the stories.

The quilt features Musical Themes from guitar chord diagrams, guitar picks and six original song titles: 'Take My Heart', 'Do Like the Robins Do', 'Easy Now', 'Yellow Room', 'Magic Pleasure' and 'For You'. All these elements are in grey, black, white, and burgundy red to blend with the home décor as well as the vibrancy of our love of music and for each other. All who enter our home will see the *Monique & Rick Story Quilt* and 'Where Loves Resides' evident in every stitch.

IN MY MIND'S EYE

As I watched the story unfold about the hardships the citizens of Dunrobin and Gatineau faced during and after the 2018 tornado disaster, I was struck with the efforts of strangers to help those who had lost so much and was profoundly touched by a media quote: "Lost their things but did not lose their hope!"

There is nothing worse than losing hope—even for the briefest moment! It can happen when you least expect it. I know. On February 2nd, 2006 my defences were down, my resolve tattered and I was overcome with stomach-churning dread about an uncertain future for Rick and me.

It had been almost two months since Rick's brainstem stroke. During that time, he had become a hostage in an unknown world both physically and mentally. So, had I. His new world was silent, lonely, and frightening. Rick was in the Intensive Care Unit at the Ottawa Civic Hospital where very sick people await a final result: Would he live, would he die or would he be in limbo?

Every day after Rick's stroke on December 22nd, 2005 I had been by his side looking for any sign of improvement no matter how small. The flickering of his eyelids, a trusting squeeze of my hand, or muted vocal sounds inhibited by a respirator tube. More than anything, I longed to hear his voice.

The doctors and the rest of the medical team saw a patient brought down by a stroke—a life-threatening brain injury. His family and his friends struggled to understand what had happened. Rick was now a different man in their eyes. They tried to make sense of it and wondered how it could have been prevented. I retained a brave face. On the outside, I was strong, hopeful, and driven to learn how to improve Rick's quality of life. On the inside, I was a mess, struggling, scared and unsure.

On February 2nd, immediately after work, I went to see Rick at the Ottawa General Hospital on Smythe Road. He was sitting in a special chair for the first time. I was surprised and happy. He was slumped over, but that wasn't surprising as his core-muscles were now weak. It was a step in the right direction. I sat down beside Rick and chatting up about anything I thought would interest him. Then the Neurologist-in-training walked in.

The Doctor took me to one side to give me a few updates. He paused and then asked this question, "Where do you see Rick and yourself five years from now?" I remembered thinking to myself: five years! Try five hours from now. That's about all I could handle but I said, "I see us doing what we can to have a normal life, with adjustments here and there. We will continue to enjoy music, family, friends and other things that make us happy."

He looked at me and then directly at Rick and stated, "What You See Is What You Get!" I was numb. I kissed Rick goodnight. I left his room and quickly rushed out and thought to myself "Oh my God had Rick heard or even understood?"

I walked towards the car. A full moon shone brightly on freshly fallen snow along a desolate trail. Each step I took was heavy and each breath painful. I dropped to my knees and wept in the moonlight. I don't know how long I languished in this state of despair. Then I heard a familiar voice behind me, Jack Balez. He was on his way to visit Rick when he had noticed me distraught on the trail. He drove me home. In between sobs, I told him what the Doctor had said.

Days later, I was being comforted by Brian Crook and his friend Laura Hunt. I told them of the hope crushing episode. "Monique, what you see in your mind's eye you will get!" said Laura. These words were like a switch and became etched in my consciousness. A lasting gift, one that has guided me each day over the past 14-years.

Rick and I have a life, as the life, I had outlined when the Neurologist-in-Training had asked, "Where do you see Rick and yourself five years from now?" My reply then is proven in our present, "I see us doing what we can to have a normal life, with adjustments here and there. We will continue to enjoy music, family, friends and other things that make us happy."

I want to go back to the hospital and show the doctor that indeed: "What I Saw Is What I Got." My vision was much stronger than his—because it was 'In My Mind's Eye!'

YOU'VE GOT A FRIEND?

As you grow older you realize there is a role for everyone you meet in life.
Some will test you, some will use you, and some will teach you.
But the ones who are truly important, are the ones who bring out the best in you.
They are the rare and amazing people who remind you why it's worth it. – Unknown

When I saw this quote on someone's Facebook page it resonated with me on many levels, As I continue to write the

Monique & Rick memoirs, I've chosen not to dwell too much on the dark periods after December 22nd, 2005. However, I know I can't continue to avoid or sugarcoat it. As I read *'Some will test you, some will use you, some will teach you.'* I can see faces and hear voices. The faces and the voices are those of family and friends who in one way or another brought me pain, disappointment, and disillusionment. These were people I thought that I and Rick could count on. I have struggled for years with their abandonment. However, there were other faces and voices—those of family and friends, even strangers, who were prepared to help us in any way that they could. Many would become my teachers.

They were there when I needed them and even when I didn't know I needed them. Not once did they judge or ignore me with responses like "I'm too busy" or "I'm not comfortable with that" and when I was being bullied, they never said, "I don't want to get involved." Instead, they acted. They embraced me with their strength, commitment, loyalty, and unconditional love. They brought out the best in me. It wasn't easy—and it took time—lots, and lots of time. Eventually, it took years, we overcame this sense of invisibility. Amazing people guided and reminded me over and over again until I started to believe, that we were not invisible—that we were part of a community of people who care about each other and, in this case, us.

Indifference was painful enough. Hectoring and belittling were excruciating. Trying to find answers to the isolation brought on by Rick's stroke while at the same time meeting the demands of my new life as a caregiver, has been a long and lonely road—at times a very rough road—with deep and ugly potholes. I bear emotional scars from the unbridled hostility to which I was subjected. I was told, "You are just the wife" over and over from relatives that I had once trusted and cared for. These words were usually a prelude to their combined efforts to shut me out from all decisions about Rick's welfare. I was just the wife as far as they were concerned as if the role of the wife was unimportant and insignificant. The fact that I had been both a partner and wife to Rick for so many years at the time of his stroke held no sway with my tormenters. Through it all, I stood firm and defended Rick and myself too. After each altercation was over, I would retreat to an empty house to nurse my emotional wounds and cry with no one to hear me. Once upon a time, Rick would have defended and protected me. Now he could not. He had a much greater challenge to face and I couldn't risk exposing him to the ugly side of our new life. As his advocate, I was his protector. I had to become my own champion and that took years of training and never letting go of hope. Fragile as that may be, hope is much better than the alternative.

At the beginning of this memoir, I indicated that this would be a story of our legacy as we have experienced it and it is. However, others have been watching and have shared their reactions to our saga. A beautiful example of a caring observer came to light in January 2017. My niece Krista asked me to read *The Story that Changed my Life* that she had written for her acting class. I didn't know what to expect or how I would feel when I read her story. It was clear her first visit with Rick, since his stroke, had had a profound impact on her. The visit had taken place on March 17th, 2006 when she was 16-years old. Now her story, years later, as witnessed through her eyes, written in her words had reminded me that Rick and I have an important role to play in this world. Rick and I are not invisible.

The Story that Changed my Life – Krista Dinel

This is the story about two musicians, my Uncle who played guitar and sang, and my Aunt who completed the duo with her powerful vocals. They were inseparable, they played many shows together and had a recording studio in their basement. This is a love story, but not like any love story. This story is to let you know how precious life is and to seize every moment before it's gone.

Fast forward to December 22nd, 2005, everything was normal and happy like any other night. They went to bed as usual. Except during the night, my Aunt had this feeling like something wasn't right, she turned to her husband and he wasn't breathing, he had stopped breathing in his sleep.

I remember getting the phone call and not knowing what to do as I was 5 hours away. I was told that when he would wake up, he would never be the same, and he wasn't. He couldn't walk on his own, couldn't do normal things like feed himself or even talk. The things we easily take for granted. I remember being afraid to walk into his hospital room, head down like I needed to hide. And then I saw him, he had suffered a stroke and he had a black-eye from trying to get up by himself to use the bathroom, which he could no longer do on his own. I remember trying not to cry because I know for him, he felt embarrassed that he no longer had these basic motor functions.

He was 48 when it happened, and he will be turning 60 on August 25th, 2017. To this day my Aunt has never left his side. Some family members couldn't take it and left. I will always be there for my Aunt and Uncle and I love the relationship they have. Even though they have been through the hardest of times. She could have left at any point, but she stayed.

My Aunt is the strongest person I know. She still takes care of him and they are still happy and very much in love. For me, I would gladly take a relationship like theirs, over a relationship where people are pushing and pulling each other. Their story is a reminder that love, can outweigh the bad. But it's not easy. Life isn't easy. Most people would have left, she didn't. Ask yourself, if you were in that situation would you stay or go?

To say I was moved by her words is an understatement. She gave me a gift that I will always cherish. I walked for an hour, reflecting on her story and how it was intertwined with the *Monique & Rick* story. Eventually, I hopped on a bus and went to Rick's room at Peter D. Clark. I lay down in Rick's single bed and read Krista's letter to him. He hugged me. No words were spoken. We didn't need them. To quote Nicholas Sparks the author of the Notebook "Silence is holy. It draws people together because only those who are comfortable with each other can sit without speaking. This is the great paradox."[26] These words ring true more so now as it is difficult for Rick to speak. But his thoughts are in his eyes and they speak to me.

There were other acts of supreme kind-heartedness from special angels, those kindred spirits who would simply show up at our door or make a long-distance call just to let me know they are there. Really there. Rick and I recently saw *Beautiful* the musical story about Carol King. We had several of her songs in our repertoire and I knew the lyrics by heart. What I didn't expect was the overwhelming emotion that took hold of me at the National Arts Centre when I heard these lyrics anew[27]:

Now, ain't it good to know that you've got a friend
When people can be so cold?
They'll hurt you, yes, and desert you

And take your soul if you let them, oh, but don't you
let them.

You just call out my name
And you know wherever I am
I'll come running, to see you again
Winter, spring, summer or fall
All you have to do is call
And I'll be there
You've got a friend
Ain't it good to know you've got a friend?

Yes, it is good to know; and I know whom I can call. Hope is in the lyrics and in the heart of those treasured souls who are truly our friends.

PAUSE THEN PLAY

"Music is therapy for the soul." This phrase is often said and heard. While I agree with that, most of the time, there was a period in my life when it was a double-edged sword. Music can be therapeutic or toxic depending on the song that life is playing.

For most of Rick's and my life music had been our touchstone, individually and as a couple. It was a sanctuary where we could be ourselves and feel free. When Rick had his stroke in December 2005, music changed its tune for me. I could barely listen to the radio or play CDs for fear that some of our cover songs would turn up and turn on the tears. Driving the car with music playing was too dangerous. I couldn't control my emotions. There are no windshield wipers for my eyes. It took several years before I could sing in the shower without feeling sad, fearful, and guilty. I put music on 'pause' on the soundtrack of my life during that time.

Despite my struggles, I needed to keep music alive for Rick. I made sure that his room in the nursing home had all his music DVD's and CD's, and I identified to the nursing staff what TV channels were his favourites—like Much Music.

In one nursing home, they had a wandering troubadour who would play his guitar in resident's rooms. His repertoire usually consisted of songs like 'Daisy a Day', 'Bicycle Built for Two' and other standards from a time before Rick and I were born. But when he walked into Rick's room and saw posters of Bob Dylan, Leonard Cohen, or Neil Young he switched to playing their songs and other standard pieces from the '70s and '80s. I remember walking into Rick's room after work to find these two having a musical bonding moment. During the early post-stroke years, it was difficult for Rick to sit up on his own let alone play the guitar. Having music present in his life in one form or another did help us. Eventually, I started to sing again.

When Rick was at Saint Vincent's hospital, (now known as Bruyère), he was only given one bath a week. This was unacceptable especially given his skin issues. On Saturday evenings, I would, therefore, bathe Rick. This broke the rules but I didn't care. While he was soaking in oatmeal and I was washing his hair, I would sing some of the songs in our repertoire. I would ask Rick for requests. The acoustics in the tub room was incredible. This became a regular Saturday night event for us both. An event that as it turned out was special for the other residents too. When we would leave the tub room we would encounter residents in the hallway. They had been listening to and enjoying our impromptu concert. Music was therapeutic for them also.

In 2008, I sang in public for the first time in four years, excluding our bath times concerts. As part of a musical tribute concert, I sang with Brian Crook. While Rick could not physically be there he was there in my heart and in every note, I sang. There are a few YouTube videos that showcase this performance and the prediction I made about Rick came true. I'll let you discover that story on your own.

Now fast-forward to August 25th, 2018 Rick's 61st birthday. I had a small party for him and luckily some of our dedicated musician friends were there to join in our celebration. Rick played his guitar, as he has off and on over the last few years. He has improved note by note and chord by chord. Bob and Doug McKenna were there to jam and helped Rick with tuning his guitar.

Rick playing guitar on his 61th birthday. Photographer: Monique Tremblay

After playing along with them I picked out a song from our Cover Tunes binder. It was Angel of the Morning a song we had not performed since 2005. When you watch this recording, you will see and hear the connection Rick and I have with music and with each other. As the song was about to end, emotions flooded into its last phrases. The Soundtrack of our lives is no longer on Pause. It is on Play!

JUST A DOOR

You open it. You go through it. You close it. It's just a door. Nothing more. Really? I often wonder if anyone truly appreciates the value of a door. It has its function to allow entry and exit. Maybe provide security from the elements of the weather. Maybe it is decorated for a special occasion—a wreath at Christmas, a Wicked Witch for All Hallows Eve, or a Lavender garland to pay homage to spring. Like many, I took the door to our home for granted. That is until it became a barrier, an obstacle stopping us from simply entering our home.

Between December 2005 and until June 2011 our front and back doors were restrictive entrances preventing Rick from coming home. Efforts were made with the help of family and friends in the early stages of Rick's stroke, but as time drew on they were less available to help, and in some cases, resentful. So much so that I stopped asking. During those periods, I could not manage to transfer Rick on my own as having help was mandatory. Rick and I lived full time at Saint Vincent's, at least it felt that way to me. Though I was able to go home and open the door and physically walk in, my heart wasn't. 'Home' as the saying goes 'is where the heart is'. My heart has been and will always be with Rick.

On a weekend visit with my Dad in April 2011, we talked about the drama surrounding Rick's care. We discussed the lack of support from his family and our friends and how frustrated I was as a result. It was my Dad, who suggested that maybe expanding the deck to the garage door might be a simple option toward getting Rick home. My Dad had a lot of experience with renovations and if it had not been for his health problems, he would have undertaken the project himself.

That's when Clyde Casto came onto the scene. My Dad recommended that I contact Clyde to see what could be done. The plans were set. Before I knew it, the deck was built with a slight ramp from the back-garage door. Since that day, a pergola was added to protect us from the rain so I can get Rick safely into the house without rushing to keep dry.

Both Dad and Clyde told me to hold off staining the deck for 4 or 5 years. Well, I waited for 7-years though not on purpose. With the help of Chris Rattray, Clyde's partner, the deck was sanded, power-washed and stained. Hot Yoga can't come close to my staining over 300 4-sided spindles in 30-degree weather.

The deck also served a greater purpose. It gave Rick and me access to the backdoor of our home. One barrier was gone. I remember the first time I took Rick home, on my own. I remember every detail of my plan to safely transfer him from the car, through the garage, up the slight ramp and then beside the back-patio door. Rick and I would then do a 'modified box-step' over the threshold and he would sit on the dining room chair, which I had previously set at the right angle. After that, it was another modified box-step to the living room, bathroom, and bedroom. Luckily, we live in a bungalow.

Rick and I have had our dance routine down pat ever since that deck was extended. I often think of my Dad and Clyde and I can only imagine that they are having a beer or two in God's workshop admiring a job well done. I think about them often. They removed a barrier and gave us the freedom for an accessible future.

There was one more barrier to conquer. The front door. I often thought, what if we could not use the back door? I had no other option to get Rick safely out of the house in case of an emergency. This was something that I'd been considering for a while.

Once again plans were set in motion and designs were drawn. Stones were laid and ramp angles measured once, twice, three times. Within 6-days, the old cement step was removed, two chipmunks were evicted (sorry Chip & Dale), a retractable screen door installed and the old interlock stones were moved to the back gate. I took pictures and each day and I marvelled at the work. Our dream was coming true. Stone by stone.

On Thursday, September 6th, 2018 I took Rick home and entered through the front door. It was just the two of us, with two hearts and four feet box-stepping over the threshold.

It's a gateway to our home, it's where our hearts reside. It's not 'just a door'!

FOUR WHEEL FREEDOM

Four Wheel-Freedom. What are you picturing? Is it the first car you owned? Or maybe it's that sports car with all the bells and whistles that you dreamed of owning and finally do?

For Rick and I, the four-wheel dream is a camping van, like a Westphalia or Roadtrek. It is just the right size for travelling across Canada with all the necessary comforts. That dream hasn't yet come true but it's still alive. We are working on it.

What we didn't imagine was that our four-wheel freedom being in the form of a Transport Wheelchair. In 2011, the year Rick moved into the Peter D. Clark Centre, I ordered a special transport chair with hand-brakes for the pusher—that's me. This is hard to find a must needed feature that is critical for our various treks around the city and to other locations.

It is lightweight at only 19-lbs. It folds down flat, fits in the trunk of our Subaru Outback, with room to spare. This allowed me to manage on my own without the help of others. I now had the freedom and ease to go places with Rick. Untethered, unbound, and unleashed we could now do what we pleased, in our way.

Having learned a new mode of travel we decided that Bluesfest would be our ultimate training ground. We outfitted the wheel-chair with a special packsack that fit perfectly. We then packed it with rain ponchos, hats, flashlights, a camera and of course our Bluesfest wrist bands. Next came a folding lawn chair for me. I had forgotten that detail the first time out and had to sit on the ground. Lesson learned. I kept the lawn chair in the car for the entire festival.

Where to park was another challenge we had to conquer. How far would we have to walk? Then I remembered the Frisby Tire store located on the corners of Somerset and Preston streets—right in front of our first apartment in Ottawa. We are their customers so I contacted them to see if we could get their permission to park there after hours. They agreed and we continue to park there to this day.

Rick and me, have our Bluesfest Routine down pat. I set up the chair, without the packsack first. Why? I had learned the hard way that a full packsack would easily tip the chair backward. Then Rick and I do our transfer dance into the chair, I attach the packsack and give Rick the folding lawn chair to hold onto. Then we begin our trek, walking down Preston Street, turning right on Albert Street then left on Booth Street until we reach the Canadian War Museum. That's 2 km of walking and rolling, trying not to clip the heels of pedestrians while maintaining momentum and at the same time watching for cracks or other obstacles that might stand in our way.

One night we learned a special trick by observing rickshaw drivers. This tip resulted in making a special modification to our freedom mode of transportation. When the festival-goers head for home, the roads are congested with people all heading in the same direction oblivious to anyone else around them. More than once people would get clipped by the footrests of Rick's wheelchair resulting in dirty looks or apologies. This is where the rickshaw moment came in. Drivers would ring their bells and within moments the crowd would part like Moses parting the Red Sea giving them worry-free passage. The very next day I bought a bike bell for the wheelchair. When I use it, people move out of the way and the look of surprise on their faces when they see a wheelchair versus a rickshaw is priceless. Yes, it is a RICK-shaw.

We broke in a new wheelchair at Bluesfest 2018 as our original wheelchair had not survived a baggage cart accident. The new chair, barely a week old, also had an accident, its footrest was broken by the owner of an electrical wheelchair who was backing up way too quickly and snapped off the bracket. Rick didn't get hurt but had to put his two feet on one footrest for the remainder of Bluesfest. Not ideal but doable.

We still have our original four-wheel freedom chair. When you compare the wheelchairs, you can see the distance travelled by looking at the threadbare tires. I wish I had attached an odometer to keep track of the mileage. But then again, it's not the mileage that counts—it's the events, the adventures, the freedom that these four wheels have brought us. Hopefully it will be a part of our next four-wheel freedom dream along with a Westphalia or a Roadtrek!

TEST FLIGHT

"Should—Could—Would—Did" reads a T-Shirt I received during a weight loss program. I'm still working on the 'did' part of that mantra.

"We should—We could—We would and We did!" These words were no longer a mantra, no longer a dream, and no longer a barrier. "We did" were the two simple words that marked a thirteen-year flight of fancy that came true on June 1st, 2018—our Test Flight!

Rick and I flew, for the first time in thirteen years, to Toronto to celebrate our 29th Wedding Anniversary. Now avid globetrotters may say, "What's the big deal?" They'd be right from an able-bodied point of view. It's another story when special assistance is required. So many details to figure out and so many 'what if's' to consider.

On May 9th, I acted. Step 1 – Buy theatre tickets. Step 2 – Book the hotel. Step 3 – Purchase airline tickets. Step 4 – Arrange visits with family and friends. Step 5 – Buy luggage.

Steps 1 and 2 were a breeze. Turns out I was able to get a package deal and buy tickets to see the play *Come From Away* at the Royal Alexandra Theatre and stay at the Sheraton Centre only a 15-minute walk away. We were very lucky to get matinee tickets as the show was sold out except for the accessibility seating. The seats were in the back row, which is not surprising but at least we were able to see the show. A bonus was that as his companion I didn't have to pay for my ticket. The Sheraton Centre was also very accommodating. We were able to get an accessibility room with a walk-in shower and a few other features that would make our stay easier.

Step 3 - I purchased our tickets with Porter Airlines. I had so many questions necessary to ensure there would be no surprises. How would I get Rick on and off the plane? Could I bring his wheelchair or would I need to use their on-site wheelchair? Would Rick's wheelchair qualify as a carry-on? Would we have assistance from the Toronto Billy Bishop City Airport onto the ferry or through the tunnel? My questions were answered but there were some surprises and lessons learned along the way.

Step 4 – Arrange to meet with family and friends. With a little juggling, Rick and I were able to meet with Audrey and Ken Peter on Friday night. Then on Saturday after the show, we had dinner with my brother Mike and his daughter Krista.

Step 5 – My ingenuity kicked in when I purchased our luggage. How was I to push Rick's wheelchair and luggage at the same time? This was never an issue when we took trips by car as most times I would have help. I wasn't too sure how we would manage to leave the cab and get inside the terminal. Then an idea struck. We would buy suitcases that were the same height as the armrests of the wheelchair. Rick could hang unto them while I pushed the wheelchair. A brilliant idea that worked!

Finally, June 1st arrived. I had everything ready. Tickets—check, Passport—check, Luggage—check and Rick—check. After all, I couldn't forget my life companion! We arrived at the airport well ahead of schedule. I was pushing Rick in the wheelchair and he was holding the suitcases with ease. We went to the Porter check-in counter and manoeuvred around the queue lines, just a little narrow for our convoy of suitcases and chair but we did it once an attendant moved the barriers. We checked in our luggage for free —which I hadn't thought about. We got our boarding passes without a problem and Rick's wheelchair was tagged.

The security check was a special adventure. Rick was treated to a pat-down or mini-massage by the security team. This was wheelchair callisthenics at its best. While I understand the reasons behind their thorough check, it is disturbing that Rick and other disabled passengers are given such a going over.

Getting on the plane was a dance involving three people. Rick's transport chair was too wide for the 3-foot metal ramp by the door. No problem. Rick and I are pros at the modified two-step. I walked backwards and Rick forwards. The only difference, the flight attendant was walking behind me with navigation. Think of the dance 'the locomotive' with two people facing the wrong direction. I never realized just how narrow the aisles were in a plane. Later, the flight attendant apologized as she had forgotten about the narrow onboard wheelchair for that purpose. Lesson learned.

Rick sat in his seat almost without incident. I forgot he was taller than me and he bumped his head on the overhead bin. Oops! I never, ever have to consider that. I jokingly said to him, "This could be Spousal Abuse." This was Rick's second time flying a commercial flight. He had done it once before his stroke but otherwise, that was it.

At 2:17 p.m. we took off in the silver bird. Rick who had the window seat and was looking at everything. When we were above the clouds, I softly sang in his ear:

> *I've looked at clouds from both sides now*
> *From up and down and still somehow*
> *It's cloud's illusions I recall*
> *I really don't know clouds at all.*

By Joni Mitchell

He turned and kissed me at 17,000 feet, our first kiss above the clouds.

As we were getting close to Toronto, we had a bit of turbulence and I realized that Rick had never experienced that before. He looked at the propeller of the plane from his window, and then glanced at me over his glasses with some surprise but not a concern. We had a smooth landing and waited to get off the plane. This time the flight attendants brought a transfer chair narrow enough for the aisle and it was also a stair climber. I safely transferred Rick into it making sure he didn't hit his head on the overhead bin. Then I watched the pros in action. One attendant was pushing and the other guiding this special chair down the stairs. There were robotic wheels that teetered down each step smoothly. It moved similar to the slinky toy we played with as kids. Impressive to watch and Rick was checking this out also as he has always been curious about how things work.

We were on our way to the Ferry and then the Taxi stand. I pushed Rick's wheelchair and the attendant rolled our suitcases and guided us through the terminal. She pointed out the intercom that we could use when we were ready to take our return flight home that would allow us to ask for help on the way back. We used it and this time went through the tunnel. That was a 'first' for both of us.

I think I surprised all of our taxi drivers during this trip. You see I've had to transfer Rick to and from our car so many times and fold the wheelchair and place it in the trunk that it has become a flawless dance routine. I'm so fast, that the taxi drivers were in awe. After many years of not having help, it has become second nature for me.

We were booked into our hotel with a view of the CN Tower. Couldn't wait for our next adventure, supper with Audrey and Ken Bell-Peter. Rick and I have known Audrey since high school and we've been in touch over the years. Audrey made a special trip to Ottawa to be at a fundraiser for Rick shortly after his stroke. Her presence at this event meant a great deal. Finally, after years of trying to plan this trip we were able to spend time with them. So many memories and so much laughter shared that evening. Looking forward to our next trip.

On Saturday, June 2nd we had breakfast and then we did a test run to the theatre. I wanted to see how long it would take to get there and what the entrance was like for accessibility. Walking at my normal pace it took me 11 minutes. I spoke to an usher who gave us a few tips about entering the theatre and all was set for later that afternoon. As we left the theatre, Rick heard live music from across the street. So as any devout musician would do, we followed the music to check it out. There was a free outdoor concert at the Roy Thomson Hall. The band called One Night Stand was playing music from the 70s. The musicians were of our age group, seasoned rock & rollers playing April Wine, Billy Joel, Eddie Money,

Bryan Adams and more. We watched them for 40 minutes on a nice summer day.

When it was over, we continued our walk towards the CN Tower. Or so I thought. I guess I was so focused on sidewalk crevices and other obstacles before I realized I had gone too far. My smartphone was set on Google maps but I hadn't been paying attention or maybe my map reading was a bit rusty. We headed back to our hotel to get ready for the show when I saw the CN Tower and said to Rick "Better luck next time."

Come From Away is the remarkable true story about our favourite province Newfoundland! This is a story written by Irene Sankoff and David Hein, Canadian playwrights. It is set in the week following the September 11th terrorist attacks and tells the true story of what transpired when 38 planes were ordered to land unexpectedly in the small town of Gander, Newfoundland. I could write several pages about this amazing musical and all the memories it conjured up for Rick and I. The people, the music, and the stories in *Come From Away* made us laugh, made me cry (I'm the mushy one) and made us want to go back to the Rock. After this test flight, we will plan another one.

We headed back to our hotel and were greeted by warm hugs from Mike and Krista. Our supper was delicious and we caught up on each other's news. I wished that Barrie and Ottawa were closer so we could see each other more frequently. Social media platforms simply can't replicate real-time or face-to-face communication. Our time together was special and way too short.

I was up early that Sunday morning, writing in my journal about our trip and marvelled at the responses to our Facebook posts. Ranging from congratulations to the unique statement, "You are stronger than you think!"

Well, it was time to head back. I used the Porter intercom to get assistance and sure enough, help was there in minutes. We went through the tunnel this time and the attendant said I'm glad you are pushing the wheelchair. As we waited for our flight in the lounge we heard that our flight had been cancelled. Why? I still don't know as the weather seemed fine. Then I heard, "Would Monique & Rick Tremblay present themselves to a Porter representative?" Off we went. We were relieved to hear that we were now booked on an earlier flight and that our luggage has been put on board. I was ready for Plan B though, just in case. I had Rick's carry-on pack sac ready with medical supplies and clothes should we be stranded.

All went well with our trip back to Ottawa with one hiccup. The attendant said, "we are ready to help you off the plane we are simply waiting for your wheelchair." As she said this, we looked out the window to see the baggage car drive by with luggage and Rick's wheelchair. Then we saw it fall off the car and a footrest landed beneath the tires and it was mangled beyond use. Porter would need to pay for damages as it turned out the part couldn't be ordered. Lesson learned to find a better way to keep the footrests from falling off when I get the new chair for our next flight.

This test flight had been an idea since August 2013 when Rick and I had updated our passports. When I glanced at my photo, I noticed how haggard and how stressed I looked. I can see the struggle etched on my face, my eyes dull and my smile doubtful. Did I dare to hope for a trip that Rick and I could take? Or would I have to accept things as they were and let the barriers keep us in a state of perpetual limbo? Back then, I didn't feel as strong and there seemed to be many forces at play that made moving forward difficult. But with each passing year the idea went from should, could, would—to We did—and We Will again to another destination and another.

TWIST OF FATE

"The best-laid plans of mice and men often go awry. No matter how carefully a project is planned, something may still go wrong with it."[28] These words were written by Robert Burns in his poem *To a Mouse* and are also quoted in John Steinbeck's book *Of Mice and Men*. I can't argue with this view as this has happened to me on more than one occasion. No matter how well I plan a project or a small task I might always be caught off guard by an unexpected twist of fate.

Here's my story of 'Mice and Woman'! I had never had to deal with mice, nor do I recall my parents having to contend with these critters. My first experience was when Rick and I moved into our Whitehill home in 1992. One pleasant morning as we were heading off for work, I heard Rick swear. He had come across mouse droppings. I had never seen those before but Rick had the first-hand experience with mice from working in the mines. When we returned home from work, we went on a mouse patrol and disinfected the house. Rick went looking for the entry point, while I cleaned up the kitchen.

I opened the oven drawer to take baking dishes out and sadly the mouse had been there too. Droppings were everywhere. More dishes to wash. I had to bend further down to get the last item at the back of the drawer. Two little brown eyes were looking back at me with fear and trepidation. I screamed like a typical movie female and grabbed a pot to cover the intruder. Rick ran into the kitchen and began laughing as I had put my full body weight on the pot. He wanted to know if I thought our tiny intruder was related to 'Mighty Mouse'? Rick coolly slipped a piece of cardboard under the pot, walked outside, and released the little fella. Rick has a big heart. The next morning, we were leaving for work again, proudly waiting for us outside was Buster the neighbour's cat. He was a handsome black tom with four white boot-like paws and a heart-shaped white-face. In between his front paws was a dead mouse. I guess he wanted us to admire his skill and his hunting prowess.

After that incident, we were vigilant and tried to prevent potential mouse invasions from breaching the walls of our fortress. But that best-laid plan took a back-seat after Rick's stroke. Little did I know that 'Monique as Damsel-in-Distress' would evolve into a fierce 'Monique the Invincible' with feline fighting and stalking instincts based in part upon Buster's example in the 1992 training session.

In December 1992 I discovered more mouse droppings. I promptly set up traps of every type to catch the intruders. I became less squeamish with each extermination and more strategic, like a cunning cat. My score—eight dead mice and one dead gerbil. The entry point via the dryer vent was blocked. I hoped that was the end of it. When spring came, I had a new problem, ants. I set up ant traps and the unwanted guests were done in. Late one night while Rick and I were almost asleep I heard a noise. It reminded me of our childhood cat. Ginger had liked to play with marbles late at night on the linoleum floor. Dad could never find these marbles. There was the sound again. I tiptoed to the kitchen and spied an ant trap moving! A mouse was playing with it! Again, I grabbed a pot and covered the intruder. This time no screams of a paranoid female but the roar of Cat Woman. Well actually, it wasn't a roar but a few choice swear words energetically delivered.

Then I turned around looking for cardboard and saw Rick in the hallway, leaning against the railing. He had come from the bedroom to the kitchen to help. Now I was in a full-blown panic. He was inches away from the basement stairs. One misstep and he could have fallen. No successful mouse-hunt is worth that. I swiftly changed my focus from offensive to defensive mode. Rick and I safely returned to our bedroom, Once Rick was back in bed my heart rate eventually stabilized. The mouse that was trapped in a pot weighed down by the *Cocktails for Two Cookbook* found its way to the porcelain-a-la martini jacuzzi.

Lesson learned if something was afoot, I had to make sure Rick stayed put. Or when you're going to morph into Cat Woman make sure your Batman is aware of the plan to trap a mouse.

That was the intent until the next twist of fate. This twist began with a loud bang and sounded like someone was breaking into our home. Rick and I both reacted but he was faster. He got out of bed opened our closet and took out an axe that he had hidden in the corner. Something I didn't know about. All I could see was the silhouette of Rick swaying to keep his balance and holding a dull axe. I got to him, took away the axe and returned him to our bed. We still don't know what that noise was but I suspect now that it was ice cracking on the roof. Back in bed, my overactive imagination, along with my crazy sense of humour created news breaking headlines "Home intruder prevents a woman from being hacked to bits by her disabled husband!" The next day the axe was safely stored in the garage.

When Rick is home on weekends or over the holidays, I always have him help me with certain chores or hire him on as 'job foreman'. On one occasion I had carefully planned that he would be sitting in his wheelchair operating a leaf blower to clear leaves off the driveway. I watched him carefully and he seemed to have everything under control. I then picked up the rake and got to work myself, still keeping an eye on him. However, a blast of wind suddenly hit the back of my head and I turned around to see Rick flipped over on his back still in the chair and with the leaf blower pointing to the sky. He had propelled the chair with his feet, the chair had rolled back on the grass and tipped. He wasn't hurt and was laughing! Enter my 'Comedienne' with another headline, 'Woman puts disabled husband at risk with a leaf blower!' My careful planning had gone awry as good ole Robby Burns might have predicted.

I always search for ways for us to do normal things with the necessary modifications intended to ensure our mutual safety. We had always enjoyed dancing. On September 25th, 2010 we danced for the first time since Rick's stroke at Ed and Chris Poisson's son's wedding. We had asked the DJ to play Anne Murray's 'Could I have this Dance', but he didn't have it and played Mac Davis's 'Oh Lord it's hard to be Humble' instead. Peculiar choice. It didn't matter. We went to the dance floor and did a swaying on-the-spot waltz step until Rick decided to get some fancy footwork in. He caught me off-guard and off-balance. Next thing I knew we were surrounded by Ryan and Angie, the Bride and Groom, and the rest of the wedding party. We then performed a group dance similar to a team-huddle. Since then we have improved our swaying-waltz. Rick's agility is getting better and I am physically stronger. I could now anticipate his moves. Or so I thought. In 2015, Rick and I went to the Toastmasters Conference and Gala where I would receive my DTM (Distinguished Toastmaster medal). We went onto the dance floor to do our improved swaying-on-the-spot waltz and signature dance routine. Because he remembered my favourite dance move, Rick decided to 'dip his dance partner'. Another best-laid plan quickly went awry. Before we went timber to the floor other dancers caught us. Later one of the women complimented Rick on his form. We have danced since then but now I have 'spotters' close by just in case Rick's inner Fred Astaire should take the lead.

Not all my well-laid plans have gone awry. I have successfully found a way to help Rick eat spaghetti. I got the idea in part from the movie *Lady and the Tramp*. One plate, two forks and four meatballs. I would twirl the spaghetti on the fork, then pass the loaded fork to Rick. This way he didn't have to struggle with dexterity glitches that might result in flying meatballs. Where there's a will there's a way.

I will continue to look for ways for Rick and me to experience life in the best way we can, despite our circumstances. All we need is a wicked sense of humour, bizarrely creative minds, and a willingness to work our way around unexpected twists of fate.

SIX PERFECT 10'S?

The camera zooms in on 111 Hemlock Street, Levack, Ontario. There is a brown one-story house and, in the driveway, a young brown-eyed girl jumping rope and counting a rhyme in measures of ten. Her voice is innocently gleeful and confident: '10, 20, 30, 40, 50, 60, 70, 80, 90, 100'. Then, she starts over again at 10. This 10-year-old girl saw these as simple numbers as she focused on not tripping on the rope. She certainly didn't imagine her skipping would become a metaphor for the decades that would mark her future life journey. I know this because I was that little girl. I still have brown eyes, somewhat natural dark-brown hair, and my voice is still gleeful and confident. Innocence has been replaced with wisdom. Guarded optimism that is buoyed up by romantic hope, hard-won from lessons learned through 60-years travelling the sometimes-rocky roads of my life. 60-years of finding out who I am and what I am capable of.

On Monday, June 17th, 2019 I turned 60-years old. The sun was shining making this day especially bright. I woke up with Rick snuggling next to me. I asked him, "Do I look different today?" He raised his eyebrows with a quizzical expression that read, "Where is she going with this? Better tread carefully!" Said I ever so coyly, "Today is June 17th." He exhales and whispers, "Happy Birthday!" There was a time when Rick would have planned a special celebration for me, as he had always done until my 46th birthday. Now I am Rick's stand-in party planner and I 'act surprised' to give the event some sense of normalcy. We've learned to celebrate in our way and each year that passes brings another special gift.

As I write I can't help but recall Facebook posts from friends and acquaintances with Happy Birthday messages, GIFs, and quotes about this milestone birthday. One message, in particular, seemed to align with the numbers in my youthful jumping rope rhyme:

> Laugh like you're 10
> Party like you're 20
> Travel like you're 30
> Think like you're 40
> Advise like you're 50
> Care like you're 60
> Love like you're 70

What about 80, 90 and 100? Maybe its author hadn't figured those out yet. Best though is when I look at the decade descriptions in this simple poem and realize that I have indeed done well in my efforts to abide by those simple but powerful instructions through thick and thin as I made my way focusing so as not to trip decade by decade.

So now I am a Sexagenarian. A person between the ages of 60 and 69. I heartily embrace this age. I found turning 40 a Quadragenarian and 50 a Quinquagenarian tougher to take. My life had gone into a prolonged tailspin when I was 46-years-old until I hit 56-years-old. I was put to many tests, beginning with Rick's stroke, and accompanied by Family drama, Job loss, Disappearing friends, Depression and Menopause, just to heat things up a bit with hot flashes and emotional outbursts to make sure I didn't get bored. Back to the skipping rope metaphor. Picture mean-spirited little girls turning the rope at 'pepper speed' when the innocent young brown-eyed little girl reached 40 and 50 in the rhyme. They'd tried their double best to trip her up. So maybe the three Fates—Clotho, Lachesis, and Atropos, otherwise known as the weird sisters, thought to test my resolve. They almost won.

But my determination, stubbornness and will to survive helped me through it all. If I tripped, I got up and tried again. I surprised myself many times. I had not known how strong I could be.

So here I am, 60-years-old, about to travel the up-swing in the U-Curve of Happiness. If the research holds then I'm keen to see what's in store. I've adopted 60 as my true middle age. Why? Google notes that the oldest person was a 120-years-old. Half of that is 60. Simple. Yes, I know it's not statistically valid. Sorry statistics geeks, I'm sticking to my position.

I heard these words of wisdom from Jenny Murphy, a Septuagenarian: "There can be nothing so magical as turning that wonderful age of sixty. This is the time when people, as they become sexagenarians, are expected to slow down a little." She continued to list my recent accomplishments in a room filled with Management Development Program for Women Toastmasters and said, "All of us in this room know that Monique has not begun to slow down—in fact, I would say she is speeding up. Monique, in your case, sixty is not some arbitrary number—it represents six perfect 10's."

What a memorable moment of validation! What a wonderful way to step into the next decade! Travelling along with this newly minted sexagenarian will be her previous selves—the little girl, the teenager, and the young woman, all instrumental in paving the road toward her 60's self. 70, 80, 90, 100—here they come, gleeful, confident, and full of potential. The camera of life will capture their adventures for future decades. Maybe even another six perfect 10's?

THE CAPTAIN & HIS FIRST MATE

The First Mate gazes with love at her Captain at the helm of yet another life journey. The wind was right, his eyes were bright, and he found serenity sailing on the Ottawa River. Well, known lyrics were ringing true for Rick and me, *"The canvas can do miracles, just you wait and see."*[29] Christopher Cross's 1979 soft rock song 'Sailing' plays on the soundtrack of my mind, I savour the panoramic scene before me, treasures that no pirates can ever steal away! If they did, this tenacious first mate would fiercely protect this memorable pearl.

It was warm and sunny on September 21st, 2019 when Rick and I drove towards the Club de Voile Grande Rivière located in Aylmer (Gatineau), Québec. Here we planned to set off on our first sailing trip since our excursion on the 28-foot *Capella*—20 long years ago in Halifax Harbour. In 2019 in Aylmer, we were greeted with warm hugs from Louise and Mike Branch. They are friends we have reconnected with over the last several months. The four of us had attended a David Wiffen tribute concert when they invited us to sail with them.

We set to work as part of their crew to ready for our sail on *The Lotus*, a sleek CS-33-foot sailboat. The first order of business was to safely transfer Rick from his wheelchair to the boat. This was a delicate dance of finding the right rhythm and the right balance to step onto Lotus's deck and then into her cockpit. It went without a hitch. No one went overboard. Rick and I now sat back and marvelled at this sailing duo masterfully manoeuvre the sailboat out of the harbour and into the buoy-marked channel that led to the open waters of the Ottawa River. I was impressed by Louise's catlike-ballet footwork as she walked along the narrow pathway from the hull to the stern and from port to starboard, doing a myriad of tasks with ropes, pullies, and clips. Rick focussed on watching Mike start the inboard engine, reverse the boat, as he gently navigated the Lotus out of the marina basin. Barely into the channel, there was an unexpected and ominous shudder. Everyone was surprised. The bottom of the 5-foot deep solid-steel keel hit an unknown obstacle below. Our hosts sprung-into-action with tag-team precision. We heard "Check the bilge! Is there water? No. All good! Call the marina they have to know!" True to their word they described what happened so that other boaters would avoid this unsuspecting jar to the bones of their vessels and passengers. Mike and Louise had taken everything in stride and reassured us that all was well. We trusted them. We were in capable hands. After all, we weren't on the S.S. Minnow. The water level in the river was particularly low for this time of year.

With the motor off, the jib sail set and the wind masterfully captured by Captain Mike, the Lotus Crew were now enjoying a scenic tour of the Ottawa River's Lac Deschenes. Ontario was on our port side. Québec was starboard. We sailed by Britannia Bay, Shirley's Bay, Aylmer Island, Alexandria Bay and finally we anchored near Pinhey's Point, a sheltered bay, just south of Dunrobin's Shore. Along the way, our hosts shared their sailing stories that spanned five decades. There was no doubt in my mind, that they truly believed what they had texted hours before "that this was their favourite spot on the planet." What an incredible gift they shared with us. For Rick and me, it was like a real vacation, definitely on par with some of our youthful adventures. Rick and I always made a point of visiting as much of Canada as possible. Now we were happily exploring in our backyard, so to speak. We had not known there was an Aylmer Island nestled on the Ontario side of the river. No clue, but then again, we hadn't grown up in the Ottawa area.

Once anchored at Pinhey's Point we shared a feast of smoked beef, ham, egg salad, fresh buns and fixings of lettuce, tomato, cheese, olives, hummus, etc. Dessert included local strawberries, chocolate turtles, and Rick's favourite chocolate bar Coffee Crisp. We savoured the bouquet of Canadian wine, Canadian scenery, and Canadian camaraderie. In the background, we heard live music emanating from Pinhey's groomed lawns. A mix of Concrete Blonde, Fleetwood Mac, and Blue Rodeo delightfully in sync weaved with Lotus's swaying motion as it rocked in the *rhythm of la rivière*. A true moment of reverie.

Living up to the Greek mythology definition, Lotus induced a dreamy forgetfulness and an unwillingness to depart for its crew. When it was time to up-anchor the Lotus's crew were eastward bound and sailing into tranquillity once more. Louise coached me, her new 'first mate-in-training', on how to chassé along the narrow catwalk towards the bow of the sailboat. I paid close attention when she told me what to grab and what not to hold onto for support. 'Wire good. Rope bad', was the mantra that echoed in my head. I didn't want to carelessly end up walking the imaginary plank. What a sensation it was, sitting on the bow with my arms outstretched (well one arm), recreating the iconic scene of the movie Titanic's 'I'm the Queen of the World' moment.

Captain Mike encouraged Rick to take the helm. I kept him steady while Mike gave him a few key pointers. It was soon apparent that the stroke had not hampered Rick's resolve, skill or sailing memory. A few seconds after he took the wheel an elated Rick noted with great satisfaction, "I still know how!" He certainly did. Mike said, "Nice move Rick, you caught the wind right on." Rick continued manoeuvring the boat through fairly gusty and changing winds without missing a beat! "You really are an excellent sailor, Rick!" said Mike. I revelled in watching my Captain sail again.

Now it was my turn at the wheel. I had never sailed before other than as a passenger. I had already watched Rick, Mike, and Louise at work. Now I did as I was told to keep the wind in the jib and flutter-free (a.k.a. full) and focussed on a fixed reference point on land for direction. I was doing pretty well until I discovered that my 'landmark' was changing. I had been aiming at a moving target—a sailboat. Yes, I was a landlubber and we all had a good laugh at my expense. Now I was on yet another 'high.' I'd learned to manage a large boat with only the wind to fuel our passage. Louise and Mike both complimented me on my handling of the Lotus. Rick smiled his smile. I think he was proud of me!

Time for some more music as we sailed along sated by our multiple experiences and in a serene state-of-mind. More was to come when Captain Mike asked if I could sing a song from the *Monique & Rick* repertoire. Of course, I would. My adrenalin was in peak form. As the sun was setting behind me, and the waves the water gently slapped against the Lotus's hull I chose Roy Orbison's 'Blue Bayou'. It's the lyrics *'Gonna be with some of my friends'* and *'with their sails afloat'*[30] were fitting. Although I had sung this song many times over the last 30-years, this time it was different. Blue Bayou struck a chord (pardon the pun) that I'd never felt before.

Six hours later, we were back in the harbour once again. The sun had set and the journey lingered in our minds and hearts. Later, while I viewed our videos, I wished I had changed the lyrics of Blue Bayou to: *'Oh, that man of mine, by my side, the setting sun on the river wide'*. The First Mate gazes with love at her one and only Captain. The serenity of this day on the Ottawa River will continue to ripple through our memories, like a treasured pearl.

WARRIORS OF HOPE

"Hope begins in the dark, the stubborn hope that if you just show up and try to do the right thing, the dawn will come. You wait and watch and work: you don't give up." Anne Lamott[31]

I had heard this quote during a romance movie. Had I heard it during the early years of Rick's stroke as I struggled with job loss and abandonment by friends seeking cheerier connections, I would not have believed this to be possible. I suffered many platitudes, many delivered with good intentions but others so insensitive, that I swallowed my rage like a heaping tablespoon of Buckley's cough syrup. Instinctively, I was not about to give up no matter how many barriers would be in my way. My barriers paled in comparison to what Rick would contend with. We became Warriors of Hope—each in our own way.

Prior to and after the derailment of our lives, we were still there for others. We opened our home when a sibling was going through a divorce and needed a place to live; when a sister-in-law was convalescing until she could be placed in palliative care; when a nephew and his girlfriend needed a place to stay until they found jobs. Rick and I never turned anyone away when they needed our help. We were staunch advocates of hope yet not knowing how our inherent strengths would play out during a major crisis of our own. I did not realize how uncommon our desire to help others was until the roles were reversed. When we needed support in our corner, those we might have counted on were often found to be few and far between.

The Hope is the Lyrics chapters capture in part our effort to latch on to and nurture that hope. After many years of carefully crafting our new realities, there are still detractors who intentionally or unintentionally challenge our determination to lead a meaningful life despite our misfortunes. I am more sensitive to naysayers than Rick is. Sometimes I am thankful for Rick's loss of short-term memory, now diagnosed as a form of dementia. It has shielded him, I hope, from the insensitive actions of others. When Rick is within earshot of a disparaging remark aimed at me, he stares the 'perp' down with his intense hazel-green eyes and admonishes them with a few curt words. Fortunately, he has not witnessed or heard everything.

"Sticks and stones may break my bones but words will never hurt me." Not so. Words can hurt to the point where they become deadly. They can erode confidence and suck out breaths of hope. Like the bullying commercial showing a girl being pushed into school lockers by words flashing on the screen, I too still get pushed around. "Your preaching again," "Get over it," "No one is interested in this stuff," and so on. Also brutal is the silence. When I have reached out to those I would like back in my life, letters, text messages, and phone calls are often not returned. Or run into a former acquaintance at a concert, try to have a simple conversation during intermission only to have her shrug her shoulders and then text someone else—this from a well-educated woman who on Facebook regularly champions the plight of victims of bullying or neglect. 'Actions speak louder than words!' A great song that comes to mind is Otis Redding's 'Try A Little Tenderness' with its soulful lyrics, lyrics that help Warriors of Hope to soldier on.

> *But it is all so easy*
> *All you got to do is try*
> *Try a little tenderness!*[32]

I have reached a turning point; I am taking my power back. I won't be silenced. I'm not preaching, I'm extremely passionate and describing my truth. I have important things to say. The Bell 'Let's Talk' campaign that started in 2010 is a step in the right direction. It's getting people to talk about mental health. But there is still a lot of work to do and to break down the stigma associated with that. As a Caregiver, it's not surprising that I struggle with all that that entails. Whether its Depression, Post-Traumatic Stress and or Compassion Fatigue. The latter term was applied only to Doctors, Nurses, etc. But recently Caregivers have been added to the mix. Those who say "Get over it!" need to do some soul searching. Walking in someone else's shoes can be very informative. Maybe I should cut them some slack because they don't know any better because they haven't travelled this road. I try to but there is merit behind my temporary tattoo that reads 'Unapologetically Me'!

I will never give up hope and I continue to treasure the help of those who understand the shoes that Rick and I are wearing. Yes, there were dreams that have had to be put aside, Rick's dreams, my dreams, our dreams, some never to be realized, some perhaps salvageable. Or there could be new dreams to enrich our lives in ways we couldn't have imagined before. I am starting to understand what Diane said to me years ago, 'You are living in a state of grace!' Yet again my spirits are lifted by another Anne Lamott quote: "I do not at all understand the mystery of grace only that it meets us where we are but does not leave us where it found us!" Words can hurt but they can also heal. These are *w*ords that can fuel the energy of the Warriors of Hope as they continue on a complicated and loving journey.

MUSICALLY YOURS

On a Valentine's Day celebration, a long, long time ago, Rick and I were sitting at a table for two, early in the evening, at a Dow's Lake restaurant in Ottawa. Although we didn't know it, we were about to become silent witnesses to a hallmark moment. On the frozen surface of Dow's Lake, bathed in the moon's glow, was the silhouette of two people. They were an older couple, arm in arm, gingerly shuffling and sliding in their boots on the ice and carefully supporting each other. Could there be love in the air? I think so. I was powerfully moved as I continued to watch this couple immersed in their private moment in the arms of Mother Nature's brisk wintry scene. They couldn't know that a younger couple was deeply caught up in their wintery tableau. They continued to move along, the unintentional stars in their own romantic drama and holding each other in a loving embrace as they backtracked into the growing darkness.

This experience became imprinted on my heart and soul, living proof that undying devotion does exist. When I reminded Rick of this memory he chuckled, "You have always been a starry-eyed romantic. You see romance in everything." That's true. I do. Years of life have been lived since that Valentine's Day, and while (I hate to admit it) we might now be closer in age to that unknown couple. We have lovingly built our own brand of undying devotion. I'm grateful for that long-ago inspiration.

Since the beginning of our story, Rick and I were in step with each other, note for note, adventure by adventure, from one treasured memory to another. We've stayed true to our silent vow 'I'm going with you!' We continue to witness our lives through all of our senses and embraced each experience in our roles as Young Musicians, the Married Duo, and the Devoted Couple.

Where do we go from here? We will continue to witness each other's lives each in our own way. Embracing opportunities and facing challenges while keeping hope alive. As noted at the beginning of our memoir *'in a marriage, you're promising to care about everything.'* We will hold true to that no matter what.

The next chapter of this legacy project is documenting our music—the soundtrack of our story. We want to share our audio and video recordings along with behind the scenes stories on our website. Then you will be a witness to the *Monique & Rick* story. You will perceive our silhouette, against a background of our soundtrack. We will perform in our own romantic movie. Watch us and understand the meaning of our metaphor 'Musically Yours'!

P.S.

THE RECORDINGS

Monique & Rick – Single Demo 1981

- Do Like the Robbins Do – M. Dinel, R. Tremblay, M. Bouchard, D. Morrisey

Monique & Rick – Soulessence Live 1991

Aurocalypse Independent studio CD release producer R. Tremblay. Cover artist M. Tremblay.

- *Hintonburgh Café Introduction*
- Early Morning Rain – G. Lightfoot

- It Doesn't Matter Anymore – P. Anka
- Dance me to the End of Love – L. Cohen
- Unsophisticated Time – B. Simpson
- Another You – T. Springfield
- Crazy – W. Nelson
- Helplessly Hoping – S. Stills
- More Often Than Not – D. Wiffen

- *Bank Street Café Introduction*
- You Turn me on I'm a Radio –
  J. Mitchell

- There's a Law – L. Cohen
- Imagine That – J. Tubb
- Stuck in the Middle with you –
  G. Rafferty
- Tears Don't Care Who Cries Them – F
  & C Tobias
- No Surrender – B. Springsteen
- Try – J. Cuddy & G. Keelor
- You Were on My Mind – S. Tyson

MONIQUE & RICK –
OTHER VOICES A MUSICAL CORNUCOPIA* 1992
(*listed only the songs performed by R & M Tremblay, not other artists.)

Monique & Rick first professional CD release.

- Wild As Eden – R. Tremblay
- She Dances to Dream – M. Dinel

- Magic Pleasure – R. Tremblay
- Yellow Room – M. Dinel / R. Tremblay

MONIQUE & RICK – RENAISSANCE 1996*
(* also known as Rational Intuition & Metaphysical Pragmatics)

Aurocalypse Independent studio CD release producer R. Tremblay.
Cover artist & photographer M. Tremblay.

- Wild As Eden – R. Tremblay
- How Many Times – R. Tremblay
- The Reception – R. Tremblay
- For Being Young and Being Free –
  R. Tremblay

- Socio-Illogical Blues – R. Tremblay
- Yellow Room – M. Dinel / R. Tremblay
- Between the Sun and the Moon –
  R. Tremblay
- Magic Pleasure – R. Tremblay

Monique & Rick with Special Guests – Christmas Wishes 2002

Aurocalypse Independent studio CD release producer R. Tremblay. Cover artist M. Tremblay.

- Santa Clause is Coming to Town – Coots / Gillespie
- Silver Bells – Livingston / Evans
- Rudolph the Red Nosed Reindeer – Marks
- White Christmas – Berlin
- Twelve Days of Christmas – Austin
- Do You Hear what I Hear? – Regney

- Christmas Song (Chestnuts) – Tormé / Wells
- Blue Christmas – Hayes / Johnson
- First Noel – Gilbert
- Oh, Holy Night – Adam
- Jingle Bells – Pierpoint
- Happy Christmas (War is Over) – Lennon
- Have Yourself a Merry Little Christmas - Martin

ORIGINAL SONGS

Rick Tremblay kept records of every Original song which were self-penned or in collaboration with Marcel Bouchard, Brian Crook and/or Monique (Dinel) Tremblay. There are also songs solely written by each individual member. For this memoir, the Top 80 out of 170 Originals are listed below.

ORIGINAL SONG TITLE	MAIN VOCALIST	ORIGINAL SONG TITLE	MAIN VOCALIST
ADELAIDE	MARCEL	ROCK M. ROLL	AURORA
APRIL AFTERNOON	RICK	RUNNING OUT OF TIME	AURORA
BEST OF FOOLS	MONIQUE	SHE DANCES TO DREAM	MONIQUE
BETWEEN THE SUN AND THE MOON	RICK	SIX PACK ROOM (PISS FOREVER)	AURORA
CHRYSLER CLOWN	RICK & MARCEL	SNOWBOUND ROAD	AURORA
DANCES TO DREAM	MONIQUE	SOBER AND BROKE	RICK & MARCEL
DO LIKE THE ROBBINS DO	MONIQUE	SOCIO-ILLOGICAL BLUES	RICK
ENDLESS WINTER	MARCEL	SOMETIMES	AURORA
EXTRA-ORDINARY MAN	RICK & MONIQUE	SUDBURY'S CENTANNIAL SONG - SUDBURY JUNCTION	RICK & MONIQUE
FIND A REASON	RICK	SUNNY SKIES	MARCEL
FONDER MEMORIES	MONIQUE	TAKE GOOD CARE OF YOUR SOUL	AURORA
FOOLS GOLD	RICK & BRIAN	TAKE MY HEART (M&R'S WEDDING SONG- THE PROPOSAL)	RICK & MONIQUE
FOR BEING YOUNG AND BEING FREE	RICK & MONIQUE	TAKING IT STRAIGHT	RICK & MARCEL
FOR TODAY	RICK & MARCEL	THANK YOU GOODBYE (EMPTY NEST BLUES)	RICK & MONIQUE
FOR YOU	RICK & MONIQUE	THE COLD THE TRUTH	AURORA
FOREVERMORE	MARCEL	THE FORUM	AURORA
GIVE IT ONE MORE TRY	RICK & MARCEL	THE FRENCH ONE	MARCEL
GOING NOWHERE	AURORA	THE REASON	RICK & MARCEL
HOW MANY TIMES I CAN BE WRONG	RICK	THE RECEPTION	RICK
I DON'T WANT TO HURT ANYBODY	RICK & MARCEL	THE VIEWPOINT OF A TRAIN	RICK
I DON'T WANT TO SEE YOU GO	RICK	THE WAY IT'S GOT TO BE	AURORA
I'LL ALWAYS COME BACK TO YOU	MARCEL	THE WHIRLPOOL AND THE SKY	AURORA
JUST ONE SHOT	MARCEL	THERE YOU GO (WHO DO YOU THINK YOU ARE)	RICK & MONIQUE
LAST CHANCE	AURORA	TOLD YOU SO	AURORA
LEARN TO RUN	RICK	TOO MUCH FOR YOU TO DO	AURORA
LEAVE ME ALONE	AURORA	WAITING TWO GENERATIONS	AURORA
LIQUOR & LOVE	RICK & MONIQUE	WE ARE REAL	RICK
MAGIC PLEASURE	RICK & MONIQUE	WHATEVER (NO PLACE TO FALL)	RICK
NATIONAL ANTHEM #2	MARCEL	WHEN I HEAR THEM ON THE RADIO	MONIQUE
NEVER COMING BACK	RICK	WHEN LOVE HAS LET YOU DOWN	RICK & MARCEL
NEVER WRITE A SONG AGAIN	AURORA	WHERE WERE YOU	RICK
NO OTHER WAY TO GO	RICK	WHO DO YOU THINK YOU ARE	RICK & MONIQUE
NO PLACE TO FALL	RICK	WHO WAS FOOLED - THE DECEPTION OF A KING	AURORA
NO THANK YOU NO GOODBYE	RICK & MONIQUE	WHY THEY CRY AT WEDDINGS	RICK
ONE FOR A FRIEND	RICK & BRIAN	WILD AS EDEN	RICK & MONIQUE
ONE MORE FOR TODAY	AURORA	WTN (WET TSHIRT NIGHT)	AURORA
ORIGINAL BLUES	RICK	YELLOW ROOM	MONIQUE
OUT OF CONDITION	AURORA	YES (DESPARATION)	AURORA
REQUIEM OF AURORA	AURORA	YOU & I	MONIQUE
ROBBERY	AURORA	YOU NEVER LEAVE HOME ALONE	RICK & BRIAN

THANKS A MILLION

WHILE RENOVATING AND DOWNSIZING our home, I found boxes of keepsakes containing various knick-knacks, photos, awards, certificates, clothes, etc., that each held memories of Rick's life, my life, as well as our life together. Then there were hundreds of 8-tracks, cassettes, reel-to-reel tapes, CDs, VHS tapes, Hi8 video recordings that captured the soundtrack of our life together. Add to that the files, binders, and post-it's of lyrics of completed and incomplete songs, set-lists, posters, and newspaper clippings. What to do with all this stuff? That's when my Legacy Project idea was born. I want first and foremost to thank our museum curator (aka: the packrat), Rick Tremblay for keeping all these items. Truth be told, I have also added similar items to our collection. The hours I spent going through and organizing it all was like taking a ride in a time machine to a place where memories were either vivid or almost forgotten. Having the Legacy Project as an idea and turning it into a memoir has been a surreal process. The experience has been both internally challenging and rewarding. I am forever grateful to the following people.

Memoir Mentors

I had been talking about the Legacy Project for years until Shelley Piercey pushed me into action. Then fate pushed a little harder. Jennifer Murphy mentioned she was writing her memoir *Our Family had Big Dreams* and that she had enrolled in a memoir-writing course. I was inspired by this and enrolled for this course in January 2017. I met Dr. Anna Rumin, who led a class of wannabee memoir writers and also, she set the foundation for us to 'get writing.' When the course was over, the Memoir Masters-in-Training writing group was formed in March 2017. Every month Carol Sutherland-Brown, Karen Crowder-Ford, Edythe Falconer, Betsy Mann, Sheila Rorke, Hendrik Siré, and Carolynn Halkett would provide their keen insight and ongoing support in bringing my stories to life. It is because of their efforts and encouragement that I am able to share our legacy with you now.

Memoir Editors

There are two incredible women who have given their gift of time and wisdom when they edited my first ever manuscript. Edythe Falconer and Claire Ball. They would not only fix my grammar but added polish to the content and structure all the while preserving this newbie author's style.

Memoir Contributors

Throughout our memoir, there have been anecdotes from various people who wanted to share their memories about our story. Thanks to Louise & Mike Branch, Nicolas Castenada, Brian Crook, Krista Dinel, Dakin Drake, Wayne Golder, Perry Guilbeault, Bob & Doug McKenna, Shirley McKey, Jennifer Murphy, Sue Potvin, Diane Laakso, and Bruce Wittet for sharing those memories.

Kindred Family

As Maya Angelou said, "Family isn't always blood. It's the people in your life who want you in theirs, the ones who accept you for who you are. The ones that would do anything to see you smile and who love you no matter what."[33] Rick and I are honoured that this Kindred Family has remained a part of our lives, especially after Rick's stroke. Our thanks for accepting us go to the following groups of people:

The CPC Gals: Judy Follet, Shelley Piercey and Debbie Stetting.

The Small Business Marketing Gang: Lynn Akerley, Bob St. Amand, Susan Jahudka, Don & Laurie Jones, Lynn Palmer & Tom Lowe, Risë Paquette, Suzanne Sweetapple and Bob & Joan Urichuck.

The MDPW Toastmasters Club: Lynn Burritt, Florence D'Eon, Shirley McKey, Janissa Reid; my classmates who enticed me to join the club. This led to new friendships Christine Coulas-O'Connor who kept me from drowning in medical expenses, Stella Castenada who told me about her son Nick, and Jenny Murphy my inspirational mentor.

Our Musical Mates: There have been many of you over the years notably: Rolly Bernier, Marcel Bouchard, Tom Connors, Brian Crook, Julie Element, Derik Fernie, Bob McKenna, Doug McKenna, Guy Morgan, Rob Rochefort, Debbie Williamson. Our thanks also go out to everyone else that crossed our musical path.

Caregivers & Health Care Advocates

This is a special group of people who have a keen front-line understanding of what it means to be a Caregiver and their wisdom and encouragement have been priceless to me. Thanks to Sandy

Bishop-Howcroft, Teri Kingston, John Newman, Kevin Newman, Risë Paquette, Dave Pitre, Pete & Valorie Pitre, Sharon Pitre, Christine Poisson and Janissa Reid. I've also had special people in my corner reminding me to take care of myself; Thanks to Dr. Anik Vandewaeter my physician, Dr. Eric Delorme my chiropractor, Shelley Featherstone my massage therapist, Dakin Drake my trainer who keeps cheering me on and Claire Ball life-coach and friend. Thanks to Ava Clark for insisting Claire come to my aid. Then there are the genuine angels who have taken care of Rick at the various hospitals and long-term care facilities. I can't possibly name them all here but there are three incredible people who have given of their hearts and humour, providing me with peace of mind, thanks to Bea Morrison, Hillary Cratzbarg, and Paul Palmer. You are our lifeline.

Acquaintances along the way and Kind Strangers

Thank you for crossing our path over the years. There are several of you who have witnessed our story in your own way. Some for a brief time only while others were there longer. We appreciate the gift of your friendship however brief. As they say 'life happens' and as you travel your road replacing old with new acquaintances, we hope it brings you the rewards you are seeking. Maybe our paths will cross again.

I wish I had collected the names of the kind strangers that we met along our journey, but since I didn't have the foresight to do so, I will put it out to the universe and say thank you for your acts of kindness. Maybe serendipity will arrange for this book to fall into your hands. You may say, "Hey I remember them!" and if that's you then please accept our thanks for seeing us as valued citizens. Rick and I also wish to thank all songwriters, authors, screenwriters, etc. whose words put to music, plays, movies and books have inspired us throughout our lives.

Devoted Friends

Your unconditional friendship has been invaluable throughout the years. You never missed a beat. You were there in your own way consistently. Some of you live nearby and others at a distance but that didn't stop you from giving a helping hand, or regularly calling, visiting, or coming to our rescue. You did so willingly with genuine loyalty in your hearts. There is no expiration date for our friendship and I'm grateful that you treasure it. Thanks to Audrey Bell-Peters, Andy Balez, Jack Balez, Brian Crook, Kevin Newman (our *Woomie* for life), Brian Crook, Ed Poisson, Wayne & Carol Golder, Bob & Joyce McKenna, Doug & Miche McKenna, Rolly & Linda Bernier and Debbie Williamson for your friendship and constancy.

There are two friends that are a special comfort to me. Christine Poisson, you have been there when Rick and I started dating and you witnessed every moment both tremendous and tragic. Not once did you leave my side and you stood up to those who tried to tear me down. Diane Laakso, you have held my hand in friendship since Grade 9. From that day, and throughout the years that followed, you have been my anchor. Next to Rick, you know me best. You've been my mentor, my champion, my kindred spirit. Christine and Diane, you are truly the *sisters of my heart* and I'm grateful that you are a crucial part of my life.

Our Family

Thank you to our parents Annabelle (*nee* Pitre) & Gerard (Gerry) Dinel and Ernest (Ernie) & Joan (*nee* Potvin) Tremblay for giving us life and doing your best to guide us along the way. As your eldest born children, we appreciate giving us the independence to find our own way. We also thank our siblings Mike Dinel & Joanne Gagne (*nee* Dinel) and Gary & Tim Tremblay. As with every family, we siblings have had our fair share of adventures, rivalries, and challenges and this is from the time we were toddlers into our adulthood. We still try to continue to learn valuable life lessons in our own way and in our own time.

Rick and I are also fortunate to have Uncles and Aunts who have been there for us in every way. This is why we want to live up to being the best Uncle and Aunt we can be to our nephews Steve, Taddrick, Tye, Nicholas, Ryan, and our great-nephews Jimmer and Nash. Last, but definitely not least, our beautiful niece Krista and great-niece Emma. In part, this memoir was written with you in mind, as well as our multitude of cousins, so that you may know the *Monique & Rick* story.

I regularly wear a fleece jacket given to me when I was an acting Manager in 1999, and the embroidered inscription continues to warm my heart. We wish to share its message with you all 'Thanks a Million' for witnessing our story.

Musically Yours

Monique & Rick

P.S. Keep in touch with us on www.moniqueandricktremblay.ca for our music and other special gems.

ABOUT THE AUTHORS

Monique & Rick 30ᵗʰ Anniversary in Québec City. Photographer: Xavier Dachez

MONIQUE TREMBLAY IS A marketing & communications entrepreneur who has a Radio & Television Broadcasting Diploma and several marketing and management certifications to fall back on. Monique is also a Distinguished Toastmaster and an avid competitor who has won several contests, as well as a singer, songwriter, aspiring voice actor and now author. She enjoys the creative process and strives to nurture the artistic side of her personality.

RICK TREMBLAY was an electronics engineering technician and an electrical apprentice. Rick has an Electronics Engineering Technicians Diploma and several continuing education electrical and electronic certificates. Rick is a songwriter, guitar player, singer, audio technician, producer, and promoter. He is the founding member of Manella Hemp, Bouchard & Tremblay duet, as well as Aurora which included Marcel Bouchard, Brian Crook and Monique Dinel.

The duet resides in Ottawa, Ontario, where Rick continues to 'live in the moment' and Monique does her best to make those moments happen.

ENDNOTES

1   Out of Africa Writer Isak Dinesen
2   Shall We Dance? 2004 film – Writers A. Wells & M. Suo
3   Shall We Dance? 2004 film – Writers A. Wells & M. Suo
4   RPM – Rotations Per Minute
5   Spinal Tap 1984 Writers C. Guest, R. Reiner, H. Shearer, M. McKean
6   Yesterday Once More Writers R. Carpenter, J. Bettis
7   I Believe Reindeer Bell poem Writer H. Reagan
8   Sudbury Junction Writers R. Tremblay, M. Tremblay (nee Dinel)
9   Canadian Broadcasting Corporation From the Vaults Episode 6
10 Oxford English Dictionary
11 On Counting Sheep Writer unknown (traditional)
12 VentureOne Trademark of Canada Post Corporation
13 The Selected Journals of L.M. Montgomery -edited by M. Rubio & E. Waterston
14 This Waltz Writer L. Cohen
15 Could I have this Dance Writers W Holyfield, B. House
16 Take My Heart Writers R. Tremblay, M. Tremblay (nee Dinel)
17 Seven Brides for Seven Brothers Music: Gene DePaul / Lyrics: Johnny Mercer
18 Ballad of Snowbound Road Writers R. Tremblay and M. Bouchard
19 Gender Representation on Country Format Radio Study 2000-2018 by J.E. Watson